the
(re-)making
of a black
american

BLACK STUDIES
& critical thinking

Rochelle Brock and Richard Greggory Johnson III
Executive Editors

Vol. 51

The Black Studies and Critical Thinking series
is part of the Peter Lang Education list.
Every volume is peer reviewed and meets
the highest quality standards for content and production.

PETER LANG
New York • Washington, D.C./Baltimore • Bern
Frankfurt • Berlin • Brussels • Vienna • Oxford

For Oral, Chloe, Carson, and Mom
my loves

Chonika Coleman-King

the (re-)making of a black american

Tracing *the* Racial *and* Ethnic Socialization *of* Caribbean American Youth

PETER LANG
New York • Washington, D.C./Baltimore • Bern
Frankfurt • Berlin • Brussels • Vienna • Oxford

Library of Congress Cataloging-in-Publication Data

Coleman-King, Chonika.
The (re-)making of a Black American: tracing the racial and ethnic
socialization of Caribbean American youth / Chonika Coleman-King.
pages cm. — (Black studies and critical thinking; vol. 51)
Includes bibliographical references and index.
1. Caribbean Americans—Biography. 2. African Americans—
Biography. 3. African Americans—Socialization. I. Title.
II. Title: Remaking of a Black American.
E184.C27C65   305.896'073—dc23   2013018779
ISBN 978-1-4331-2074-9 (hardcover)
ISBN 978-1-4331-2073-2 (paperback)
ISBN 978-1-4539-1161-7 (e-book)
ISSN 1947-5985

Bibliographic information published by **Die Deutsche Nationalbibliothek**.
Die Deutsche Nationalbibliothek lists this publication in the "Deutsche
Nationalbibliografie"; detailed bibliographic data is available
on the Internet at http://dnb.d-nb.de/.

CONTENTS

CHAPTER FOUR

CHAPTER FIVE

CHAPTER SIX

Converging Identities and Realities: Finding One's Place in the Home, School, and World 173

CHAPTER SEVEN

The (Re-)Making of a Black American:

Introduction

Tables

Headmaster a come, make has'e! Si-down,
Amy! Min yuh bruck Jane collar-bone
Tom! Tek yuh foot off o' de desk,
Sandra Wallace, mi know yuh vex
But beg yuh get off o' Joseph head.
Tek de lizard off o' Sue neck, Ted!
Sue, mi dear, don bawl so loud,
Thomas, yuh can tell me why yuh a put de toad
Eeana Elvira sandwich bag?
An, Jim, whey yuh a do wid dah bull frog?
Tek i' off mi table! Yu mad?
Mi know yuh chair small, May but it not dat bad
Dat yuh haffe siddung pon di floor!
Jim don' squeeze de frog unda de door,
Put i' through de window—no, no Les!
Mi know yuh hungry, Mary yeas
Won' full yuh up, so spit it out.
Now go wash de blood outa yuh mout.
Hortense, tek Mary to de nurse.
Nick tek yuh han' out o' Mary purse!
Ah wonda who tel all o' yuh
Sey dat dis class-room is a zoo?
Si-down, Head master comin' through de door!
"Two ones are two, two twos are four"
—Valerie Bloom

For me, being born in the United States to Jamaican parents has felt like being of two worlds simultaneously, but not belonging completely to one or the other. This ambiguity—the inability to locate one's membership in a particular group or space—marks the experiences of 1.5- and second-generation Caribbean American youth. As I matriculated through the K–12 public school system in New York City, I felt myself invisible in the school curriculum, not fully internalizing the history of Black or White Americans. I desired to know more about the Caribbean, a history and culture to which I felt connected but rarely had an opportunity to explore in the formal school curriculum. It was not until I travelled to England as a senior in college and was a student teacher in a primary school in southern England that I encountered a resonant diasporic representation of Caribbean people. While perusing the shelves of a British bookstore, I came across the work of Afro-Caribbean-descended individuals whose work spoke to a number of diverse Black experiences. The poem "Tables," written by Valerie Bloom, a Jamaican-born poet who had resided in England since 1979, reflected something I desired but that my schooling experience and the consciousness of mainstream America lacked. Bloom's poem, documented by Grace Nichols (1988) in an anthology called *Poetry Jump-Up: A Collection of Black Poetry*, gave me a space that was my own, a space outside of the Black-White dichotomy wrought by U.S. hegemonic ideology. It allowed me to be fully Black and, though absent from America's social and cultural radar, present in the consciousness of many people like me.

The last line of the poem "Tables"—"Two ones are two, two twos are four"— especially spoke to my experiences as a second-generation American. Although my mother—my first teacher—held high academic expectations for me and diligently worked with me at home, once I became school age we sometimes struggled to speak the same "academic language." I vividly recall my mother attempting to teach me multiplication tables as a 4-year-old kindergartner. She was appalled that my elementary school had yet to teach multiplication tables, a skill most 3-year-old children in Jamaica acquire. But I could not understand what my mom meant by "Two twos are four." I cried, frustrated and confused, and never did learn to say my multiplication tables at home. I mark this memory as one of my most distressing early learning experiences. I learned my multiplication tables eventually—years later, along with my peers in elementary school.

My mother instilled in me a deep respect for education. Most of the learning experiences she provided were engaging and rewarding. The traumatic experience of learning my multiplication tables was an exception. As Jamaicans who held strongly to their ethnic and cultural values, my parents expected me to measure up to children reared in Jamaica. Growing up in the rural countryside of Jamaica, my parents and their siblings engaged in laborious daily chores and sought to replicate for their U.S.-born children a similar level of accountability for household responsibilities. My extended family was strict, yet loving.

Living in a Caribbean enclave in Queens, New York, made my first school experience all the more dissonant. School marked the beginning of my exposure to non-Caribbean-descended individuals, including Blacks who had resided in the United States over generations, descendants of enslaved Africans brought to the United States between the 1600s and 1800s. In this book, I interchangeably use the terms *native-born Blacks* and *Black Americans* to describe this group, and *Caribbean immigrants* and *Caribbean Americans* to describe previously enslaved African descendants from the English-speaking Caribbean.

My parents rarely noted distinctions between Black Americans and Caribbean immigrants, but upon entering elementary school I experienced ruptures in my schematic understanding of the world as I engaged my Black American peers, who spoke in ways that were foreign to me. I distinctly remember a classmate asking me to borrow what sounded like "a pin." After several attempts at clarification, I said, "Oh, you want a "p-e-n!" Cultural *mis*communication occurred frequently in my school life. Social experiences in grades 3–5 proved very difficult as my Black American peers teased me, "Get back on your banana boat, you Jamaican beef patty!" and berated me for the complicity of *my people* in the drug trafficking that had been occurring in the mid- to late 1980s. This taunting reflected larger social discourses on Caribbean immigrants.

These early experiences—at school and at home—undoubtedly shaped my understanding of myself. Recurring encounters and miscommunications alienated me from my Black American counterparts. Although I loved to learn and rarely missed a day of school, social tensions marked my days. I felt I could not relate to children at school because my home and my community context were distinctly Jamaican and Caribbean. My family experiences promoted a framework for Jamaican identity development through immersion in various cultural and ethnic discourses. These home experiences often did not resonate with the world I knew at school. I was an outsider to the Black American majority within my school. My ostensibly inherent difference shaped my perspective on the social world. I saw myself as "other" because of my home experiences; my Black American peers reinforced this identity by bringing to the fore my difference and citing me as other.

Despite these early conflicts, things began to shift in the early 1990s. Caribbean immigrants became increasingly *populous* and *popular*. During my years in middle school, it became *cool* to be Caribbean, and especially Jamaican. A comingling of cultures, ethnicities, and worlds strengthened formerly tenuous relationships. In middle school, my best friends were Latinas and Black Americans who were deeply interested and involved in New York's Caribbean culture.

These experiential and contextual differences, which occurred over time, have shaped the lens through which I examine the experiences of Caribbean American immigrants and their children today. While an increasing number of researchers seek to document and theorize the experiences of Caribbean American youth, their outsider lens, though arguably more objective,[1] limits their analysis of the experiences of Caribbean immigrant families and their children. As an insider, I have personally experienced the nuances that shape the public and private lives of Caribbean American people and therefore can apply these multifaceted perspectives to my research and analyses. This book gives voice to the experiences of Caribbean American youth buttressed by the analyses of an insider, one whose lens adds insights to the current body of literature surrounding the experiences and identities of 1.5- and second-generation American children of Caribbean immigrants.

My defining ethnic identity as a Caribbean American or Jamaican American individual, however, does not preclude my additional identities as Black and American. Instead, I am sometimes "either" or "both-and" Caribbean and Black American among other categories with which I identify. In my blackness, the experience of American racism deeply resonates with me, and as a person of Caribbean descent my experience is often marginalized and misunderstood. Researchers who examine the experiences of Blacks in the United States tend to study race without regard to ethnicity or national origin, leaving the experiences of those who exist within multiple racial *and* ethnic spaces underexplored. My teachers did not know the struggles I endured adapting to life at school, nor were they aware of my desire to learn about the history and experiences of Africans in the Caribbean. Teachers were unaware that I had needs specific to my racialized experiences *and* my ethnic and cultural background. The U.S. Black-White binary excluded those who were indeed "Black like [*me*]."[2]

Background and Problem

Though racism stemming from the effects of slavery has left a lasting impact on many parts of the world, the aftereffects of slavery varied tremendously, depending on location. The abolition of slavery in the English-speaking Caribbean created a ruling Black and mixed-race (Black and White) majority as Whites fled to their native countries (Vickerman, 1999). Though Whites maintained colonial rule over many Caribbean islands and continued to exploit Caribbean inhabitants and pillage resources (Memmi, 2006), African descendants had extensive control over local affairs, cultural practices, and social norms (Rogers, 2006). In the United States, however, the legal abolition of slavery did not change the power structure or the racial makeup of the land. The White majority maintained political, social, and economic power through legal and social means of marginalizing Blacks. The experiences of Afro-Caribbean people stand in sharp contrast to the persistent legal and social marginalization of Black Americans after the legal abolition of slavery (Rogers, 2006).

Today, the histories of Blacks from many parts of the world collide with the vast increase in migration from Africa and the Caribbean to the United States (Rong & Brown, 2002; Vickerman, 1999). Recent immigrants and longstanding residents of the United States experience a plethora of complex social relations as each group attempts to understand the others and their relative positions in social, political, economic, and often newly emphasized racial classifications (Waters, 1999). Black immigrants in particular must often renegotiate their identities to include race and ethnicity in new and complex ways, given exposure to U.S. racial classifications and the hierarchical positioning of racial groups.

Researchers identify historical differences, the immigration process, and current attitudes and practices regarding race as contributors to the development of distinctive racial and ethnic identities among Black immigrant groups (Ogbu, 1991a, 1992; Ogbu & Simons, 1998; Rong & Brown, 2002; Waters, 1994, 1999). In a study of second-generation Caribbean American youth, Waters reported:

> Three types of identities are evident among the second generation—a Black American identity, an ethnic or hyphenated national origin identity, and an immigrant identity. These different identities are related to different perceptions of and understandings of race relations and of opportunities in the United States. Those youngsters who identify as Black Americans tend to see more racial discrimination and limits to opportunities for Blacks in the United States. Those who identify as ethnic West Indians tend to see more opportunities and rewards for individual effort and initiative. (Waters, 1994, p. 795)

In addition to links between identity and the perception of opportunities in the United States, researchers have also found a link between racial and ethnic identity and educational achievement and attainment for immigrant groups (Waters, 1999; Rong & Brown, 2002; Massey, Mooney, Torres, & Charles, 2007; Miller, 1999). These findings are significant in light of trends in research and policy designed to close the Black-White achievement gap.

While identity theories provide valuable insight into the school achievement of minority students, a host of additional theories have existed for some time. Some scholars attributed Black underachievement to genetic inferiority.[3] More recently, researchers have recognized a cultural mismatch between racial minorities' home culture and the Eurocentric culture of schools and cite this incongruity as an impediment to Black students' success in academic institutions (Karunungan, 2001; Ladson-Billings, 1994; Perry, Steele, & Hilliard, 2003).

Although researchers have increasingly taken up issues pertaining to Caribbean immigrants and their progeny, this area of study remains underexplored. Researchers such as anthropologist John Ogbu (1991a, 1992) and sociologists Milton Vickerman (1999, 2001) and Mary Waters (1999) have attempted to shed light on the integration experiences of Black immigrants and how these experiences are compounded by the sociopolitical nature of blackness in the United States. This book builds on previous work by expanding the exploration of the intersections among race, ethnicity, nationality, socioeconomic status, and historical context. For example, Mary Waters documents the adoption of anti-Black American sentiments as central to the identity formation of Caribbean immigrants. She argues that Black immigrants distance themselves from U.S.-born Blacks, thereby elevating their group to model minority status in an attempt to buffer the effects of U.S. racism. She does not consider, however, the ways in which class background, the social rejection of Caribbean immigrants on the part of Black Americans, and historical context interface with Caribbean American identity formation.

Additionally, John Ogbu's work characterized "voluntary immigrants"—those who came to the United States on their own and not by conquest—as uncritical about U.S. race relations and savvy in circumventing the effects of racism. However, his work does not consider the ways in which voluntary immigrants from the Caribbean have currently and historically resisted White hegemony and the oppression of Blacks. Nor did he take up the pervasiveness of institutionalized racism that has stymied Blacks' attempts at upward mobility. The work of Vickerman, though more thoroughly conceived, does not address the intersections between identities and the educational experiences of children born in the United States to Caribbean immigrant parents (second generation) or children born in the Caribbean who migrated to the United States between the ages of 6 and 13, known as the 1.5 generation (Zhou, 1997). Previous research has not comprehensively examined the ways in which three factors work together to shape the identity formation processes of Caribbean immigrant youth: (1) the history of racism in the United States, (2) the distinction between experiences of race in the United States and the Caribbean, and (3) colliding perspectives on racial and ethnic identity. While existing studies highlight trends in academic performance and differences in the racial and ethnic identity of Caribbean immigrant populations, studies have not explored the micro-level processes that contribute to Black immigrant youth's perceptions of race and their position within U.S. society. More important, the impact of contextual differences on parents' racial socialization practices has not been qualitatively examined. This study contributes to research on Black immigrant populations by elucidating socialization processes that influence the racial and ethnic beliefs of 1.5- and second-generation Caribbean American students, as well as how these ideas reflect youth's identities and understanding of themselves as they embark upon the processes of integration, Americanization, and ultimately racialization.

Guiding Questions

The key factor for the youth I studied is race. The daily discrimination that the youngsters experience, the type of racial socialization they receive in the home, the understandings of race they develop in their peer groups and at school affect strongly how they react to American society. The ways in which these youngsters experience and react to racial discrimination influences the type of racial/ethnic identity they develop. (Waters, 1994, p. 802)

As supported by Waters (1994), evidence suggests that racial socialization and other ecological factors influence the identity development of youth. However, little research has aimed to describe how these processes occur and how they might be connected to students' experiences in educational institutions.

In an effort to further current research on immigrant identity and educational experiences, I will explore the process of racial socialization practices across two distinct contexts. This study will examine the racial socialization practices of Caribbean immigrant parents and how their children come to understand these messages in the face of racialized school experiences. The study sample consisted of two 1.5-generation and eight second-generation Caribbean American students attending middle school in a middle-class, mixed-race, suburban community outside of a large city in the northeastern United States.

This study supplements the seminal work that exists pertaining to the experiences of Caribbean immigrants and their children by answering the following questions: (1) How do Caribbean immigrant parents socialize their children with respect to race and ethnicity? (2) What do Caribbean American youth learn about U.S. racism through experiences in a mixed-race, middle-class school? (3) How do socialization experiences at home and school influence youth's understanding of themselves as racial and ethnic minorities in the United States?

In addition to these larger questions, the following related questions will also be taken up:

1. How do historical legacies and life narratives inform parental racial and ethnic socialization practices?
2. In what ways does integration into U.S. society shift the race salience of Caribbean immigrants from majority-Black countries?
3. What strategies are immigrant students given to navigate educational institutions as racialized individuals within the United States?
4. How do contextual issues regarding racial mixing and socioeconomic status shape the issues with which youth must contend?
5. In what ways are Caribbean American students implicated in race dynamics at the school?

Guided by these questions, research on the experiences of 1.5- and second-generation Caribbean immigrant children helps to situate the racial and ethnic identity development of youth within a larger historical and context-specific framework. In other words, I examine the trajectory of racial politics in the Caribbean as central to understanding the race consciousness of Caribbean immigrants upon arrival in the United States. While many studies have focused on immigrant adaptation to the United States, relatively little work explores the intersections between immigrants' experiences in their native countries, adaptation to U.S. society, and the characteristics of the host community as inextricably intertwined. This study explores the ways in which integration into particular communities—whether hostile or supportive—also helps to shape immigrants' perspectives regarding race in the United States over time. Additionally, these questions take into account the ways in which the social-class background of parents and means of self-identification within the Caribbean influence perceptions of race and racism in the United States. This study regards these experiences as instrumental to Caribbean immigrants' parenting practices and describes how these experiences influence the messages parents send to their children, further shaping their identities.

A more complex understanding of immigrant experiences reframes assertions that Caribbean immigrants' identities are formed mainly in opposition to Black Americans, but instead views intra-racial contention as one small piece in an intricate system of identity development and integration processes. This work links the history and perspectives of Caribbean immigrant parents to the identity development of their children, but also acknowledges that Caribbean American youth have their own unique experiences with race and racism. Their parents' interpretations, teachings, silences, actions, and inactions relative to issues of race and racism complicate these understandings, however.

A transnational framework for understanding Caribbean immigrant families challenges deeply held assumptions embedded in traditional analyses of the perspectives and experiences of Caribbean American youth. Transnational theory highlights the ways in which psychological realities are not always rooted in a particular space but can exist across spaces that particular histories, locations, and experiences inform and re-form. Charles (1992), argues that "analyzing international migration from a transnational perspective implies a redefinition of social context" (p. 101). In essence, any attempt to understand the perspectives and identities of immigrants without consideration of the historical and social processes of their native country is problematic. The identity development of Caribbean American youth is not static or entirely uniform, but shifts over time and succumbs to the push and pull of factors such as individual characteristics, historical legacies, politics, and class background. A transnational perspective allows us to move away from deterministic and static notions of blackness to incorporate a wider array of diasporic realities.

Previous studies have identified variations in self-identification that exist for 1.5- and second-generation youth, and researchers seek to explain why these variations exist. However, these analyses fail to situate immigrant experiences within a larger sociopolitical framework. Rather, they highlight the types of identities youth form and offer anecdotes for why identities develop as they do, although few researchers have closely examined the nuanced processes that lead to particular self-identities. This study centers on this broader context—how experiences and messages shared at home and school as informed by multiple historical and sociopolitical spheres shape understandings regarding race, racism, and ethnic identity.

Morristown Middle School and the Issue of Diversity

This study took place in a suburban school district outside a large city in the northeastern United States. For the purposes of the study, I'll refer to the suburb as Morristown and the adjacent urban community as New Kensington (both pseudonyms). While major cities along the East Coast of the United States such as Miami and New York have historically attracted a large contingent of Black immigrants (Bryce-Laporte, 1979; Rong & Brown, 2002), more recent demographic trends demonstrate a shift in earlier patterns of migration. Recent trends show that New Kensington has re-emerged as a major gateway for immigrants from various regions of the world (Singer, Vitiello, Katz, & Park, 2008). However, recent immigrants are going beyond New Kensington to settle in neighboring suburban communities. In the 21st century, newcomers have been branching out beyond the center of New Kensington into peripheral spaces, ultimately shifting the traditional landscape of suburbia.

According to a Brookings Institution report (Singer et al., 2008), New Kensington experienced the following formative trends over the last several decades:

1. As compared to similar regions, New Kensington had the largest and fastest-growing immigrant population.
2. New Kensington has attracted immigrants and refugees from Asia (39%), Latin America and the Caribbean (28%), Europe (23%), and Africa (8%). The 10 largest source countries are India, Mexico, China, Vietnam, Korea, Italy, Ukraine, Philippines, Jamaica, and Germany.
3. Sixty percent of immigrants arrived after 1990 and show positive levels of employment and educational attainment

as compared to migrants in other metropolitan immigrant communities.

4. The population growth of immigrants in the surrounding suburbs has even outpaced that of New Kensington. In particular, the suburb of Morristown, where this study took place, has the largest number of immigrants.

5. Of labor force growth since 2000, 75% is attributable to spikes in migration to the New Kensington Metro Area.

Mirroring trends across the United States, immigration to New Kensington reflects a significant drop in migration from Europe. In the 1970s European immigrants made up over 80% of the immigrant population in New Kensington; today, 76% of recent immigrants to New Kensington hail from places mainly populated by people of color (Brookings Institution Center on Urban and Metropolitan Policy, 2003). Immigrants from majority-Black countries in the Caribbean did not constitute a significant percentage of immigrants living in New Kensington during the last few decades of the 20th century. By 2006, however, Jamaican and Haitian immigrants were among the top 10 immigrant groups in the area, comprising 4.3% and 3.5% of the total foreign-born population respectively (Singer et al., 2008). Jamaicans also ranked as the fifth-largest source of the area's immigrants in 2000. While the area has gained Black, Asian, and Hispanic residents in the last decade, many of them immigrants, New Kensington simultaneously lost 180,000 White residents (Brookings Institution Center on Urban and Metropolitan Policy, 2003).

Despite the loss of many White residents and the changing racial makeup of the district, the middle-class base of the community has been maintained. On average, families in the Morristown School District earn $72,183 per year (Trulia, 2007). According to local residents and Morristown teachers, Morristown is one of the few middle-class communities in the area that embodies such diversity, which makes the neighborhood sought after by many liberal White families. At Morristown Middle School, the racial makeup is 47.6% White, 41.8% Black, 3.2% Hispanic, 7.1% Asian/Pacific Islander, and 0.3% American Indian (SchoolMatters, 2007).

As demographic trends have shifted, the Morristown School District has been touted as one of the most diverse middle-class school districts in the region. However, this increase in diversity has brought challenges as the district has struggled to mitigate achievement disparities between Black and White students—a daunting task in the face of No Child Left Behind (NCLB) standards. While Morristown students of all racial groups made Adequate Yearly Progress (AYP) (SchoolDigger, 2007), Black students performed at or above the state target in reading and math approximately—63% and 57% respectively. In comparison, White students performed at about 90% and 85% in reading and math, respectively (Pennsylvania Department of Education, 2006–2007).

The parents of Black students were outraged by achievement discrepancies between the groups, and the local chapter of the National Association for the Advancement of Colored People (NAACP) became involved. In an effort to address the simmering issue—or assuage the concerns of irate Black parents, as some local teachers and parents contend—Morristown Middle School administrators invited two professors from the school where I did my PhD work to assist in closing the achievement gap. The "Can We Talk?" (CWT) research intervention was instituted as a supplement to academic remediation and other efforts to boost Black student achievement. The project consisted of a series of after-school sessions designed to encourage academic success by promoting healthy racial identity development and teaching students how to cope with racial stressors. CWT also focused on teaching critical consciousness and racial negotiation skills to Black students. The CWT research project introduced me to Morristown Middle School as a research site.

The Caribbean Presence at Morristown

My study, which serves as the basis for this book, grew out of my role as a researcher and group facilitator with the CWT project. CWT yielded access to school administrators, teachers, and students, but it also influenced the ways in which these constituents perceived me. I was able to gain the trust of a number of teachers and students, including several White teachers committed to examining the role of race in their pedagogical practices. However, those who either had little interest in exploring racial dynamics or for whom addressing racial issues seemed too risky often kept me at a distance. Nonetheless, my "in" with key players in the school—especially the guidance counselor who was assigned to work with me—generally granted me privileged admission to community spaces and many classrooms.

As I increasingly participated in various aspects of the school community, I became acutely aware of a Caribbean presence within the school building. Oftentimes I would encounter groups of students, girls in particular, who were either taunted by their peers because of their Caribbean heritage or banded together around interests central to their Caribbean identity. I began to actively seek out Caribbean American students and to document instances where issues of Caribbean national origin and ethnicity were brought to the forefront of student interactions and discourse.

In an effort to connect with Caribbean American students further, I visited classrooms throughout the school. I introduced myself, shared information about my research interests, and asked students if they were either born in the Caribbean or had parents who were born in the Caribbean. After compiling a list of approximately 35 students, I invited the parents of those students to attend an information session. Among the 35 students who self-identified as being of Caribbean descent, seven of their families attended the meeting, and five families volunteered to participate in the study. An additional seven students whose parents did not attend the meeting requested consent forms to participate in the project, bringing the total to twelve students—four boys and eight girls.

Out of approximately 320 Black students at Morristown, 11% of those students were identified as having Caribbean heritage. This number is proportional to the overall percentage of Caribbean Blacks in the total U.S. Black population (Rong & Brown, 2001). However, as I documented the background of Caribbean American students throughout the school, there seemed to be an overwhelming Haitian American presence.

Two Haitian American families attended the initial parent meeting, but neither family chose to participate in the project. The lack of participation on the part of Haitian students prompted me to consider whether French- and Creole-speaking Haitian immigrants perceived themselves as being connected to the other mostly English-speaking, majority-Black countries in the Caribbean.

Nonetheless, I was able to recruit a diverse group of students in terms of class background, gender, and academic achievement levels. According to Weiss (1994), when a diverse body of research participants is taken together, the group displays the variations that can occur within a population. By recruiting a diverse group of students who had experienced a variety of socialization experiences and perspectives, I was able to maximize the range of possible findings and potential generalizability of the study (Hammersley & Atkinson, 1995; Weiss, 1994).

Caribbean American families who took part in the study mostly hailed from the island of Jamaica. Of the ten Caribbean American students who participated in the study, five students had parents who were both from Jamaica. One student's parents were both from Trinidad and Tobago, and another student's parents were both from Antigua. The other three students in the study had parents whose origins included these pairings: Jamaica-Guyana, Jamaica-Dominica, and Bahamas-United States. Thus, seven out of ten students had at least one parent from the island of Jamaica. The overrepresentation of Jamaican-descended participants in the sample is consistent with demographic trends in the region; Jamaica sends more immigrants to the New Kensington Metro Area than any other country in the English-speaking Caribbean. In the year 2000, Jamaica was the fifth-largest source of immigrants to New Kensington (Brookings Institution Center on Urban and Metropolitan Policy, 2003).

Eight out of ten participants were born in the United States; the other two immigrated at ages 2 and 9. Additionally, four out of ten came from families where parents held professional-level jobs; others' parents were entrepreneurs or worked in the service sector. All of the high-achieving students except one came from households with professional parents. However, a significant number of non-professional parents owned homes in the Morristown community and earned enough money to access the luxuries of a middle-class lifestyle, despite lower levels of formal educational attainment as compared to others in their community.

Race and Social Class Politics in the Larger Morristown Community

Morristown Middle School is buried in an enclave right at the border of New Kensington, a sizable city in the Northeast. As you approach the intersection of Wyndham Boulevard and Merrick Avenue, there is a bustling shopping center and several store-lined streets. The shopping center houses a major supermarket, several fast-food restaurants, a pharmacy, a few gas stations, and other low-end stores commonly found in lower-income and working-class communities. At first glance it appears that only a barrier of wild trees, shrubs, and weeds stands between the supermarket and the Morristown community. However, nestled in the shrouds of foliage, a 20-foot-high fence reveals the intention of maintaining a physical border between Morristown and New Kensington.

Beyond the 20-foot fence, a large expanse of slightly elevated grass further separates the shopping center from the Morristown school building off in the distance. Visitors have to enter the campus by way of one-way streets located in a residential community, as the 20-foot fence obstructed direct access to the school. You can't see it from the side that faces New Kensington, but the campus has several tennis courts and a rather large parking lot designated for teachers and support staff.

While metropolitan New Kensington has a reasonably good public transportation system, taking the bus to Morristown requires getting off near the intersection of Wyndham and Merrick and walking about half a mile to get around the fence. In this very practical way, the presence of the 20-foot fence kept Morristown separate from New Kensington, purposely shielding the neighborhood from the perceived blight of the adjacent urban locale.

Distinctions between the socioeconomic statuses of Morristown and New Kensington are immediately apparent. Morristown has moderately sized single-family homes with well-manicured lawns, in stark contrast to the sometimes ill-kept row houses in New Kensington. The proximity of Morristown to New Kensington makes the disparity between the "haves" and "have-nots" all the more evident.

The Morristown Middle School building—a large brick edifice that is more flat than it is tall—appeared to be a run-of-the-mill school building from the outside, but the amenities and resources housed inside of the building told another story. At the time of my study, a large, partially carpeted lobby provided cushioned benches along windows that run from the ceiling to the floor. A courtyard offered flowerbeds and outdoor seating. The ceiling of the main hallway boasted student artwork dating back several decades, as students had painted images directly onto ceiling tiles. Similarly, artistically designed ceramic tiles made by students decorated portions of the hallway. The halls were always impeccably clean and bright, and fully functional lockers served students on the academic wings of the first and second floors.

On any given day, the Morristown campus and school building appeared orderly. It was hard to believe that several hundred adolescents used the building. Floors were always shiny and relatively free of litter. The walls were nicely painted, and banners of colleges and universities adorned the school hallways in sections labeled "The Ivy League," "Big Ten Schools," and "Historically Black Colleges and Universities." Teachers' first and last names appeared outside their doors with uniform placement, font, and paper. Banners representing the colleges and universities they had attended were posted on teachers' classroom doors. Most classrooms displayed several banners, since many teachers had at least one advanced degree.

Beyond the physical organization of the building, there was a wealth of course offerings at Morristown Middle School. An entire wing of the building was devoted to the arts. There were classrooms dedicated to band, chorus, orchestra, woodworking, fine arts, and a brand new Macintosh lab with large, 27-inch-screen desktop computers was used for music composition. A language corridor housed French, Spanish, German, and Italian instruction, among other languages. The school library boasted approximately 40 Dell PCs in addition to two separate, general-use computer labs—one for PCs and another for Macs. In the school's basement, a home economics classroom offered stoves and other essentials. Academic classrooms brandished dry-erase boards, smartboards, several computers, laptop carts, and other equipment. The school allotted students two sets of textbooks—one for school and another that remained at home—to protect students' backs and ensure against forgetting the books they needed to study or complete assignments.

As a former teacher in a low-income, Title I school, I was struck by the small class sizes at Morristown Middle School even more than the physical resources. Classes generally consisted of no more than 15–20 students, sometimes fewer. Teachers had aides and other resources to assist students with special learning needs. There were approximately five full-time special education teachers on staff at Morristown Middle School at a time when urban schools struggled to find enough special education teachers to serve their students. Despite their focus on students with special needs, aides and special education teachers provided assistance with classroom management, grading papers, and overall classroom instruction, thereby relieving overburdened teachers of responsibilities that in some districts led to teacher burnout.

"Challenge" students (otherwise known as gifted students) received additional resources, including one-on-one and small-group instruction with a Challenge teacher in a resource room specially designated for gifted students. Classroom teachers were also expected to provide more rigorous academic instruction for designated Challenge students during their time in mainstream, heterogeneous-ability classrooms.

In addition to the academic and administrative support offered to the Morristown teachers, it appears that the Morristown School District handsomely compensated teachers for their work. One Morristown teacher in her early 30s, who had been teaching for approximately 10 years and had earned a master's degree within the last 3 years, reported earning approximately $85,000 a year. According to New Kensington's official published salary scale, she earned approximately $20,000 more per year than a teacher with similar credentials in the New Kensington public schools. The Morristown district never made public an official salary scale, but my informal conversations with teachers and others reflected general agreement that teachers in the Morristown district were well paid.

Parents in the Morristown community held high expectations for Morristown schools. While some parents carefully monitored whether those expectations were being met, others simply assumed that Morristown County schools would meet them. Morristown encouraged parental engagement through the use of technology. Parents could access their children's grades online, including grades for homework, tests, and quizzes as teachers recorded them throughout the school year. Additionally, the school encouraged parents to maintain open communication with teachers through email, telephone calls, and periodic teacher conferences.

Middle- and upper-middle-class parents who wanted their children to live in a racially diverse community and attend racially diverse schools strongly favored Morristown schools. While Morristown drew most of its students from a solid middle-class community largely comprised of single-family, owner-occupied homes, a subset of students who attended Morristown lived in local apartment buildings. According to students and teachers at Morristown, students who lived in particular apartment complexes were viewed less favorably. There seemed to be a general sense of disdain for those who lived in the Marple Meadows apartment complex, which was known for zoning students from working-class families into the school district.

The Marple Meadows apartments were located directly on the border of the Morristown community, with Wyndham Boulevard, which ran between Marple Meadows and New Kensington, dividing the two communities. Marple Meadows apartments were significantly more affordable than Morristown's single-family homes. However, these same apartments were more costly than renting or owning a home in the adjoining New Kensington area. Many working-class families (who were also disproportionately families of color) often chose to pay more in rent for an apartment in Marple Meadows and gain the benefits of the suburban school district rather than owning a home or renting in New Kensington.

The presence of Marple Meadows residents at Morristown Middle School often stirred controversy among teachers and administrators. There seemed to be a question as to who truly belonged at Morristown. New Kensington residents' attempts to circumvent zoning laws as a means of gaining access to Morristown schools compounded these sentiments further. According to one teacher, a full-time staff member was hired to track down students who did not reside in the district and have them removed from the school. The district also required these families to reimburse thousands of dollars to the school district for tuition.

In many ways, the district's zeal to bar New Kensington residents from the school served as one of the many mechanisms for addressing issues related to race and disparities in student achievement. By ridding the school of this mostly Black, mostly lower-income student population—families in search of alternatives to New Kensington's underperforming schools—Morristown Middle School could maintain an environment that thrived off of the social, cultural, and economic capital of its mostly middle-class constituency.

Morristown's relationship to New Kensington and the disparities between the two in wealth and school funding mirror larger societal inequities involving not just social class, but also race. Although Morristown residents boasted of the district's racial diversity, only certain kinds of people of color were made to feel welcome in Morristown. Morristown Middle School and the larger community reflected a type of liberal hypocrisy wherein middle-class *professionals* of color fit the standard, but other kinds of folks did not. These racial and class politics are not unique to Morristown but reflect larger systemic issues that people of color—and Blacks in particular—contend with daily. An understanding of the larger community context helps to situate Black, Caribbean-descended youth's experiences within a web of longstanding politics that ultimately color their racial and ethnic identities and notions of self.

Caribbean American Youth
and the (Re-)Making of a Black American

Many researchers agree that Black immigrants to the United States tend to do well in terms of education and employment as compared to their Black American counterparts (Bashi & McDaniel, 1997; Ogbu, 1992; Kao & Tienda, 1995; Massey et al., 2007; Sakamoto, Woo, & Kim, 2010; Vickerman, 1999; Waters, 1999). However, some scholars also challenge this sentiment by showing why these findings are misleading (Foley, 2005; Foster, 2005; Kalmijn, 1996; Pierre, 2004). I contend that the picture of Black immigrants' success is neither black nor white, but instead an intricate and nuanced reflection of great successes counterbalanced by hardships, sacrifices, and failures.

Assessing and understanding the experiences of Black immigrants in the United States is intensely complicated by the issue of race and racism in addition to matters regarding social class and sociohistorical distinctions. What is most striking, however, is that rather than achieving upward mobility over the course of several generations (as White immigrants do), the progeny of Black immigrants experience a downward trend (Kasinitz, Mollenkopf, & Waters, 2002; Zhou, 1997). Their increased integration into the U.S. social milieu stymies immigrants' optimism, work ethic, and ability to thrive within a system deluged by social barriers.

For Black immigrants, the process of Americanization is synonymous with racialization. Black immigrants not only become Americans; they become *Black* Americans. While membership in this group is not inherently negative, it engenders various psychological and material threats that ultimately affect the well-being of the group and its ability to prosper under oppressive conditions. Black youth of Caribbean descent stand at the intersection of this quandary.

In this book, I examine that dilemma by seeking to understand the process of U.S. racialization for Caribbean immigrant youth. As these adolescents begin to think more about their identities within a context such as Morristown, where they are deluged by race and class politics, they are forced to assess and re-assess the messages of pride, optimism, and perseverance shared by their parents as they contend with structural and interpersonal racism and class barriers. Even as these youth reject negative depictions of Blacks, they are concurrently positioned within these negative portrayals as Black Americans. Previous studies have shown that with time, Black immigrant groups succumb to these pressures as they are made into "Black Americans" and forced to exist at the margins of society.

Blacks all over the world suffer from marginalization and oppression; however, there is something distinctly different and heinous about being Black in America. Morristown, like many places across the country experiencing a surge in immigrant population, must determine ways to address the intersectionality of immigrant status, race, and class. The rising influence of immigrants of color in the New Kensington Metro Area has tremendous implications for K–12 education as well as to the social integration of immigrants, access to employment, and other public policy concerns. The immigration of increasing numbers of persons of color implores us to examine the needs, experiences, and means of adaptation to American society by these groups.

The complex tangle of race, class, and citizenship requires a more nuanced analysis than the reductive binary that post-racial or not-post-racial provides. Without question, this is a difficult cluster to disentangle (if such a thing is even possible), made so by the fact that race, class, and national identity have been bound up together in complicated and shifting ways across American history.

Book Overview

The introduction and first two chapters of this book lay the foundation for understanding and analyzing the data collected at the Morristown Middle School field site. In this introduction, I have highlighted personal experiences that piqued my interest in the intersections of race, ethnicity, and immigrant status, which subsequently developed into the research questions that guided this study. I also present a snapshot of immigration demographics and highlight critical aspects of immigrant research that others have failed to take up in their work and describe the site, pseudony-

mously named Morristown Middle School, in the equally pseu-
donymous New Kensington Metropolitan Area, where I undertook
my research.

In Chapter 1, I present and critique literature regarding historical distinctions between issues of race in the United States and
the Caribbean, the perpetuation of racism, and differences in how
race and racial identity have played out across groups and over
time. I also discuss literature that marks the transnational experiences and identity formation of Caribbean immigrant youth.

Chapter 2 focuses on the life narratives of several parents
whose children participated in the study. These life narratives depict the parenting and socialization practices of these parents,
which greatly influence the next generation and the familial sense
of what it means to be Black and Caribbean. These narratives also
trace the socioeconomic trajectories of parents and their integration into U.S. society as central to their perceptions of race and racism in the U.S. context. Furthermore, I examine values these
parents espoused and the ways they engaged their children in dialogue around issues of race.

Chapters 3 and 4 give a closer look at parental perspectives
that guided socialization messages and practices. In particular,
Chapter 3 documents the way parents' transnational perspectives
shaped their analysis of how they were able to "make it" in the
United States. These scripts were often devoid of racial interpretations, relied heavily on perceived ethnic competencies, and were
deeply woven into the stories parents told their children. Chapter
4 explains how parents came to their individual understandings of
race in the United States through early immigration experiences
and the extent to which they shared these ideas with their children.

Chapter 5 documents the ways in which Morristown Middle
School served as a site for learning about race and racism. First,
the chapter describes the institutionalized practices teachers and
administrators supported that reinforced racial hierarchies. These
practices include academic tracking, disparities in discipline by
school officials—whom they disciplined and how they disciplined
them—and the ways they communicated academic expectations to
Black youth. Chapter 5 describes the racialized experiences of

Black students more broadly, thereby demonstrating the salience of race in the Morristown context regardless of ethnic and class background. Caribbean American youth's analyses of race and racism at Morristown were informed by their observations of disparate treatment between Black and White students.

I bring the home and school together in Chapter 6 as I analyze how these two distinct sets of experiences shaped the perspectives, identities, and behaviors of 1.5- and second-generation Caribbean American youth. The chapter starts by underscoring how students self-identified and the ways in which, for them, race, nationality, and ethnicity were inextricably linked and uniquely negotiated. I also describe the challenges students faced as they made attempts at merging their racial and ethnic identities and how home and school contexts as well as larger social and political norms sometimes rejected or complicated their modes of self-identification. Following Chapters 2, 3, 4, 5, and 6 which are organized to contextualize racial and ethnic socialization practices leading to identity development and negotiation as part of the larger historical landscape, institutionalized structures, and transnational experiences, Chapter 7 concludes the book with implications for these findings on teacher practice, education policy, and research regarding the lives and experiences of Caribbean immigrant families in the United States.

Permission to reprint is acknowledged for: Numbers, © 2000 Valerie Bloom, from *Poetry Jump Up: A Collection of Black Poetry*.

Notes

1. See Kusow (2003) for additional information on the insider/outsider debate.
2. See Gladwell (1996), p. 74.
3. See Jensen (1969).

CHAPTER ONE

Historical Contexts, Transnationalism, and Race in the United States

When debates regarding the experiences of Black immigrants enter the public sphere and academic circles, they cause quite a bit of contention. On the one hand, many would argue that the success of Black immigrants, at least in comparison to their Black American counterparts, proves that the United States has transcended racial inequity. On the other hand, some contend that Black immigrants have limited potential for upward mobility because of a "triple disadvantage"—racial discrimination, xenophobia, and lower-class status (Rong & Brown, 2002). In many respects, research studies on the success and struggles of this population have been inconclusive, even contradictory. However, many researchers agree that racial and ethnic identity are central to the adaptation and mobility of Black immigrants.

This study illuminates the complex realities faced by Black immigrants as they adjust to life in the United States across generations, at the same time leaving aside the question of group-wide success or failure in favor of a more nuanced depiction of the Black immigrant experience. Attempts to dichotomize the experiences of Black immigrants as either the epitome of immigrant success or the essence of immigrant struggles have been detrimental to gaining a richer understanding of the continuum of experiences that characterize the Caribbean immigrant journey. Variations in country of origin, class background, sending and receiving community contexts, and personal experiences with race and racism inform Black immigrants' identities and influence opportunities for success. To neglect the impact of these variables creates an incomplete picture of how immigrants are faring in light of the obstacles they face in their journey to becoming American. By examining these variables, I've sought to complicate understandings of Caribbean immigrants' relationship to issues of race and ethnicity.

In this chapter I'll frame the topics addressed throughout the book and highlight key terms and contexts for analyzing the data collected throughout the study. I start with a history of racial politics in the United States and the Caribbean. This history contextualizes the ideology of many Caribbean immigrants upon arrival in the United States and the dissonance that occurs as they enter a country colored by its own unique legacy of slavery, racism, and oppression. Specifically, these accounts demonstrate the ways in which the unique history of the Caribbean has shaped Caribbean immigrants' analyses of and responses to the experiences they face in the United States. This history provides a framework for understanding the nature of racism across space and time, its implications for Caribbean American youth, and the transnational lens applied to the socialization messages conveyed by their parents.

Following my explication of race in the United States and the Caribbean, I delve into more recent manifestations of racism, focusing on how the process of migration and then daily experiences in U.S. institutions such as schools implicate Caribbean immigrants in institutionalized racism. I conclude by describing how Black American parents use racial and ethnic socialization practices to prepare and protect their children from the harsh realities of U.S. racism. The racial and ethnic socialization practices of Black American parents serve as an important point of reference as the rest of the book explores how Caribbean immigrant parents prepare their children for success in a racially hostile climate.

Slavery, Capitalism, and the Social Construction of Race

As early as the 17th century, Europeans began to chronicle the existence of what they deemed the "monstrous races," eventually marking the beginning of racial taxonomy dividing the human race into *homo sapiens* and *homo monstrous* (Willinsky, 1998). *Homo monstrous* referred to those with real physical disfigurements (such as dwarfs and giants) and imaginary ones (such as those with one eye or no head). Although early studies of race sought to be scientific, over time philosophers, historians, and anthropologists expanded notions of racial hierarchies. These trends marked the development of a continuum along which hierarchically organized groups of people deemed some civilized and others savages on the basis of physical and cultural distinctions (Willinsky, 1998).

Despite the established continuum of racial categorization, Bonilla-Silva (2002) argues that a more accurate representation of racial classification is one that recognizes the line drawn between Whites and non-Whites as groups, which positions Whites as superior and individuals of color as inferior. This dichotomization of Whites and non-Whites has served as justification for innumerable tragedies and holocausts throughout history, as well as the enslavement, colonization, and domination of non-White groups (Willinsky, 1998; Césaire, 2000).

This racist ideology helped to justify the transatlantic slave trade, which trafficked 12 million Africans to foreign shores throughout the Americas. As the property of White slaveowners, these Africans endured horrific working conditions for the financial gain of their "masters" (Willinsky, 1998). A common past marked by slavery continues to bind together African descendants across the globe. However, contextual distinctions in the evolution of the institution of slavery and the racial politics that it generated continue to influence the centrality of racial categorizations and racism experienced in different parts of the world.

Slavery in the Caribbean and the United States

The geography and climate of the Caribbean made it suitable for the production of sugar, a crop that required more intensive labor than cotton, tobacco, or cattle rearing (Stinchcombe, 1995). Sugar production was also more lucrative than other forms of agriculture, producing five to ten times more political and economic power per acre as compared to other crops. According to Franklin and Moss (1994), the Caribbean became "the scene of the first serious effort to develop a lucrative agricultural economy in the New World" (p. 42). They argue that economic capital garnered from the sugar plantations sparked what we know as modern-day capitalism.

Over time, areas with climates conducive to the growing of profitable crops became increasingly susceptible to the institution of slavery in the Caribbean, just as in the United States. Crucial distinctions in the institution of slavery evolved between the two places, however. Variations in climate, the type of crops harvested, and systems for managing slave labor proved integral to how race relations developed and continue to affect the respective regions today.

According to Franklin and Moss (1994), two aspects of Caribbean slavery distinguished it from its U.S. counterpart. First, Caribbean slaves were treated more harshly. Inadequate food and rampant disease resulted in higher death rates. Newly transported slaves experienced a particularly high risk of death, as approximately 30% died within 4 years of their arrival. The slave trade provided an uninterrupted flow of new Africans to the Caribbean in an effort to maintain the labor force. Second, many White plantation supervisors made seasonal visits to the Caribbean instead of living there year-round, in part because many found the tropical climate unpleasant. In the United States, most slavemasters lived on their plantations year-round. This distinction had a profound impact on the racial balance of plantations. In the Caribbean, enslaved Africans increasingly outnumbered the White "landlords" present on the islands (Franklin & Moss, 1994).

The low ratio of "landlords" to slaves gave rise to fears of slave uprisings, which subsequently resulted in the enactment of more severe slave codes in the Caribbean. However, frequent slave uprisings persisted in spite of these codes. Distinct maroon (runaway) populations often terrorized White landlords (Franklin & Moss, 1994). These uprisings came to improve the social and political conditions of Blacks in the Caribbean. Over time, Caribbean slaveowners experienced difficulty establishing religious and educational institutions, the profitability of sugar decreased, and insurrections and miscegenation became increasingly prevalent. This led Caribbean slaveowners to get rid of their slaves, selling them to Whites in other areas of the Caribbean and the United States.

Slave uprisings in the Caribbean inspired measures to prevent similar events in the United States. The United States enacted harsh slave codes of its own and legally closed the slave trade with the Caribbean and Africa. U.S. slaveowners deemed Caribbean slaves too resourceful and revolutionary, and African-born Blacks "raw and unruly" (Franklin & Moss, 1994, p. 91). As the institution of slavery began to unravel in the Caribbean, the conditions for slaves in the United States worsened. By the 1830s slavery was abolished in many regions of the Caribbean but continued in the United States for approximately another 30 years. Over time, the United States had developed an impenetrable "one-drop" rule that positioned individuals of mixed race as non-White and therefore exempt from the privileges granted to Whites. Individuals with a trace of Black ancestry were generally denied the right to participate in political, social, and economic enterprises. In the Caribbean, however, a growing number of Blacks produced children with Whites as well as with Chinese and Indian laborers. This higher rate of miscegenation in the Caribbean complicated notions of race and led to the development of a fluid racial continuum rather than a fixed demarcation between Whites and non-Whites (Vickerman, 2001).

With the blurring of racial boundaries in the Caribbean, individuals of Black and mixed ancestry were granted privileges that were designated only for Whites in the United States. Even though lighter-skinned individuals still maintained an advantage over their darker counterparts, dark-skinned individuals could improve their social standing through educational attainment and professional status (Vickerman, 2001). In the Caribbean, social class became the determinant of power and access, and, though it correlated with skin color, access was not exclusively denied to one particular group.

As the number of Whites in the Caribbean dwindled even further, the population of Black and mixed-race individuals burgeoned. Individuals of African ancestry increasingly participated in the social and political development of the Caribbean, even as slavery continued in the United States. Yet after slavery was abolished in the United States, the Black Codes and Jim Crow laws restricted the full incorporation of Blacks into the larger society.

Two historical distinctions are paramount to understanding some of the sociopolitical distinctions between the experiences today of Blacks in the United States and in the Caribbean. First, the United States developed into a majority-White country, and the

English-speaking Caribbean maintained a Black (and mixed-race) majority. Second, non-Whites eventually gained control over local affairs in the Caribbean (in spite of its past experiences with imperialism) as Blacks in the United States struggled for decades and continue to struggle today for equal rights and opportunities. These two distinctions have had profound implications for how one's blackness shapes life experiences, the perceived salience of race, and the development of racial identity in the United States and the Caribbean.

A Closer Look at the Effects of Macro and Micro Race Politics

The historical legacy of slavery and racism continues to impact individuals and nations across the world. Namely, First World countries have derived massive amounts of wealth from imperialistic relationships, and previously colonized countries live with debt and little control over their own natural resources (Césaire, 2000; Stewart, 2012; Willinsky, 1998). Populations of color residing in developed, majority-White countries suffer under racialized systems of oppression while Whites monopolize wealth and social privilege (Bell, 1995a; Heath & McMahon, 1997; Sue et al., 2007). These institutionalized systems have led to disparities in the overall functioning and well-being of each group. Similarly, in developing countries—mostly occupied by people of color with a relative absence of Whites—individuals continue to struggle with attempts at modernization, economic independence, and securing daily necessities such as food, adequate shelter, and satisfactory health care (Gafar, 1998; Gasparini, Gutierrez, & Tornarolli, 2007; Leipziger, 2001). The parallels between the disenfranchisement of people of color in developed and developing nations are quite striking and are grounded in the same racist ideology that has led to a world system fraught with socioeconomic stratification that places Whites in positions of power and reinforces the marginalization of Blacks and other people of color (Kellecioglu, 2010).

The parallels between the experiences of people of color throughout the world also mirror the conditions of Blacks in America and the Caribbean. The lack of opportunities for upward mobility in places like Jamaica, Guyana, Trinidad, Antigua, and the remainder of the Caribbean has prompted many to seek opportunities in the United States, Canada, and the United Kingdom. However, immigration policy has also served to erect barriers along the lines of race. Prohibitive policies have worked to restrict the flow of Blacks from developing countries to developed countries (Bashi, 2004; Bashi & McDaniel, 1997; Bryce-Laporte, 1979). Bashi (2004) traces the transnational nature of anti-Black immigration policies that operate on a global level to ensure the exclusion of Blacks. Both Blacks in the United States and the Caribbean suffer under systems of oppression that maintain distinct differences in their manifestation but similarly restrict power, access, and mobility.

Immigration policy that determines access to U.S. visas has also worked in favor of U.S. capitalistic gains and self-interest. In instances where skilled labor has been needed, the United States has rapidly issued visas to people of color from developing countries, in some instances contributing to the "brain drain" of particular countries. Similarly, when the U.S. agricultural market necessitates an increase in laborers, immigrants are admitted into the United States, albeit temporarily, to work at menial jobs. Today, seasonal guest workers leave behind their families and flock to communities across the United States to fill jobs in hotels and on farms. Over the past 5 years, it is estimated that approximately half a million jobs have been filled by guest workers even during a time of economic crisis and high unemployment in the United States (Seminara, 2010).

Obtaining a visa to travel abroad is the first race- and class-based barrier faced by non-White immigrants from developing countries who have hopes of entering the United States. It is argued that "implicit and explicit racial biases still pervade all four major arenas of legal immigration: family-sponsored, employment-based, diversity and refugee" (Ogletree, 2000, p. 761). Despite seemingly race-neutral immigration guidelines, quotas have been applied, resulting in fewer visas being issued to people of color relative to the number of people that apply. Blacks face more barriers than most people of color.

Immigration policy on this side of the U.S. border is also

fraught with racial inequities. Today, evidence suggests that despite the prevalence of undocumented immigrants from Canada and Poland residing in the United States, undocumented immigrants from countries populated predominantly by people of color emerge as the focus of deportation efforts (Ogletree, 2000). Immigrants from the Dominican Republic, Haiti, Mexico, and Jamaica have been among those most targeted for deportation (Bryce-Laporte, 1979; Johnson, 1997).

An uncanny resemblance exists between current deportation laws and historical attempts to remove fugitive slaves from particular jurisdictions within the United States. Slave catchers seized fugitive slaves from the Caribbean wherever they found them, took them before a magistrate to obtain a certificate ordering removal of the individual from the state, and returned them to the jurisdiction from whence they had come (Franklin & Moss, 1994). Verbal accusation by a White person served as sufficient proof of fugitive status. In a similar vein, law enforcement officials have the right to hunt, detain, and deport Haitian refugees, while the state provides Cuban refugees protection under immigration laws (Ogletree, 2000).

Caribbean Blacks leave their homes in hopes of gaining access to better opportunities and resources in America, but they encounter social and structural limitations once they arrive in the United States (Baptiste, Hardy, & Lewis, 1997). Unlike the structural racism that affects Blacks in developing countries on a broader international scale, Black immigrants in the United States face glaring disparities between Whites and Blacks within the same nation. Black immigrants go from living in a country where resources are scarce to living in a country where resources are abundant—but only available to certain groups. As Blacks in America, immigrants contend with structural racism on the national level, as well as social stigmatization and racial microaggressions in their day-to-day experiences (Papademetriou & Jachimowicz, 2004; Rong & Brown, 2002; Waters, 1994).

Immigrants acknowledge the costs of leaving behind family and the natural beauty of their balmy Caribbean homelands in search of better opportunities, but they rarely understand the price of being subject to racism in the United States. According to

Feagin and McKinney (2003), the costs of being Black in America are vast. Racism in the United States negatively impacts the educational achievement and attainment of Blacks, creates stressful encounters leading to psychological and physical illnesses, contributes to subpar medical services, exposes individuals to unhealthy living conditions, and blocks access to jobs, promotions, and equitable pay (Conley, 1999; Feagin & McKinney, 2003; Harrell, 2010; Suárez-Orozco, 2000).

Race and the Integration of Black Immigrants in the United States

Research shows that more recent waves of White immigrants follow a path of straight-line assimilation. Scholars posit that White immigrants lose their ethnic distinctiveness over time; the White mainstream sweeps them in and they profit from the benefits of White social access and power. However, the mobility patterns of Black immigrants show a marked distinction from that of their White counterparts.

Immigrants become subject to the U.S. system of racial classification, which leads to the inequitable treatment of Black immigrants and other immigrants of color (Kao & Tienda, 1995; Rong & Brown, 2002; Sokamoto, Woo, & Kim, 2010; Waters, 1994). For instance, the poverty level of immigrants from many Asian and Latin American countries decreases or remains stable over time. However, Black immigrants experience a 26% increase in poverty levels between the first and second generations (Zhou, 1997). The integration of Black immigrants into low-income communities plagued by under-resourced, low-performing schools contributes to increased poverty levels in subsequent generations. Such disparities reflect the cost of being Black in America despite one's country of origin.

Vickerman (1999) argues that despite differences in culture and the historical manifestations of racism, African ancestry and phenotype are the most significant bases for discrimination in the United States. According to Vickerman (1999),

West Indians' encounter with racial discrimination is an integral part of their lives in America...because negative stereotypes regarding individuals who have been socially defined as Blacks are deeply engrained in society.... West Indians...feel their impact...[i]n their pursuit of upward mobility in this country.... (p. 91)

Bonilla-Silva (2002) argues that non-Whites have shared experiences of colonialism, oppression, exploitation, and racialization and therefore are not privy to privileges afforded to Whites. Still, Rong and Brown (2002) posit that Black immigrants face more than just racism and argue that they face multiple levels of disenfranchisement upon migrating to the United States. Immigrants of color often contend with racial discrimination, xenophobia, and lower-class status resulting from their integration into low-income communities of color and their lower-class status in their native country.

Research also suggests that despite higher levels of educational attainment for Black immigrants as compared to their Black American counterparts, Black immigrants enjoy only a 1% advantage in income. This demonstrates that Black immigrants are subject to inequitable wages despite their higher levels of education (Kalmijn, 1996). In some instances, Black immigrants are positioned as model minorities, a misleading depiction given their lower levels of educational achievement and attainment in comparison to Whites (Bashi & McDaniel, 1997). A comparison of Caribbean immigrants to White immigrants (Kasinitz, Mollenkopf, & Waters, 2002) showed that Whites were more likely to obtain undergraduate and graduate degrees and were less likely to drop out of college. Although some Caribbean immigrants demonstrate a slight advantage over Black Americans in the areas of education and income, the gap between White immigrants and Black immigrants is substantial (Rogers, 2006).

The dissonance that migration and subsequent experiences with racial discrimination create has historically led Caribbean immigrants to advocate for racial equity. However, the widespread engagement of Caribbean immigrants in U.S. racial politics has waxed and waned over time. Lara Putnam (2009) argues that a disproportionate number of pan-African thinkers came from the Caribbean in the early to mid 1900s. These pan-Africanists believed that racial oppression was widespread across the world, and only unified efforts could bring about racial parity. In supporting this notion, Putnam (2009) argues that

> voices across the Caribbean public sphere were speaking out about the common experiences of African peoples around the globe, about their common suffering and common aspirations, and about the need for collective action to make shared dreams a united reality. (p. 108)

Similarly, Black Power movements emerged from the Caribbean in the 1960s and 1970s, urging Blacks worldwide to unite against forces of oppression (Meeks, 2009).

While past iterations of racism made it clear that inequities were a function of racial discrimination regardless of immigrant background, more recent and insidious forms can be allusive and confounding. Limited exposure to racism in the Caribbean, coupled with more ambiguous forms of racism in the United States, has made it increasingly difficult for Caribbean immigrants to acknowledge the salience of race in the United States and in their own lives. During this time, within a context marked by aversive racial politics, it has become increasingly difficult for Caribbean immigrants to grasp the nature of U.S. racism and to recognize a need for racial solidarity with native-born Blacks.

Scholarship suggests that Caribbean immigrants in the United States have more recently come to reject a racialized identity, preferring to define themselves by nationality or ethnicity (Waters, 1999). Research in this area has often failed to acknowledge the complexities of racial identity development, particularly for individuals who were not reared in the U.S. context and have different ideas about and experiences with race. Racial identity development is deeply tied to an individual's personal experiences around issues of race. Evidence shows that racial politics are multifarious, fluid, contextually specific, and change over time (Suárez-Orozco, 2001). The rise of pan-African and Black Power movements occurred at times in history when migration to various parts of the world exposed Caribbean immigrants to overtly racist, institutionalized practices and personal affronts, as well as global economics that perpetuate poverty in countries densely populated by people of color (Meeks, 2009; Putnam, 2009). However, the changing face of racism has led to more subtle manifestations of racism that are more difficult to identify today than they were in past decades. Ac-

cording to Derald Wing Sue and fellow researchers (2007), contemporary racism

> (1) is more likely than ever to be disguised and covert and (2) has evolved
> from the "old fashioned" form, in which overt racial hatred and bigotry is
> consciously and publicly displayed, to a more ambiguous and nebulous
> form that is more difficult to identify and acknowledge. (p. 272)

These scholars argue that such manifestations of contemporary
racism play out in the form of racial microaggressions that are
"brief, everyday exchanges that send denigrating messages to people of color..." (p. 273). Sue and colleagues (2007) describe these
racial microaggressions as microassaults, microinsults, and microinvalidation. Microassaults are explicit forms of derogation like
verbal and non-verbal attacks and purposeful discrimination; microinsults are subtle snubs the perpetrator commits by accident;
and microinvalidation seeks to exclude or negate the experiences
of people of color (Sue et al., 2007). Microaggressions are often invisible to the perpetrator and easy for observers to ignore or diminish, which makes the dynamics around them complex.

In an article regarding the increasing migration of Caribbean
individuals to New York City in the late 1970s, Bryce-Laporte
(1979) asked, "Given their ambition, Protestant ethic, and Euro-
pean-colonial acculturation, what would have been their progress,
status, and power in the United States were they not Black or
brown and of neocolonial background?" (p. 223). She further posited, "In this sense these particular immigrants represent a special
prism of American racism." An underlying assumption of this
query is that Black immigrants bring with them the background
and skills that have typically ensured the success of White migrants; however, the complexities of both their race and colonial
history situate them within a unique social milieu. For Caribbean
immigrants, their immigrant status often makes them vulnerable
to workplace exploitation, irrespective of their educational attainment; they generally reside in racially segregated communities,
and as a result also attend racially segregated and underfunded
schools.

U.S. racism often depends on an identifiable African phenotype
and U.S. rules governing race. Americans perceive Caribbean im-

migrants as Black first, making them susceptible to the same interpersonal and institutionalized racism experienced by native-born Blacks. Under the "one-drop" rule, U.S. society erases Black immigrants' history with colonialism, shifting ideological notions of inequity, and ecological difference (Davis, 1991; Vickerman, 2001).

Black Immigrants, Identity Development, and School Achievement

The growing population of immigrants in the United States and the prevalence of first-, 1.5-, and second-generation immigrants in U.S. classrooms have led researchers in various fields to seek to understand the educational experiences of these groups. Findings in anthropology, sociology, and psychology suggest close ties between the identities of immigrant groups and educational outcomes (Chang & Le, 2010; Crosnoe & López Turley, 2011; Ogbu, 1991a, 1992; Waters, 1994, 1999; Yoon, 2012). However, research examining the ways in which identity development informs the education experiences and outcomes of the Black immigrant remain limited. The absence of such research is most profound in the field of education. This section highlights some of the foundational work of anthropologists and sociologists who seek to deconstruct the interrelated workings of immigrant status, identity formation, and educational outcomes of Black immigrant youth.

John Ogbu's Contribution to Understanding the Identities of Black Immigrant Youth

Over the last several decades, the work of anthropologist John Ogbu has been pivotal in inspiring scholarly debate that (1) acknowledges Black immigrants as an ethnically distinct group, (2) recognizes the unique positionality of Black immigrants who are striving for upward mobility in a country inundated with racial discrimination, and (3) maintains the salience of racial identity in determining upward mobility and school success.

Ogbu's work involved a comparative analysis of data on the school and community lives of racial minorities of immigrant and non-immigrant status, and his research brought recognition to ethnic and cultural variation among African descendants, something scholars long overlooked in favor of more monolithic and racially determined categorizations (Bashi & McDaniel, 1997; Foster, 2005). Ogbu separated the overarching umbrella of minorities into two groups: voluntary/immigrant minorities and involuntary/non-immigrant minorities. Voluntary minorities migrate willingly and for the purpose of economic gain and overall opportunities. Involuntary minorities, such as the descendants of American slaves and Native Americans, "are a part of the United States society because of slavery, conquest, or colonization, rather than by choice" (Ogbu, 1992, p. 290).

Ogbu found striking differences between voluntary and involuntary minorities (Ogbu, 1991a, 1992; Ogbu & Simons, 1998). His work reveals the connection between the history of a group, the current treatment of that group, and specific types of cultural models and identity development. He argued that these differing cultural models and identities determine various groups' engagement with mainstream society's values, expectations, and institutions.

Ogbu maintained that the "initial terms of incorporation" of a minority group into a society, as well as "subsequent discriminatory treatment," lead to differential responses, some more adaptable to the mainstream context than others (Obgu, 1991a, p. 10–11). Mickelson (1993) argues that involuntary immigrants tend to view their circumstances in comparison to their White counterparts, while voluntary immigrants compare their circumstances to those they have left behind in their native countries. Because of this, voluntary immigrants are more likely to feel financially stable. In contrast, native-born Blacks more readily discern race-based inequities between Blacks and the White majority. Unlike involuntary minorities, who are quite adept at recognizing racial discrimination, voluntary immigrants often attribute discrimination to xenophobia (Ogbu, 1991a; Rong & Brown 2001; Vickerman, 1999). As a result, involuntary minorities view racism as a more formidable obstacle.

John Ogbu analyzed historical, cultural, and environmental characteristics to determine how minority groups develop particular cultural models and identities and how culture and identities affect a group's ability to gain access to mainstream America (Gibson, 2005; Ogbu, 1991b). Ogbu theorized that cultural models, community forces, and group identities are central to understanding the adjustment and mobility of immigrant groups. He called the resulting framework a "cultural-ecological model." This model considers what Ogbu called "system factors" ("the way…minorities are treated or mistreated in education in terms of educational policies [and] pedagogy") and "community forces" ("the way minorities perceive and respond to schooling as a consequence of their treatment") (Ogbu & Simons, 1998, p. 158). Ogbu's theory postulates that system factors such as the treatment children receive in schools, as well as the historical and current societal treatment of minority groups, impact communities' and groups' attitudes and behavior toward learning, school, and school officials (Gibson, 2005). In other words, minority groups experience system factors and consequently develop strategies and coping mechanisms for dealing with them.

Ogbu focused on how specific minority communities developed "community forces" as a response to minority status and how well those community forces meshed with the values of mainstream America. His initial work explored a variety of ethnic and racial minority groups, but it became increasingly controversial as he applied this theoretical model to Blacks. Ogbu argued that distinct perspectives and experiences regarding race and cultural strategies used to cope with American racism determine the academic success of voluntary and involuntary Black immigrants.

However, despite the seminal insight offered by Ogbu's work, his analysis of immigrant identity and upward mobility is not immune to critique. Ogbu used his cultural-ecological framework to argue that oppositional coping strategies of Black Americans lead to their underachievement in schools as compared to Black immigrant groups. However, numerous scholars argued that Ogbu's work did not account for variables such as self-selection in immigrant groups (Thomas, 2012) and the pervasive deleterious effects of American racism (Morris & Monroe, 2009). Ogbu's work sparked immense controversy in the research world and has prompted some researchers to study further the ways in which various groups of Blacks respond to issues of race and inequity in America.

Moving Beyond Ogbu

Drawing upon many of Ogbu's concepts, Mary Waters conducted an ethnographic study of 83 second-generation Black immigrant adolescents in New York City. In this study, Waters explored how identities shape perceptions of race and racism and influence school achievement in the children of Caribbean immigrants. She found that second-generation Caribbean American youth adopted one of the following identities: Black American identity, ethnic or hyphenated identity, or an immigrant identity. Waters argued: "For most of the respondents their self-identification...entailed their coming to terms with how they were different from Black Americans" (Waters, 1999, p. 64).

Waters's findings paint a somewhat different picture than do those of Ogbu. Data from her research show that 28% of respondents embraced an immigrant identity, 30% held a hyphenated-ethnic identity, and 42% adopted a Black American identity (Waters, 1994). In all, 70% of participants who reported Black American and immigrant identities either saw themselves as similar to Black Americans or held neutral opinions of Black Americans.

The typologies Waters developed of each ethnic identity and the links between these identities and educational profiles represent a significant contribution to our understanding of Caribbean immigrant youth. Caribbean American youth who identified as Black Americans showed more signs of assimilating to Black American culture in their speech, choices of attire, and music. This group also tended to perform less well in school (Waters, 1994, 1999). Waters attributed the academic underachievement of these youth to the development of an oppositional identity that embraces anti-school behaviors. Waters claimed that immigrant youth who identified as Black Americans experienced more academic challenges as a result of their oppositional identities. She maintained that West Indian students who identified closely with their parents' country of origin and ethnicity and separated themselves from native-born Blacks tended to do better in schools (Waters, 1994, 1999). She attributed better educational outcomes to the fact that these youth embraced their families' cultural values, including hard work and desire for socioeconomic mobility.

Ogbu and Waters recognized the ethnic heterogeneity of Blacks in America. While their work has contributed greatly to this field, many researchers have extended their findings and offered new insights regarding the experiences of Black immigrants. These successive pieces offer great contributions to understanding the educational experiences of Black immigrants.

To expand on Waters's analysis on identity, Rong and Brown (2002) provide alternate explanations as to why Black immigrants may adopt a Black American identity. Drawing on research conducted by Bashi and McDaniel (1997) in their explanation, Rong and Brown state that U.S. society thrusts Black American identity upon Black immigrants despite their attempts to avert a loss in status. Racial classifications are forced upon all immigrants as they assimilate into society and are subject to the system of racial stratification in the United States.

Immigrants do not merely choose their racial and ethnic identities. Instead these identities are shaped by multiple factors that lie within the immigrant community as well as the context into which immigrants migrate. When Black immigrants do not adhere to stereotypical notions of blackness, they often face harsh criticisms from Black and White Americans alike. As cited in Rong and Brown (2002), Vickerman shared the experience of a college student, arguing, "Jamaican students found themselves being referred to as 'oreos' by White students. A Jamaican student interpreted this as his White classmates' efforts to 'quell the cognitive dissonance that resulted from encountering Blacks who outperformed them'" (p. 260). This quote reveals, among other things, the pressures Caribbean immigrants are often under to conform to dominant notions of blackness.

More recent research on Black immigrants has also taken a closer look at the way generational status impacts the experiences of Black immigrants. According to Rong and Brown (2001), differences in how successive generations of immigrants fare in America reflect the importance of how identity develops in successive generations and its impact on educational attainment and socioeconomic mobility. Some evidence suggests that second-generation

Americans (children born in the United States to immigrant parents) often surpass their parents in terms of educational attainment and income gain. While data show that first-generation Black immigrants may perform better than their children in mathematics, their children often outperform them in reading because of better proficiency in Standard English. Rong and Brown found, however, that by the third generation, the achievement of Black immigrants is on a par with native-born Blacks (2001). They theorize that these distinctions exist because second-generation Americans still hold to their parents' belief system and work ethic and identify closely with their parents' immigrant status, while third-generation Americans identify more closely with Black Americans and thus lose ground in terms of the educational achievement and economic gain acquired by their predecessors.

Race and Education in the United States

For decades the intersection of race and formal education in the United States has been at the forefront of scholarly debate. Scholars agree that education—which should lead to social and economic mobility—continues to perpetuate the marginalization of people of color and disproportionately propel Whites into positions of power (Bowles & Ginits, 1976; Feagin & McKinney, 2003; Freire, 2004; Solorzano, 1995). Education has long been used as a tool for control and the inculcation of White supremacist hegemonic ideology. According to Willinsky (1998),

> Education is no small player in giving meaning to...differences. We are schooled in differences great and small, in borderlines and boundaries, in historical struggles and exotic practices, all of which extend meaning to these differences. We are taught to discriminate in both the most innocent and fateful ways so that we can appreciate the differences between civilized and primitive, West and East, first and third worlds. We become adept at identifying and distinguishing features of this country, that culture, those people. We are educated in what we take to be the true nature of difference. (p. 1)

Beginning with European imperialism and colonialism, formal education has been used as a tool to legitimate the domination of various groups of people and support ideas regarding race, culture, and nationality used to divide and "educate" the world (Willinsky, 1998). Today, education still inculcates values that distinguish the civilized from the primitive and sort people based on race, culture, and nationality. In particular, educational institutions teach young people to loathe that which represents the primitive—people of color—and appreciate the civilized—Whites. Schools pathologize marginalized students of color as lazy and incompetent and therefore in need of redemption by way of integration into and acceptance of White values and norms (Freire, 2004). School officials carry out these practices in the name of "peace" and "freedom," refusing to call it domination or oppression (Freire, 2004).

While in the past Blacks were denied access to educational institutions, more recent forms of institutionalized racism lead to subpar schools and school conditions for Blacks (Kozol, 1991; Peller, 1995), racially stratified classes within racially diverse institutions (Yosso, 2002; Bell, 1995b), and unequal treatment between Blacks and Whites within the same classrooms (Freeman, 1995). Often grounded in state and federal policies, these practices perpetuate disparate educational experiences and outcomes between students of color and Whites (G. Lopez, 2003).

On a local level, schools also support racially charged practices perceived as neutral, objective, and even merit based (Lynn, 1999). In schools across the country, Black students suffer the consequences of macro-level institutionalized racism as well as commonplace microaggressions. While many schools continue to be segregated along racial lines due to *de facto* protection under the law (Bell, 1995a, 1995b; Freeman, 1995; Lynn, 1999; Peller, 1995), Blacks who attend integrated schools are often marginalized within those spaces. According to Bell (1995b), "racial balance measures have often altered the racial appearance of dual school systems without eliminating racial discrimination" (p. 25). Even in well-resourced, racially diverse schools, Black students are subject to a second-rate education (Oakes, 2008). In a national debate early in the 20th century, W. E. B. Du Bois attested, "A mixed school with poor and unsympathetic teachers, with hostile public opinion, and no teaching of truth concerning Black folk, is bad" (cited in Bell, 1995a, p. 18). Du Bois argued that conditions in diverse schools can be such that issues concerning Black students are exempt from the curriculum or poorly represented in the curriculum, and students could be subject to harassment by White teachers.

Additionally, the exhaustive reliance on standardized tests as a measure of academic ability has successfully kept Black students from accessing high-level academic courses (Bell, 1995b; Lynn, 1999; Yosso, 2002). Similarly, tracking—a practice that "has been critiqued for providing inadequate and inequitable education to students in low-level courses, for separating students in integrated schools along race and class lines, and for perpetuating unequal access to a college-bound curriculum" (Rubin, 2008, p. 647)—also restricts access to quality education for Blacks. Wells and Serna (1996) argue that over time tracking practices have reinforced *de facto* segregation within school buildings, relegating poor students and students of color to classes for those of lower ability and thus providing them with a lower-quality education.

Though educational policies eventually called for "detracking" public schools, no funding was allocated, and schools received very little direction on how to offer instruction in detracked schools and classrooms (Loveless, 1999; Oakes, 2008). Ultimately, schools rarely executed detracking policies—instead they merely hid tracking (Oakes, 2008). No Child Left Behind (NCLB) legislation nominally sought to lessen race and other gaps in achievement by holding schools "accountable" for educating all children as measured by results on standardized tests; however, the policy failed to examine tracking as a problematic practice (Oakes, 2008). Instead, NCLB legislation has reinforced tracking practices as schools offer instruction to groups of students based on their perceived academic needs, restricting curriculum in lower-level classes to rigid test prep while high-level classes engage in complex enriching instruction (Watanabe, 2008). Similarly, Oakes (2008) asserts:

> Test-based accountability approached in separate classes designated for "gifted" and "regular" students worked against their achieving [racial parity]. As teachers adjusted their instruction to help students score well on high-stakes, "standards-based" tests, the teachers offered subtle, but powerful differences in students' educational opportunities. Students in the "academically gifted" classes read and wrote more widely, tackled more thought provoking assignments, and got more feedback than their

peers in the "regular" classes where test-preparation occupied the lion's share of instructional time. Intended to narrow the achievement gap, these differences between the "regular" and "gifted" classes helped to widen that gap. (p. 706)

Institutionalized tracking practices disproportionately affect Black students (Oakes, 2008; Rogers & Freelon, 2012; Rubin, 2008).

Research links experience of racism to symptoms of depression and risky behavior in Black American and Caribbean American youth (Seaton et al., 2008), which pose detriments to educational success. Several studies have documented the ways in which internalized notions of academic inadequacies—commonly referred to as *stereotype threat*—can negatively influence the identity and academic functioning of marginalized groups (Steele, 1997; Suárez-Orozco, 2000). As a consequence of tracking and consistent dismissive and pejorative messages of Black students' place in schools, Black students often expect to do poorly and thus help to reinforce their own underachievement. They also diminish the appeal of academic success by ridiculing high achievers. Woodson (1933) described the internalization of inferior status:

If you control a man's thinking, you do not have to worry about his action. When you determine what a man shall think, you do not have to concern yourself about what he will do. If you make a man feel that he is inferior, you do not have to compel him to accept his inferior status, for he will seek it himself. If you make a man think that he is justly an outcast, you do not have to order him to the back door. He will go without being told; and if there is no back door, his very nature will demand one. (p. 154)

Research regarding the experiences of Black youth in schools seldom identifies whether students come from an immigrant background. However, one could assert that Black Americans and Caribbean immigrant youth experience racism directed at Blacks in similar ways. Blacks as a whole face discrimination related to low academic expectations, and inferior, racially segregated schools in low-income communities or low-level classes in racially diverse schools (Portes & Rumbaut, 2005; Portes & Zhou, 1993). Though the experiences of Black immigrants may differ slightly in relation to their Black American counterparts, Black immigrants are in no way exempt from race discrimination in educational settings. Educational trends that promote White, middle-class values at the expense of other racial and ethnic groups marginalize all non-Whites. Furthermore, the culture of schools and nature of the curricular content taught in schools seldom address the interests and lived realities of students of color (Suárez-Orozco, 2000; Suárez-Orozco, Onaga, & Lardemelle, 2010; Pinder, 2012).

According to Zhou (1997), "neither valedictorians [nor] delinquents are atypical among immigrant children regardless of racial and socioeconomic backgrounds" (p. 72). These distinctions in school success depend on the immigrant group, their class background in their native country and the United States, the extent to which they live in highly segregated communities, and whether families maintain their native culture and child-rearing practices (Portes & Rumbaut, 2001). While some students perform well, others perform at rates similar to their native counterparts, and some below. Although some researchers argue that Black immigrants typically outperform their Black American counterparts (Massey et al., 2007; Rong & Brown, 2002), Suárez-Orozco (2001) argues that the patterns of achievement for immigrant students vary more widely than their counterparts. Nonetheless, race remains a significant issue for Black immigrants as institutionalized forms of racism mark their school experiences.

A New Paradigm for Understanding Links Between Parenting, School Experiences, and the Identity of Caribbean American Youth

As highlighted in the previous section, studies on Black immigrants overwhelmingly argue that racial and ethnic identity informs the educational outcomes of immigrant youth. Researchers hypothesize that youth who do not hold to their parents' immigrant ethic risk experiencing downward mobility and that in subsequent generations, the progeny of immigrants lose rather than maintain an advantage. In essence, over time, the racial politics of the United States overcomes Black immigrants and strips them of the energy, motivation, and rich ideas that often prompted their migration to begin with. They lose the ability to move about their daily lives with little consideration of race and become increasingly aware of the racial stigma their mere presence engenders.

For Black immigrants, Americanization is tantamount to racialization as immigrants shift from ethnic and national identities to become both Black and American. Newfound experiences with racial trauma not only change the identities of immigrants and their children; they also cause changes in parenting strategies and how parents teach their children to understand and cope with U.S. racism. As a result, transnational identities, racialized experiences, and socialization practices coalesce for Black immigrants.

Researchers have determined that identity informs mobility, but research lacks an in-depth analysis of the intersectionality of race, class, ecological factors, and immigrant status on the various types of identities adopted by Caribbean immigrant youth. Together, perceptions of and experiences with race, class, and community context inform the racial and ethnic socialization messages shared by parents and thus shape the identities of Caribbean American youth.

Racial Socialization: Preparing and Protecting Black Children

Coleman describes socialization as the way in which "children come to internalize and conform to societal expectations and become productive adults by acquiring the necessary competencies to do so" (2006, p. 4). Socialization also includes the "process by which young people learn to negotiate, and participate in, multiple, and existing worlds" (Stanton-Salazar, 1997, p. 20). In other words, children learn the rules of the society in which they live through socialization.

Today's society exposes children to a litany of socializing agents (i.e., media, peers, educators, etc.), but parents and family generally play a crucial role in socializing children and youth. Parents of Black children in the United States assist their children in learning the unwritten rules of participation in a world where their race and ethnicity pose risks to healthy growth and development. Black American parents bear a burden that parents of White children do not.

Black skin has long made individuals vulnerable to numerous atrocities and discriminatory sanctions. Black parents continuously fear that their children might experience teacher bias and police brutality and harassment, and might internalize notions of racial and ethnic inferiority. Psychologists have studied the ways in which parents have responded to these concerns (Caughy, Randolph, & O'Campo, 2002; Stevenson & Davis, 2004; Stevenson, Reed, Bodison, & Bishop, 1997; Thornton et al., 1990), finding that Black parents attempt to mitigate the ill effects of racial minority status and racism by employing specific socialization strategies.

Researchers refer to socialization practices designed to help children navigate race relations and racial identity as *racial socialization* (Stevenson et al., 1997; Thornton, Chatters, Taylor, & Allen, 1990); some researchers also use the term to refer to any ethnic or cultural socialization (Bentley, Adams, & Stevenson, 2008). According to Peters (1985), racial socialization is "the responsibility of raising physically and emotionally healthy children who are Black in a society where Black has a negative connotation" (p. 161). Bentley and colleagues (2008) refer to racial socialization as strategies that seek to "counter and protect [Black] children from malicious stereotypes that may limit their opportunities [and] to promote healthy functioning through adulthood" (p. 255). Racial socialization messages help Black children adapt to environments in which they must function outside of their cultural frames of reference, develop strategies for dealing with discriminatory experiences, and learn to interact with others across racial and ethnic boundaries.

Researchers break down racial and ethnic socialization practices into the categories of racial pride, mistrust of racial outsiders, preparation for discrimination, and emphasis on the equality of all people (Hughes & Chen, 1999). Racial socialization may constitute a parent telling a daughter that she does not need to straighten her hair to be beautiful, or telling a son not to wear a hooded sweatshirt at night to avoid harassment by police. Expressed preferences for darker or lighter skin also send messages to children about race. Children may also prompt racial socialization messages by telling their parents that the teacher yells at the Black students in their class but not at the White students, and research to date fails to measure this process. Parents employ these racial socialization practices in a variety of ways and to differing degrees depending on the characteristics of children, the surrounding environment, and parental experiences. Just as parents employ diverse approaches, children receive and utilize these strategies in diverse ways.

According to Stevenson and his fellow researchers (2002), protective, proactive, and adaptive processes are central to "providing youth a healthy psychological approach to the world..." (p. 88). Again, this demonstrates variation in the intended purposes of racial socialization practices. Stigmatized groups utilize protective measures as a means of shielding themselves from abuse directed at individuals or their respective group. On the other hand, proactive measures of racial socialization serve to instill in children a sense of pride and self-worth in the face of discrimination. Proactive racial socialization would include the tendency to tell children "that they are special and ought to be proud of their cultural heritage" (Stevenson & Davis, 2004, p. 360). By using proactive measures, minority parents employ tools to buffer racism experiences before the incidents occur.

Racial socialization research is mainly situated in the field of psychology, where quantitative analyses prevail as the dominant mode of inquiry. Consequently, very few studies demonstrate the processes by which racial socialization occurs. Several mixed-methods studies employ the use of open-ended interviews as a qualitative component of data collection (Thomas & Speight, 1999; Thornton et al., 1990), but these data do not fully capture the delicate nuances of how racial socialization evolves from day to day. Quantitative measures ask questions such as "How important do you think it is to discuss race with your child?" or "How often do you tell your child that he/she must work harder than Whites to succeed?"

Racial socialization research tends to focus on what parents say to their children about race and how often they share these messages. However, parents may employ other forms of racial socialization such as depictions of race in the home environment (Caughy et al., 2002), parental modeling of intraracial and interracial interactions, and adult conversations about racial experiences.

Factors That Shape Racial and Ethnic Socialization Messages and Their Influence on Youth

The quantitative thrust of racial socialization research carries many benefits, but also limitations. Nevertheless, racial socialization remains a dynamic concept with the potential to capture the interplay between the traits of youth, perspectives of parents and other adult influences, and various ecological factors. Things like neighborhood characteristics, socioeconomic status, gender, and age shape the messages youth receive and, in turn, youth's responses to those messages. Quantitative research has been instrumental in helping to determine the relationship between various racial socialization messages and their impact on the identities, development, and school achievement of youth.

Given the wide array of characteristics that inform racial socialization messages and responses, parents rarely employ proscribed racial socialization practices. Instead, racial socialization messages respond to the vicissitudes of children's racialized experiences coupled with parents' notions of perceived needs and threats. These factors add to racial socialization's complexity. Parents' knowledge of how race and racism operate, the perceived effectiveness of specific coping mechanisms, and the messages parents themselves received during their childhood all create variation in parental practices.

Neighborhood demographics arguably play a key role in determining the racial and ethnic socialization practices of parents. Scott (2003) found that in racially diverse communities, parents recognize an increased possibility of experiencing interracial and cultural conflict and therefore direct socialization practices at assisting youth in finding supportive networks. Typically, these networks take the form of racially homogeneous groups where youth find acceptance and shared experience of racial challenges. Such networks can play a key role in mitigating symptoms of depression and other risk factors that result from culturally hostile environments and prolonged exposure to discriminatory treatment.

In another study, Stevenson and colleagues (2002) discovered that parental responses to racism vary depending on the gender of the child *and* the degree of neighborhood diversity. In areas with low cultural diversity, parents respond differently to perceived threats directed at boys as compared to girls. Parents expect boys to be the targets of harassment and therefore use racial socialization messages to help them cope with antagonism. On the other hand, they give girls messages about racial pride and cultural identity. Stevenson and fellow researchers hypothesize that variations in racial socialization messages between boys and girls in contexts with low cultural diversity reflect the expectations that boys will become protectors and girls will become nurturers. Parenting strategies prepare youth to fulfill these assumed gender roles. Antithetically, however, high diversity communities bring about different racial socialization messages. In these settings, boys tend to receive more messages of self-pride and strategies for dealing with discrimination. These findings give evidence to the ways in which the demographic characteristics of a community can shape parental perceptions of children's needs and hence the thrust of racial socialization messages.

In addition to community demographics such as neighborhood diversity, the culture of the surrounding community and the home environment have implications for racial socialization. According to Caughy and colleagues (2002), if a neighborhood has a "negative social climate" characterized by delinquency and crime, parents generally prepare their children to cope with racism and discrimination and promote the mistrust of others. The researchers found that depictions of Africentric culture in the home environment and culturally appropriate toys, clothing, and pictures correlated with better cognitive competence. However, gender and neighborhood context affected this correlation. Girls produced better scores on cognitive measures regardless of neighborhood, but there was stronger association between cognitive scores and an Africentric home environment in higher-risk neighborhoods. Boys only showed better cognitive performance related to Africentric items in the home if they lived in high-risk communities.

These findings suggest that boys and girls respond differently to racial socialization messages and that parents may also make decisions about racial socialization that reflect children's responses to discrimination. As suggested by Caughy, Randolph, and O'Campo (2002), boys and girls receive different types of racial socialization messages. Such multifarious aspects of the relationship between racial stimuli and individual responses add complexity to homogeneous notions of how groups develop coping mechanisms.

In a study on the racial socialization practices of both mothers and fathers, McHale and colleagues (2006) employed a within-family design to determine whether parental and child gender, parenting styles, and children's age influence racial socialization practices. They hypothesized that even within the same family, racial socialization experiences would vary. Data from the study suggested that mothers engaged in more preparation for bias and the cultural socialization of older children in the family than younger children. Findings also demonstrated that fathers engaged in more racial socialization practices with their sons than their daughters. Researchers hypothesized that fathers engaged in racial socialization with their sons because of their experiences with discrimination directed at Black males in particular. They found that when fathers engaged their children in cultural socialization, children demonstrated fewer symptoms of depression.

A litany of findings from racial socialization research suggests that racial and ethnic socialization is an iterative process informed by a multitude of dimensions. The aforementioned studies illustrate several key ideas: (1) the neighborhood and community contexts play an integral role in determining parental racial socialization messages; (2) racial socialization messages occur in explicit forms (e.g., verbal promotion of mistrust of others) and implicit forms (e.g., parental choices of Black or White dolls); (3) the characteristics of youth (e.g., gender) influence the messages parents share and the results of these messages (e.g., cognitive performance, evidence of depressive symptoms); and (4) parental characteristics (e.g., gender) and experiences with race and racism (e.g., fathers' experiences with racial discrimination) inform the extent to which parents engage in racial socialization and the types of messages embedded in racial socialization practices. These themes illustrate the multidimensionality of racial and ethnic socialization and have potential to inform our limited understanding of the factors that contribute to Caribbean immigrants' process of racialization in the United States.

Caribbean American Youth and the Benefits of a Qualitative Understanding of Racial & Ethnic Socialization

Although scholars in the fields of sociology and anthropology have begun to explore the racial and ethnic identities of Caribbean immigrants (Ogbu, 1992; Rong & Fitchett, 2008; Vickerman, 2001; Waters, 1999), racial and ethnic socialization research stemming from the field of psychology has historically focused on the experiences of Black Americans. Only recently have a few scholars in the field of psychology begun to parse data to identify trends related to Blacks of immigrant origin.

Racial and ethnic socialization research shows that native-born Blacks have extensive experience with the workings of U.S. racism that guides their assessment of what children need in order to adapt healthy identities and successfully function in a majority-White country. Caribbean immigrants often lack this context or knowledge of the history of U.S. racism and its changing manifestations over time, but still seek to raise emotionally and psychologically healthy Black children in a country that despises blackness. Caribbean immigrant parents' transnational notions of race—ideas they bring with them from their respective countries—constrain this ability. Caribbean immigrant parents' limited exposure to interpersonal racism, however, does not mitigate the impact of racial minority status on their children. According to Suárez-Orozco (2000), the costs and pressures of migration, structural barriers, and racist encounters place overwhelming stress on their developing psyches. With parents who don't quite understand U.S. racism, 1.5- and second-generation Caribbean American youth must often assume the responsibility of navigating the rough terrain of U.S. racial politics with little parental support.

Despite Caribbean immigrants' absence from racial socialization research, racial and ethnic socialization frameworks can offer provocative insight into not only how Caribbean youth identify, but also how socializing agents such as schools and parents shape the development, dispositions, and academic engagement of youth. Unlike previous studies that examine the various identities adopted by youth and support broadly conceived collective identities (Ogbu,

1991a; 1992; Waters, 1994, 1999), a racial socialization framework highlights the assistance individuals faced with particular contextual demands receive in making meaning of the world and their role within established racial and ethnic hierarchies. This allows for a more complex analysis of how diverse groups of Blacks navigate experiences around race, and it further evidences the usefulness of racial and ethnic socialization frameworks in examining how Caribbean American youth conceive of and respond to race and racism in a multiracial school environment.

Socialization research has had a pronounced impact on our understanding of the symbiotic relationship between ecological factors and the developmental characteristics of children and youth. Such a framework moves us beyond gross generalizations of the Caribbean immigrant experience to consider individual complexities. Children act not as passive recipients of socialization practices, but instead as active participants in a relational interplay between environments and individuals. This interplay deeply impacts the experiences of Caribbean American youth as ecological implications of the U.S. context and transnational discourses on race and ethnicity influence socialization messages and youth's responses to these messages.

Researchers expand the benefits of a racial and ethic socialization framework when we utilize qualitative modes of inquiry to examine nuanced processes such as how the interplay between what happens at home, in school, and the larger community shapes youth's understanding of their place in the U.S. system of racial classification; how youth understand their racial and ethnic identities and the relationship between them; when and how youth rely on ethnic and racial identities; how youth understand their parents' attempts at racial and ethnic socialization; how youth utilize their own agency in determining their identities; and day-to-day experiences that shift and shape identities.

While quantitative methodologies have added to our understandings of the dynamic interplay between various child, parent, and community characteristics and racial socialization, the field lacks a richly textured analysis of how racial and ethnic socialization processes evolve and how parental transnational notions of self also shape these processes. A qualitative approach to racial and ethnic socialization research can help us to examine what happens in the daily lives of youth and how school experiences and other environmental factors work together to inform youth's identities and strategies for self-preservation and upward mobility.

I approached this project with the understanding that "individuals seek understanding of the world in which they live and work. They develop subjective meanings of their experiences [and]...these meanings are varied and multiple" (Creswell, 2004, p. 8). In this work, I aim to capture how Caribbean American parents and children make meaning of their experiences. In studying the experiences and perspectives of 1.5- and second-generation Caribbean American youth, it is important to understand how they negotiate their subjective meanings of the world through social, historical, and cultural norms. For this project, I focused mainly on the socialization messages Caribbean American youth receive from their parents, teachers, and peers, which shape their subjective meanings pertaining to race, class, ethnicity, and education in the United States. Students' realities of living and attending school in a racially and ethnically diverse middle-income community further complicate these meanings. I have attempted to describe ways in which students' understanding, their individual perspectives, and realities within the school environment mediate parents' realities and socialization practices.

Using qualitative research methods, I crafted a research design best suited to address the aforementioned foci of the study. In particular, ethnographic observations within the school context and a series of in-depth and informal interviews with parents, their children, teachers, and administrators constituted the bulk of the data collection process. I also used questionnaires to identify consistencies and possible areas of disjuncture regarding socialization messages transmitted to children about race, ethnicity, and education. In addition, I collected artifacts representing participants' perspectives on race and ethnicity. By using an array of qualitative methods, I was able to justify themes by identifying ways in which these themes were presented across various categories of data. According to Hammersley and Atkinson (1995), "data source triangulation involves the comparison of data relating to the same phenomenon but deriving from different phases of the fieldwork"

(p. 230). The triangulation of data was central to ensuring the accuracy and depth of the analysis.

Moving Forward: Transnationalism, Racial and Ethnic Socialization, and Identity Negotiations

This study is the first of its kind to embark upon a rich qualitative examination of two primary socializing agents—parents *and* schools—and their impact on the racialization process for Caribbean American youth. Together, an examination of messages and experiences from school and the homes of Caribbean American youth unearth the various facets of "Becoming a Black American." This study reconceptualizes racial and ethnic socialization, as the field of psychology understands it, by treating racial and ethnic socialization as two distinct categories that are informed by the transnational lens of immigrant parents and youth. Additionally, this work goes beyond the typical focus on the racial and ethnic socialization practices of parents to include the ways in which educational institutions engage forms of racial and ethnic socialization. Caribbean immigrants do not arrive in the United States as clean slates. Although immigrants often lack experience with U.S. notions of race, Caribbean immigrants bring their own ideas about what it means to be Black and of a Caribbean nationality. Prominent works on Caribbean immigrants describe their ethnic identity as mostly grounded in their disdain for Black Americans, or, to put it another way, they emphasize an ethnic identity because of internalized racism (Rogers, 2006; Waters, 1994, 1999). This premise holds little regard for the meaning that Caribbean immigrants give to their ethnicity and culture prior to migration. Transnationalism, the concept that an individual can both physically and mentally "live" in two spaces, helps us to understand that Caribbean immigrants' perspectives on U.S. politics of race are not simply grounded in what they see, hear, or experience on U.S. soil. Instead, realities outside of the United States inform what Caribbean immigrants do in the United States and how they perceive the United States. Acknowledgment of this opens up possibilities for understanding and analyzing Caribbean immigrant parents' ideas about race and ethnicity and hence the socialization messages they transmit to their children.

Fouran and Glick-Schiller (2002) define transnational migration as "a process of movement and settlement across international borders in which individuals maintain or build multiple networks of connection to their country of origin" (p. 171). This process may include travel between countries, sending remittances back home, being involved in political processes in both places, and maintaining social and familial ties, to name a few. Growing evidence shows that these transnational processes are not limited to first-generation migrants; 1.5- and second-generation youth also maintain transnational ties (Perlmann, 2002). Perlmann (2002) also argues that second-generation transnationalism might be shaping the future ethnic identification of individuals who reside in the United States. If today's youth have more connections to their parents' country of origin through transnational ties, they are all the more open to multiple, fluid interpretations of their racial and ethnic selves.

Transnationalism as an analytic underpinning of this work forces us to acknowledge the role of the host community and the relationship between experiences and perspectives grounded on both sides of international borders. The pervasive notion that Caribbean immigrants embrace ethnic identities as a means of distancing themselves from Black Americans does not account for the relationships between Caribbean immigrants and Black Americans in the U.S. context. Whether the Black American community readily accepts Caribbean immigrants or shuns them and positions them as outsiders has critical implications for whether individuals seek to maintain ethnic distinctiveness. It forces us to look at notions of belonging outside of ethnic enclaves and participation in broader U.S. networks as central to a transnational existence.

Caribbean immigrants' views, informed by transnational experiences, also guide their engagement with racial and ethnic socialization of their children. While the racial and ethnic socialization framework is useful in broadening our conceptualization of the process of racialization and Americanization for Caribbean immigrants, it blurs the distinction between racial and ethnic socialization (Hughes et al., 2006). Although both terms are rather broad, and ethnic groups receive racial socialization and racial groups experience ethnic socialization, in this study I make a clear distinction between the two. Ethnic socialization pertains to parental guidance around cultural traits, religious practices, and values germane to a group of people connected to a particular region. In the case of Caribbean immigrants, ethnic socialization describes processes attributed to cultural traits derived from immigrants' Caribbean background and perceived as distinct traits of those who possess membership in this group. Racial socialization, on the other hand, speaks specifically to the correlation between one's ancestry and skin color and how membership in a particular racial group impacts individuals' identities and how outsiders perceive that group. I argue that racial and ethnic socialization influence one another, and at times intersect, but in the case of Caribbean immigrants should be considered separately.

Understanding ethnic socialization practices of Caribbean immigrant parents is key to identifying how Caribbean immigrants and their children experience and interpret the world and how that results in certain responses and identities. As previously stated in this chapter, past studies have demonstrated that ethnic identity is closely tied to academic success. However, research rarely asks how people derive these particular identities. By looking at how transnational lenses shape racial and ethnic socialization practices of children who also receive messages about race in schools, we get to understand how two major socializing agents work together to inform the racial and identity negotiations of Caribbean American youth.

In this chapter I've attempted to bring together ideas from multiple disciplines to create a more dynamic framework for understanding the experiences and perspectives of Caribbean immigrants and their 1.5- and second-generation Caribbean American children as they become fully enmeshed in Black America. I have brought together works from anthropologists (Ogbu, 1991a; Waters, 1994, 1999), sociologists (Vickerman, 2001), psychologists (Bentley et al., 2008), political scientists (Rogers, 2006), and historians (Perlmann, 2002) to inform this multidisciplinary work and its implications for identity, the incorporation of Caribbean immigrants into U.S. society, and for education. Given the limited attention paid to this population, I have taken the most foundational frameworks available to date to push my understanding to another level and propel forward my conceptualization of how identities form and how parents and citizens can pursue healthy identities and positive educational outcomes for Black children. The information presented here helps to frame the experiences of Caribbean immigrant parents and youth presented in subsequent chapters.

CHAPTER TWO

Life Narratives: Identities in Transition

After wrapping up the CWT ("Can We Talk?") project in June of the prior school year, I began the next school year by exploring only the experiences of Caribbean American students. My comfort with students, teachers, and school personnel made my transition to working with Caribbean American students and families rather smooth. I solicited the contact information of Morristown students who expressed interest in participating in this study and began calling Caribbean parents to further discuss the parameters of the study. Calling the homes of children whose families hailed from various regions of the Caribbean, I heard a multiplicity of accents and languages indicative of distinct cultural and ethnic backgrounds. In several instances, I reached Creole-speaking parents and grandparents from Haiti, whose thick accents and inability to speak English created barriers to communicating. I also spoke with parents from the English-speaking Caribbean, and while I could understand these parents very well—they shared marked similarities to my family's dialect—their accents, as much as the language barriers in other cases, bespoke the intersections and tensions often endemic to the amalgamation of several distinct cultures under one roof.

Although it was often difficult to distinguish Caribbean American and Black American students from one another at school, the first meeting with parents of Caribbean American students reflected a very different reality. The following vignette demonstrates the ways in which parents' ethnic and cultural markers came alive in the midst of their Caribbean comrades.

> As parents entered the school library for our meeting, I could identify the areas of the Caribbean from which each migrated. The first parent to arrive was a man with a very smooth, dark-skinned complexion, with a broad nose and a nice smile. He was dressed flawlessly in a blazer, dress shirt, and slacks and entered with a cool swagger. I knew he was Haitian even before his thick Haitian accent gave him away.

Shortly thereafter, two women—one who appeared to be in her mid- to late thirties and the other early thirties—walked in. Observing their facial features, hairstyles, and overall appearance, I marked them for Jamaican. As several other parents walked into the room, they began to coalesce into groups based on their respective places of origin without saying a word to one another.

As the groups sat together they engaged one another in their respective languages and dialects. The Jamaicans laughed heartily as they spoke in Patois and exhibited less formal and uninhibited body language. The Haitian parents spoke Creole and engaged each other in a more formal tone, and the other parents talked among their families.

Almost immediately after I opened the floor for questions, one parent asserted, "The fact of the matter is, our kids are not Jamaican." And in response, another Jamaican parent asked, "How can we get them to buy into the fact that yes, you are Jamaican?" As the conversation took a course of its own, parents spoke freely about the ways in which their children's lives were much easier here in America, and inevitably they went on to grapple with the ways in which they were introduced to the concept of race as they became enmeshed in American life and culture.

During this meeting, each parent shared something that was central to the experiences of Caribbean immigrants to the United States. They grappled with questions of identity and the tension between their desires to raise Caribbean children who—by legal and social definitions—would never be considered Caribbean. They noted the ways in which their children's lives as "Americans" were markedly distinct from their childhood experiences. The parents wrestled with the notion of "race," how they encountered race, and whether race had become central to their daily lives. They revisited life in the Caribbean and the sorrow they felt in reflecting upon all they had relinquished to migrate to the United States. Each person had a story that, while distinct, mirrored many similar stories of Caribbean immigrants across the nation.

Caribbean immigrants bring with them the history of their experiences in the Caribbean and their abrupt shift to life in America. They often neglect to recognize the unique history of America itself and how that history shapes their current experiences in the United States. Instead, they use their histories from the Caribbean to inform their understandings of modern-day experiences in the United States, histories that often precluded the use of critical racial analyses.

In this section I share the life narratives of four parents— narratives that capture both the variations and similarities embedded in the Afro-Caribbean experience. Parents used their life narratives to teach their children important lessons, mostly from their childhood, that reinforced the values they hoped their children would internalize. These individuals, though all from Jamaica, shared life narratives that illuminated nuances in the life trajectories of Caribbean immigrants from various islands throughout the region. Jamaican parents were overrepresented in the sample but were also more responsive to interview requests. I triangulated findings from these interviews with other students' reports of narratives shared by parents who hailed from Trinidad, Guyana, Dominica, Antigua, and the Bahamas. In sum, these narrative discourses inform understandings of (1) Caribbean family and community structures, (2) the impact of social class on the experiences of immigrants, (3) circumstances under which individuals migrated to the United States, and (4) integration into American society and initial experiences with U.S. constructions of race and racism. These four components of Caribbean American parents' experiences greatly influenced the racial and ethnic socialization messages they conveyed to their children.

From Rags to Riches: The Life Narrative of Kerry Ann Fisher, Mother of Bryce

Kerry Ann moved to New Kensington at the age of 16 from a rural community in Jamaica, West Indies. After Kerry Ann lost her mother at age 5, her father migrated to the United States and left Kerry Ann and several of her siblings for their grandparents to raise in a poor community of subsistence farmers. Many families encouraged their children to stay home to assist with farmwork as opposed to attending school. Kerry Ann noted distinctions between literate and illiterate families: literate parents often chose to send their children to school, while illiterate parents often chose to keep their children at home.

Kerry Ann's grandmother was literate and her grandfather illiterate. While her grandmother endorsed formal education, her grandfather often requested that the children remain home to tend the crops and care for the animals. Kerry Ann recalled attending school regularly, in part because she was "defiant" and chose instead to go to school against her grandfather's wishes. One of Kerry Ann's brothers was less defiant, as she recounted:

> My brother below me doesn't read and write that well because he would always be the willing kid and go [plow the fields] and me and my youngest brother [were] defiant.... Yeah, so he in a way...he would be the obedient child, because he obeyed and my younger brother and I, we said no, we wanna go to school so we are better readers and writers for that reason and up to this day you can see the impact it has on my brother and I feel almost, we both feel like we have to do everything for him...what happened to him...happened...because he was the obedient child and if you look at it, we were the disobedient children.

While Kerry Ann expressed gratitude for the opportunity to attend school, she also possessed a great deal of guilt for the benefits she reaped by being "disobedient" and choosing to attend school rather than assist her grandparents with their farming responsibilities. More importantly, she felt responsible for taking care of her brother, whose "obedience" led to illiteracy.

The memories of growing up without a mother or father in a poor rural community were pivotal aspects of Kerry Ann's life story and instrumental to the life narrative she shared with her son. Kerry Ann wanted her son Bryce to recognize how fortunate he was to have parents and the luxuries of a middle-class lifestyle in suburban America. Instead of positioning his blackness as a source of marginalization in America, Kerry Ann taught Bryce that he was extremely fortunate. According to Mickelson (1993), Black immigrants tend to define success and socioeconomic mobility by comparing their current conditions to the conditions of individuals back home in their respective countries. Kerry Ann and several other parents in my study relied heavily on their life narratives of poverty and hardship to motivate, encourage, and communicate expectations to their children.

While Bryce, the oldest of Kerry Ann's two sons, often argued that his mother's "hard life" was derived solely from not having parents, Kerry Ann argued that Bryce took for granted common U.S. luxuries such as running water, indoor bathrooms, and motorized cleaning tools. Daily tasks in Jamaica required arduous physical labor.

> Before I go to school in the morning, I had to go get water at the spring, bring it back, full the drum up so my grandparents can cook, wash, and do whatever they needed to do at home while we're at school. I gotta pick the bread fruit lea[ves] up out the yard everyday and we had what you call red floor, you had to shine it and leave no mark when you going to school in the morning, every morning. And then...I had 3 uniforms.... I had to come home every day and [hand] wash my uniforms, iron them so they can be ready for the next day and if I need water to go get water, I gotta go get them, but my brothers they mostly go look the wood, they help tie out the goats, feed the pigs, wash the pig pen, yuck! I grew up in a very country lifestyle.

Kerry Ann, a Certified Public Accountant (CPA) and real estate investor who lived in a rather large home in the Morristown community, was unable to disentangle her humble beginnings from her current middle-class lifestyle. She used her "rags-to-riches" narrative to encourage her son to overcome obstacles and take advantage of the opportunities afforded to him as a U.S. citizen.

In speaking with her son, Kerry Ann generally emphasized the abbreviated version of her story—rags to riches. But the full story reveals a complicated path to success. Kerry Ann's father had been granted a visa to work on the plantations in Florida picking oranges. After his wife died, he decided not to go back to Jamaica and instead risked living in the United States as an "illegal alien." It was years before he received his green card and could petition for his children to join him in the United States. After being without her father for approximately 10 years, 16-year-old Kerry Ann had to adjust to a new life in the United States away from her grandparents.

Soon after Kerry Ann's arrival, she sought to return to Jamaica to escape the challenges she faced in her New Kensington-neighborhood high school. Life in the United States didn't live up to what she'd heard in Jamaica, and Americans' less-than-sophisticated knowledge of other people and places across the globe astounded her. Kerry Ann recalled being asked, "[Do] you speak English? Did you come on a boat?" She added:

> At that age, I thought that everyone read history, everyone read books that tell them about different civilizations, different countries and stuff like that and I just never understood why I was bombarded with these questions like, "Did you learn English?".... I'm thinking, I'm from a British colony, English is our official language, couldn't understand that so I went back home.

After graduating from high school in Jamaica, Kerry Ann returned to the United States and the same mostly Black high school, where her peers harassed her about her presumed affiliations with Jamaican gangs, and teachers and counselors gave her little guidance on how to navigate life beyond post-secondary education. The part of Kerry Ann's story that came between the beginning and the end revealed harsh realities of triple disadvantage—poor, immigrant, and of color—that stood in her path to upward mobility. According to Rong & Brown (2002), today's immigrants of color often migrate to cities, which provide easy entry into the lower strata of U.S. society. This, along with racial minority and immigrant status, constrains attempts at upward mobility.

Kerry Ann noted:

> [I] went to school; I realized there was no guidance in the schools. I went to George Washington High School. I didn't have a counselor to say, okay, here's what you need to do to succeed. I just went to school. I took the SATs, but I didn't know why I was taking them, but once I took them, a recruiter start[ed] coming to my house and my dad sign[ed] me up at 17 years old and I joined the United States Air Force.

Although Kerry Ann had been in the Air Force reserves for approximately 20 years at the time of the interview and viewed her time in the military as integral to her growth and upward mobility, she also recognized that her father's ignorance and school personnel's neglect had served to steer her toward military service. In Kerry Ann's estimation, this would not have occurred had she been in Jamaica. She argued, "In Jamaica your neighbor would have told you, your church would have told you, everyone would have

[said], Oh Ms. Fisher you have a bright kid, let's see what we can do for your daughter to get a scholarship to go here and there." Kerry Ann added:

> My father didn't know, he was functionally literate [chuckles]. He didn't understand schools and stuff like that so basically, I had to fudge my way through and I think my first job kinda set the tone for what happened to me because a lady I work for, she recognize my talents very quickly and she said, you know, I think you should go to college. But, I didn't know. I already signed up…to go to the military so [afterward] I join[ed] the reserve[s] and I said look, I want to go [to college].

After attending Clinton University for a year, Kerry Ann could no longer afford the tuition. The following summer, she worked to pay off the money owed to the school, collected her transcript, and transferred to a university where her record at Clinton merited a full scholarship. Kerry Ann reflected, however: "What really help me [was] that, that lady was out there because my dad 'til this day doesn't know how I made it through college. He had no clue. His whole thing [was], go to school, but *HOW*?"

While the narrative Kerry Ann often related to her son contrasted humble beginnings with her climb to success, it omitted the struggles and disadvantages she faced as a result of race, class, and immigrant status. For Bryce, Kerry Ann's account of her life focused on the loss of her mother early in life, her father's inability to advocate for her, and her attendance at a high school that did not equip her to experience socioeconomic mobility. However, Kerry Ann did not relate these experiences to larger systems of institutionalized racism. Instead, she marked herself as a poor child, without a mother, from a relatively uneducated family, who "made it" with the assistance of one stranger. While all those things were true, Kerry Ann's framing and interpretation of her early experiences in the United States were informed by how she was taught to understand and organize the world as a child growing up in Jamaica. Her limited exposure to conceptualizations of racism allowed her stories to circulate without the critical analysis she might have adapted after years of exposure to U.S. racism.

While Kerry Ann noted that, for her, the road to upward mobility was quite tenuous, she also believed that her gender afforded her an advantage. According to Kerry Ann, being born a woman gave her the socially constructed privilege of being able to find someone she could expect to take care of her. Kerry Ann argued that men's calling to be providers kept them from marrying to gain class privilege. Kerry Ann's husband, Bryce's stepfather, was also Jamaican, in the military reserves, and a CPA. Though Kerry Ann noted that she owned several investment properties that were all her own, she also credited her gender privilege as central to her current socioeconomic status. However, gender expectations from the Caribbean context informed this view. Black women in the United States have diminished expectations of upward mobility through marriage (Dickson, 1993; Gibson-Davis, 2011). Like a number of people in the study, Kerry Ann used analyses that reflect Caribbean realities rather than realities common in the African American community of the United States.

Kerry Ann's narrative of making it in America centered around her academic ability, her having been sent into the military with little understanding of or desire to commit to it, her having someone who encouraged her to attend college, her perseverance through struggles to pay for college, her desire to move out of New Kensington into a safer community, and her ability to secure a husband whose socioeconomic status enhanced her ability to attain a solidly middle-class lifestyle.

In narrating her life, Kerry Ann didn't emphasize the importance of navigating the racial inequities she faced on her journey toward upward mobility. The implicit messages she conveyed to Bryce as a means of socialization reflected this analysis. She thought her life narrative would provide a roadmap to academic success and the attainment of life goals. She also beckoned Bryce to adhere to her guidance, given the likelihood that he would eventually be expected to provide for his own family. However, these stories did not account for the presumed role of race or racism in regulating the opportunities made available to her. The socialization messages she provided for Bryce implied that individual wherewithal determined life success without regard to the impact of structural barriers.

Hustling for Success: Life Narrative
of Marcia Young, Mother of Charles and Elyse

Like Kerry Ann's, Marcia's life story did not situate race as central
to her experiences, nor did she note how the particular intersections between race and class in the U.S. context shaped her initial
experiences in the United States.

Marcia's mother migrated to the United States from Jamaica,
leaving Marcia to live with her grandmother at the tender age of 3.
Like Kerry Ann, Marcia lived in a rural community in Jamaica.
Unlike Kerry Ann, however, Marcia noted that her grandmother
spoiled her, exempting her from many chores.

Marcia recalled living in a one-room house with her sister,
grandmother, her grandmother's husband, and her adopted uncle,
all of whom slept on one full-sized bed. Despite these circumstances,
when I asked Marcia what her family's class was, she said:

> Middle class. I think we were the better off people because my grand-
> mother used to always help people out, she took them in, we had no
> space, but she took them in, but after a while we um, we built another
> house, a four bedroom house now, which is on the same property. My
> mom has 4 bedrooms, 2 bathrooms so my grandmother started and my
> mom finished it so now we're you know [middle class].... My grand mom
> always help people, she um, she um, for living, you know what she did
> for a living, am I allowed to say what she did for a living?

I responded that I hoped she would, and Marcia's husband, Mark,
indicated that Marcia's family had grown marijuana. Marcia continued:

> I didn't see nothing wrong with it until I came here and she would sell it
> and she was the better off of people and she used to help people and, um,
> every Sunday a whole group of people used to come to our house, who-
> ever didn't have food, come and eat, even during the week, who didn't
> have food, oh come on over, we'll give you food, you understand so that's
> how my grand mom was, she was um...she was the main house in the
> community where people [you] know um....

Mark added: "Back then they call it the big yard."

Marcia's understanding of the meaning of "middle class" reflected the fact that her grandmother could provide for the needs

of immediate and extended family and the larger community. Providing food and shelter for those less fortunate implied good fortune even in the absence of much formal schooling, resources, or skills. Marcia's respect for her grandmother was central to her life narrative and gave her faith in entrepreneurship as a means of survival.

Family and community were central in Marcia's narrative. Marcia also noted that she came from a highly insulated community, mostly made up of family members—all descendants of her great-great-grandmother's 12 children. "Strangers" could enter the community only with family members. Marcia spoke nostalgically of her family and childhood experiences in her small rural community.

However, the mood of our conversation shifted abruptly when Marcia recalled the day her grandmother told her that her mother was coming to visit. Marcia explained:

> In Jamaica I was living with my, um, my grandmom, cause, um, my mom came to America when I was like 3 years old and that part of my life I don't really remember. I just remember, um, being 9 and being with my grand mom, 6, 7, 8, 9 [years old] and then one day she say, um, to me that, your mom is coming to see you. I said, "My mom coming to see me?" I said, "You're my mother." She said, "No, I'm not, I'm your grandmother." I said now, so you know, I didn't really know that I had a mom, I thought [my grandmother] was my mom.

Marcia left Jamaica at the age of 9 but had vivid memories of her life there. Her father stayed in Jamaica, and she would often return during the summer to spend time with him. She also described living on the west side of New Kensington directly beneath the elevated train line of a run-down, low-income community. As Marcia recalled her initial reaction to the United States, she explained:

> I was like oh my goodness, this is America. I had a View-Master, you know View-Master, they show you all these pretty pictures of America, the street so wide, it's big and pretty, and when I came I was like, "Oh my God!" The school was dirty, all the kids were mean, it was cold for me 'cause it was March. I was like oh no. We cried every day, take me back home, take me back home. My sister even threaten[ed] to jump out the window if my mom didn't take her back home.

Not only was it difficult for Marcia to transition from life in a rural town in Jamaica to an urban community in the United States; she also had to leave behind the grandmother she loved dearly to live with a mother she had only recently learned existed. Her mother didn't spoil her like her grandmother had, and Marcia never described the same closeness to her mother that she had with her grandmother. She did, however, note that her mother's expectations of her sparked her independence and desire for self-sufficiency.

> I was always ambitious, at 14, I wanted my own. My mom wasn't giving me enough money. My allowance, she give me $12 a week and that was a lot of money back then, but by the time I buy my tokens out of it, it was $5.50 and you know...whatever for lunch money, I didn't have [any money left]. I said, "Mom, I wanna go to work." She said, "No way, no way!" so I said to her, I said to her, "If I go to work you won't have to give me any money." She said, okay and I was 14 and I started working at Burger King in Millersville.

> I started working when I was 14 and I would take the bus from Main Street Station every Friday. I work[ed] Friday, Saturday, and Sunday because those were my hours. I was underage and um, took the bus from Main Street Station all the way down to um, Millersville, it's like an hour ride [and then] I started working and from that day my mom never gave me a penny after that.... I got my first car by myself when I was 17, you know, so one job led to another.... I was very ambitious, I know what I wanted, I had to go to work, the time was cold, I was freezing so I said I wasn't gonna stay here, I wasn't gonna keep on taking the bus in the cold, so I worked towards a car.

Marcia's description of herself as hard working and "ambitious" from a young age was integral to her narrative of her transition to life in the United States. Leaving a community in Jamaica where her needs were met in abundance for a low-income community in the United States propelled Marcia toward exerting increased control over her life.

While Marcia began working at a young age, she also became pregnant and elected not to complete her senior year in high school. She never earned her high school diploma or even high school equivalency. However, Marcia provided for her family by owning a day care center and working as help for an elderly White woman and her son. Marcia had moved herself and her two children out of New Kensington and into the Morristown community. Like her grandmother, Marcia strategically found ways to ensure that the needs of her family were met with little formal education or technical training.

Marcia's life story taught her children about the ability to create opportunities while circumventing mainstream approaches to mobility. Marcia achieved success without conforming to traditional pathways; she emphasized providing for her family by entrepreneurial means and personal drive. To her children, Marcia's life served as a testimony to the possibility of securing middle-class status regardless of race or educational background. Her narratives reflected an enduring reliance on values derived from her ethnic background. Marcia's children internalized the currency of their mother's espoused ethnic values over time.

Street Smarts and Skilled Labor:
The Life Narrative of Mark Young,
Father of Charles and Stepfather of Elyse

Marcia's husband Mark was also born in Jamaica, West Indies, and described his background as middle class. However, unlike Marcia, Mark grew up mainly in Kingston, Jamaica's capital, where he resided with his mother, stepfather, and brother. His mother had hired help—a housekeeper who did cooking, cleaning, and laundry. However, Mark's mother required the housekeeper to set aside his school uniforms so that he could hand-wash and iron them on his own. Mark's biological father owned a home in Portmore, a newly developed, middle-class community at the time. Mark spent most of his time in Kingston with his mother but also spent weekends with his father in Portmore.

In addition to consistent visits between the homes of his mother and father, Mark also spent a great deal of time with his paternal grandmother in rural Montego Bay, which he loved.

> Montego Bay...that's the life, to go to country. That's where you go shoot the birds and you climb the tree go look mango and fish and all the good stuff, so I couldn't get the bag packed fast enough to go, ah, I wanted to go.... I get to carry the water, go look the firewood, 'cause that's fun,

yeah, that's fun for me, you know, 'cause in Kingston everything is there, you know.

In spite of his solidly middle-class roots, Mark had no immediate plans after high school. After a year of hanging around with his friends and smoking marijuana, his mother prodded him to seek a career. He had learned hairdressing from her, but he feared being "called names" if he went to beauty school. He tried being a mechanic with a friend of his mother's, but that only lasted a day. Then he decided on culinary school.

Mark's experience attending culinary school sparked the beginning of a career and entrepreneurial journey. By this time his mother had migrated to the United States, and Mark landed a job as a chef at one of the top hotels in Kingston. He eventually decided to open a jerk chicken stand on weekends. The following is an excerpt from Mark's retelling of his transition to becoming a businessman.

> I'm not book smart, but I'm ambitious and...I get tired of people telling me what to do, so, what I do, I tell my mom, I say, "Can you send me $100 U.S., I want to start a business." She said, "What kind of business?" I said, "I want to sell some jerk chicken." She said, "No, they gonna obeah you. They gonna obeah you and they will kill you. No, no, no, no, no, just gwan go work fi people." I said, "Nope," so what I do, I go back and work and I save up that money and when I get enough I go, you know those drum, the big drum, I buy one and I bring it 'round my friend...the same mechanic guy [for whom he'd worked for one day] and he do welding, he used the welding torch to cut it open for me and make me a jerk pan and I went and I have a bicycle and I say okay, so the first time um, on a Friday I went and buy everything, jerk chicken and I season it up and I put it out and then at least half an hour, the whole bucket of chicken finish, and I say, "What [is] dis? Is [this] a dolly house thing or what, you doing business? [Meaning he should have had more chicken if he wants to be taken seriously.] The next week I buy two buckets and it gone, the next week I buy three bucket, and then when my mom come from America and she come she say, what you doing with so much money, where you get so much money from?

Mark's entrepreneurship led to his migration to the United States.

> I say, I work. I work from Monday to Friday or Monday to Thursday and then for Friday and Saturday, I do my jerk chicken. I do roast fish, jerk chicken, save my money, you know, and so forth until [my mother] say,

okay, you ready to come to the State[s]. [I] say, I don't want to come, [but] I don't have no choice, she already file for me....

Mark migrated to the United States when he was 21 years old and had not experienced formal schooling in the United States. This was in marked distinction to the experiences of Kerry Ann and Marcia. In many ways, their school experiences exposed them to inequities in segregated, low-income schools regardless of whether they had a meta-analytical awareness of these structures.

After arriving in the United States for what Mark initially deemed a temporary stay during which he could make money and leave, he struggled to find a job using his Jamaican credentials. Emphasizing the importance of hard work, Mark explained that he took jobs as a dishwasher at restaurants and subsequently worked his way up to becoming a chef, owned a restaurant that later went out of business, and started a catering business. Mark proudly noted that as a result of his work ethic he had amassed enough money to purchase a house outright for his mother. Like his wife, he emphasized entrepreneurship over formal education.

Mark contrasted "book smarts" with "street smarts."

I never go to college and university, but trust me, if you give that guy a million dollars and give me zero and put me on the street, I guarantee... his million [is] gonna finish and I probably end up mak[ing] a million...because I'm street smart. I'm not book smart, but I'm street smart, yeah.

Mark finished with a sly chuckle as he reflected upon his business acumen. This quote reflects Mark's mantra, an essential component of his life story: *"I'm not book smart, but I'm street smart."* Mark's endorsement of this message was pivotal to the socialization his children received from him regarding means of upward mobility.

Mark's analysis of his trajectory toward upward mobility also informed his perspective on the Black Americans he encountered upon migrating to the United States. His assessment of his ability to enter the country with what he deemed to be nothing and achieve middle-class status left him confounded about the social class disparities he often witnessed between Blacks and Whites.

Antagonistic relationships he'd had with Black American males soon after migrating to the United States cemented his negative perceptions of Black Americans. Mark jokingly asserted that he hoped to place a billboard at the airport warning new immigrants of potential interactions with Black Americans. Twenty years later, Mark vividly recalled feuds he had had with his Black American counterparts and reluctantly described his dream of writing a book about his initial encounters with difference. However, he also noted:

> It's not just about [Black Americans], I mean likkle of everything. I mean Caucasians, just the ways and things I see when I just came here. You go to the supermarket and they [Caucasians] grabbing up they bag, [when] you [Black people] going by. Or, you going to the market and you see a Black American and both of them, husband and wife, and the [groceries] come up to a hundred dollar and your wife taking out fifty, that one taking out fifty to complete the hundred, where in a Caribbean family you don't see that, the man go in his pocket and pay the hundred. You know, little stuff. And, as far as bank account, they...they scared to open a bank account, you know stuff like that. You know...just tell a story of...you know, little experience of what I go through....

Mark's desire to tell a "little story" revealed that he did not view these incidents as derived from the country's historical legacy. Mark thought it odd that a White woman would grab her purse in the presence of a Black man and assume that he is inclined toward criminal behavior. He scoffed at the idea that Black Americans were reluctant to bank at financial institutions. Although Mark was accurate in his assessment that Black Americans are less likely to have a bank account when compared to other groups (Aratani & Chau, 2010), he did not consider the historical legacy of mistrust between Black communities and banking institutions caused by redlining and other discriminatory practices, or that low-income communities of color had fewer banking options. Mark did not understand the widespread marginalization of Blacks in America and failed to examine the ways in which legacies of racism continued to play out in U.S. society. He was also miffed by unfamiliar gender roles. Like his wife, and like Kerry Ann, Mark's life narrative and distinct history served to color the lens through which he examined and analyzed race relations, racial identity, and social mobility, to name a few.

Privilege Begets Privilege:
The Life Narrative of
Craig Thompson, Father of Jeffrey

Craig Thompson was raised in one of the more prominent communities in Jamaica, an upper-middle class community called Red Hills. Where other participants recollected having to "work hard" growing up, Craig noted that his only responsibility was to attend school.

> I can't recall having responsibilities, you know, the ah, I think ah what we did we'd go to school, come back home, I mean, it's so much different because we had like a nanny or a helper who lived-in and ah I just can't recall having a great deal of responsibilities, you know like doing house work and house chores, which is bad because I make sure my sons have chores to do, you know.

Although Craig did not recollect having responsibilities of his own, his father was a model hard worker, and Craig determined not to take his family's elite status for granted. Craig also explained that his father maintained social relationships with people whose background spanned socioeconomic levels. Craig used these experiences to temper the abundance of his relatively comfortable life. He remembered distinctly that his father taught him to value and respect all people despite their class backgrounds.

Craig's housekeeper lived in and took care of all the domestic responsibilities. Upon graduating from high school, Craig went on to attend college in Trinidad and later moved to the United States to pursue an MBA. Regarding this decision, Craig said nonchalantly:

> Well...you want to know the honest truth to that [laughs] because ah, I could have probably attended graduate school in um...in Jamaica honestly, but they didn't have a MBA program so...the U.S. is the closest place to do a MBA, you know. I could have gone to London, but they were expensive and you know, nobody does a MBA in London, you go to the, at that time anyway, you go to...where capitalism reigns. But the honest

truth is my buddies were up here and I wanted to party so you know, I
came to Washington and...you know that's what I did.

Craig's class privilege supported his leisurely choices. He encountered few hardships on the path to an upper-middle-class lifestyle
in adulthood. He lived completely differently from other parents in
the study. After completing graduate school, Craig decided to move
back home to Jamaica, but he later returned to the United States
to marry a woman from Dominica whom he had met in graduate
school. He would have preferred to live in Jamaica, and his wife
had promised that eventually they would.

Craig claimed not to believe that racial disparities in socioeconomic status are rampant throughout the United States. His experiences in the United States shielded him from these realities.
Upon his arrival in the United States, Craig was immediately integrated into the Black middle class. As a graduate student, he
recalled being a member of the National Black MBA Association,
through which he encountered many upwardly mobile and accom-
plished Blacks. His lack of exposure to people and places plagued
by economic disenfranchisement supported his analysis that socioeconomic disparities between Blacks and Whites did not exist.
While Craig noticed some differences in terms of the expectations
of Blacks and in the integration of Blacks into leadership positions
in top-tier institutions, he dismissed the existence of a deeply entrenched, institutionalized racism that historically precluded Blacks
from attending school, owning property, and participating fully in
society.

However, Craig also noted disparities as he took a step down
from his position in Jamaica to take a job here in the United States,
where he encountered very few Blacks in high positions at one of
the nation's leading financial institutions. Nonetheless, Craig maintained that American Blacks had just as much wealth as Whites.
When asked what he thought led to the socioeconomic disparities
between the two groups, Craig argued, "You know, I've heard that,
but I'm telling you and people keep saying [it], but I meet so many
ah, especially in the National MBA Association and around, just
going around, that I meet so many well-off, you know, educated

Black people, that I'm like, you know, I don't buy into that myth too much."

Craig acknowledged racial *discrimination*. He believed the scarcity of Blacks in high-level positions reflected racial prejudice at the core of American life, but his analysis of the extent to which racism affected Blacks teetered on the brink of naiveté. He claimed to believe that racism did not have to impede the socioeconomic mobility and overall well-being of Blacks in America. Craig believed that racial discrimination was surmountable and that with education, cooperative economics, and hard work, Blacks had the power to counterbalance the impact of racism. He believed that upper-middle-class Blacks had figured out how to circumvent racism. However, people's high socioeconomic status does not account for how much more they might have been able to accomplish had they not been subject to racism.

Conclusion

The four parents whose journeys are described in this chapter represent a range of immigrant experiences and trajectories toward upward mobility. The parents came from varying class backgrounds, had distinct experiences integrating into U.S. society, and had different levels of exposure to and perspectives on issues of race and racism. Each parent's narrative is imbued with unique perspectives and experiences but is also representative of the diverse narrative profiles of many Caribbean immigrants to America.

Parents' beliefs and experiences greatly influenced the racial and ethnic socialization messages communicated to their children. Despite variations in class background, each of the parents interviewed attained middle-class status, some by way of formal education and the procurement of professional jobs and others on the basis of entrepreneurship and little formal schooling. All of these parents placed their life narratives at the center of the socialization messages conveyed to their children, messages grounded in their ethnically oriented analyses of their histories and realities. According to Rong and Brown (2002), "ethnic sentiments derive from interactions occurring within specific economic, political, and historical contexts" (p. 253). These ethnic narratives reflected the ways in which the economic, political, and historical context of the Caribbean informed immigrants' notions of upward mobility, which precluded more U.S.-centric understandings of the role of race in complicating attempts at upward mobility.

Overall, the absence of a race-centered framework or consistent efforts to resist a race-centered framework affected the degree to which Caribbean American parents viewed racial socialization as important and necessary. Given their ability to achieve middle-class status without means of critically examining ways to navigate the racist terrain of the United States, Caribbean parents relied heavily on ethnic socialization and their life narratives to encourage their children's social and economic mobility.

Parents in my study rarely used socialization messages that reflected the historical realities and legacies of Blacks in America or how they were implicated in structural disparities. Instead, Caribbean parents used preexisting frames of reference to lend understanding to the contextual realities of life in America. Though some immigrants acknowledged racial inequities, others insisted that racism did not seriously impede the socioeconomic mobility of Blacks. In their minds, inherent qualities and opportunities afforded to them by hard work, family support, and in some instances sheer providence produced their upward mobility. It is through these psychological distinctions and tensions that racial and ethnic socialization practices were born. Parents' perspectives on race and racism that inform their racial and ethnic socialization practices were not derived in opposition to Black Americans, as some contend, but instead reflect Caribbean immigrants' schematic understandings of the world.

E(race)ing Socialization: Transnational Scripts, Ethnic Socialization, and Getting Ahead in America

I didn't know I was Black until I came [to America]. First of all, I thought I was a Jamaican and I was a human until I came here. I figured out that wait a minute, I'm Black. Somebody told me! Because, when I was growing up, my race wasn't defined. I never knew there was a difference in how I'm supposed to act or what I'm supposed to achieve based on my race. It only occurred to me when I came here.

—Kerry Ann Fisher, mother of Bryce

In the United States, it seems odd to claim to be unaware of racial distinctions and ridiculous to pretend not to know your own race. After all, isn't it obvious? Can't everyone determine their own race by a simple glance in the mirror? At the very least, official forms make Americans aware of their racial categorization by pressuring people to check the appropriate box. Notions of race have long been entrenched in the culture and history of the United States and often seem inextricable from the daily lives and lived realities of Americans; however, people outside the United States have histories marked by different narratives, values, and means of self-identification. Many of the Caribbean parents in this study did not see race as an aspect of self-identification prior to migrating to the United States. This chapter centers on the conundrum of assimilating U.S. notions of racial identity with a schema that generally lacks such a basis for identity.

The unique positionality of Caribbean parents as both insiders and outsiders to U.S. cultural norms created both challenges and opportunities for engaging in racial and ethnic socialization processes. On the one hand, Caribbean parents were often unaware of the extent to which race shaped their children's daily experiences; on the other, their divergent perceptions of race afforded their children a unique space for interrogating essentialist notions of blackness.

As the parent quoted in the epigraph above describes, a Caribbean upbringing does not teach immigrants to consider race as central to their identities and daily experiences prior to migration. This distinction profoundly affects their ability to engage in racial socialization practices. While racial socialization scholars contend that Black parents who have lived in the United States for multiple generations have used racial socialization strategies to help prepare and protect their children from the harsh realities of interpersonal racism (Harris-Britt et al., 2007), Black parents from the Caribbean lacked opportunities to develop such knowledge and skills over time, given the relative racial homogeneity of their countries.

In contrast to the well-researched racial socialization practices of Black American parents, the racial socialization practices of Black immigrants to the United States get little attention. Further, the roles of ethnic socialization and the intersections of racial and ethnic socialization for this group go largely unexplored.

The process by which Caribbean parents came to recognize and understand race—through integration into American society—has shaped the ways in which each parent has come to conceive of him or herself as a racialized individual, as well as how they consciously and subconsciously rear their children to conceptualize race in the U.S. context. Though parents of Caribbean American youth had very little control over their children's experiences as they pertained to issues of race and ethnicity—particularly in schools and the larger community—their socialization practices shaped their children's perceptions of and responses to these experiences. Caribbean immigrant parents tended to privilege the transmission of ethnic socialization messages over racial socialization messages. (Chapter 1 distinguished between ethnic and racial socialization. Ethnic socialization refers to parents' attempts to instill within their children the values they considered to be specific to the Caribbean; racial socialization in this context relates to the specific ways in which phenotype and associations with individuals of a particular phenotype impact individuals' experiences and self-perception.)

While ethnic socialization messages appeared fairly consistent across families, racial socialization seemed to vary on the basis of parents' experiences with race, racism, and socioeconomic mobility in both U.S. and Caribbean contexts. Caribbean immigrant parents adhered strongly to constructions of Caribbean ethnic identity that defined Caribbean people as hardworking, family and community oriented, well mannered, and invested in education. However, socialization around racial identity development proved more complex for Caribbean immigrants and varied among participants on the basis of their class background, modes of incorporation into U.S. society, and exposure to racialized experiences.

This chapter focuses on the multiple ways in which parents' histories, experiences, and perspectives regarding race, class, and ethnicity shaped their endorsement of particular socialization practices. I identify three dominant means by which these processes occur: (1) examining the ethnic socialization practices of parents and their investment in promoting ethnic socialization messages among their 1.5- and second-generation American children; (2) exploring the types of racial socialization practices endorsed by Caribbean parents, as well as limitations in their conceptualization of the socialization needs of Black children in the United States generally and in schools specifically; and (3) addressing the ways in which the class backgrounds of parents often shaped their perspectives and intentionality regarding racial socialization and the educational needs of their children.

The United States as a Training Ground for Learning Race

Although every parent recalled a distinct transition to life in the United States, not one respondent had been raised to consider race. Like Kerry Ann Fisher, quoted in the epigraph, Caribbean parents identified as "human," with a nationality—until they migrated to the United States. Craig, another parent, asserted: "When I was growing up you, you didn't necessarily understand that there is a difference between Black and White. I mean, in Jamaica you're just, you know, just Jamaican."

While Jamaica's national motto—"Out of Many, One People"— is indicative of some racial diversity on the island, Jamaica is mostly racially homogeneous. About 75% of the population is of African heritage. However, the racial and cultural diversity that does exist is glossed over in favor of a common national identity and culture. Students in the study whose families hailed from Trinidad and Antigua expressed similar notions of nationalistic identity. Geneva, a 1.5-generation American student who migrated to the United States at age 2 and who described her background as multiracial, expressed that her national identity as Trinidadian would take precedence over racial distinctions in the Trinidadian context.

Despite nationalistic means of self-identification, many Caribbean immigrants described their African heritage as essentially distinct from "race" or nationality. In an interview, Marcia— Charles and Elyse's mother—described conversations with her dad as the catalyst for understanding her diasporic relationship to Africa. She explained:

> I think I was asking my father about our background and that's when he told us about the ship and how they grab people from, multiple family from different places and then take them to different islands and drop them off. That's when I realize I am African. I am from Africa, my ancestors so you know, um, Black you know, is just too, you know, out there, but you know, I can't say I'm African American cause I wasn't born here, you know, I'm just you know, African descent, um, African Jamaican, I don't know if there's no such thing, but, you know, that's how I come to that conclusion, we are from Africa. Our ancestors are African.

Marcia understood herself to be a descendant of Africa. Her identity as African was a historical fact that did not undermine or diminish her sense of being fully Jamaican. While there were associations that could be made between African ancestry and phenotype, Marcia was not considered to be more or less Jamaican than someone with Asian heritage and phenotypic characteristics who was born and reared on the island. Americans, whose histories have long associated race and phenotype with citizenship and belongingness, have trouble comprehending the framing of race in other parts of the world. The United States reserves full citizenship to those who are both White and American (Jacobson, 2006; Martinez, 2006). However, non-White Americans have historically been perceived as second-class citizens or "hyphenated" Americans such as African Americans, Asian Americans, or Latinos (whose classification is generally devoid of the defining "American" tag line).

For many Caribbean immigrant parents, the process of learning race—as distinct from their understanding of ancestry or physical descriptors—proved quite tumultuous. Many Caribbean immigrants said that they had been ignorant of American notions of race prior to their arrival in the United States, having thought of ancestral and phenotypic distinctions mainly as descriptors of one's physical traits or historical lineage and devoid of stringent social implications. The following conversation between Mark, Marcia, and me demonstrated the ways in which they understood racial difference in the Jamaican context, understandings that shifted upon migration to the United States.

Marcia: Race, well, of course you have, well, you know Caucasian Jamaicans, but not where we're from. Where we're from originally, there's all our people so we never had a race issue and then, when um, we didn't know about racism until we came to this country 'cause we never used to call White folks White in Jamaican. My dad always said brown, brown man, cause my dad said, "Marcia, nobody in this world is White cause White is the color of your shirt, you understand?"... So he said...the brown man, but we were never taught racism. I wasn't taught racism; I was taught everyone is one.

Mark: In my...case, because I was [in] Montego Bay and that's a tourist resort [area] when I go down to spend time with my dad, cause that's where he's from, and he used to work in the hotels, so when I go to visit him, I see a lot of Caucasians, they always talk [to] me and my dad [and say], "Oh, can we have a picture?" and they [ask about] food or stuff like that, so you know, I never at no time feel uncomfortable 'til when I get here, that's when I start realize, you know....

Marcia: We were different.

Mark: Yeah, in their eyes we're different, but me, we go to the beach, they there bathing, we bathing, they talk, they speak to me, I speak to

them and um, you know, and so forth so I never really experience, 'til
when I get here, that's when I realize....

Marcia: People calling me names.

Mark: You know I didn't...even know [those] name 'til when I get here.

Hierarchy has infused race and racial categories since their
most nascent stages. These hierarchical underpinnings are imbued
in U.S. notions of race that Caribbean immigrants had not known
prior to migration. Ashley Montagu (1997) suggested that the concept of race intrinsically implies that people with particular physical traits have inferior intelligence. U.S. society justifies
discrimination in education and employment through reference to
this intellectual inferiority (Herrnstein & Murray, 1994; Jensen,
1969), and Blacks in America suffer the resulting barriers to upward mobility, social integration, and economic success. Blacks in
the Caribbean may have some sense of historical discrimination
and racial stereotypes, but they lack awareness of current forms of
racism and racist ideology.

For many Caribbean immigrants, migration to the United
States exposed them to both racial hostility *and* xenophobia. My
respondents experienced dissonance when they encountered the
categories "Black" or "African American" to which the outside
world assigned them and with which they did not identify. Because U.S. society ties Black as a racial category to negative
stereotypes and lower social status (Rong & Brown, 2002), their
desire for upward mobility conflicted with the category. They
tended to embrace the ethnic and nationalistic modes of identification they had brought with them from their respective homelands
in response to that dissonance.

Black immigrants' desire to maintain ethnic and nationalistic
identities in lieu of American conceptions of blackness has been
regarded as "oppositional" to Black Americans (Waters, 1999)
and indicative of unhealthy racial identity (Hall & Carter,
2006). However, reading Caribbean immigrant ethnic identity as
mainly oppositional misses several key points: (1) transnational
notions of self do not simply eviscerate upon migration and (2)
immigrants make sacrifices to migrate to the United States seek-

ing social and economic gains, associations with groups or categories linked to downward mobility conflict directly with these goals.

Early experiences with Black Americans also complicated Caribbean immigrants' understanding of blackness within the U.S. context. In particular, Kerry Ann, Marcia, and Mark's initial experiences placed them in low-income, majority-Black communities where they reported experiencing hostility from Black Americans. Kerry Ann resented zoning stipulations that required her to attend the predominantly Black George Washington High School, even though Morristown High School, a more diverse and well-equipped school, was closer to her home. Kerry Ann wanted to return to Jamaica soon after her arrival in the United States, partly because of the xenophobia she experienced at the hands of her Black American peers. Initial negative experiences regarding race alienated people like Kerry Ann from U.S. notions of Black identity and encouraged a more ethnic and nationalistic orientation among Caribbean immigrants.

Additionally, ruptures often occurred during attempts at communicating solidarity on the basis of African ancestry. Mark recalled being challenged to a fight after he asserted that his coworker, a Black American, was indeed *African* American." Mark recounted the story, stating:

Mark: When I used to work at Holiday Inn, remember I told you, um, you know, couple Americans was in there working so, I don't know what get into me....

Marcia: Black Americans?

Mark: Yeah. I start talking and you know, for some reason, I go say, I say it to them, "You know you['re] African American...." He say, "What? What you just say to me?" I say, "You [are] African American." He say, "No!" "No!" He say, "I'm not no African, I'm not no African, I'm American, you don't ever say that again, I take you outside."

According to Mark, this incident occurred before Blacks in America generally accepted the term African American. It reflected an overall rejection of Africanness on the part of Black Americans, which baffled him. According to Mark, African heritage was inherent in his knowledge of himself as a person and distinctly different from the notion of race and the social implications related to this socially constructed category. This incident also demonstrates the experiential and political differences between Caribbean immigrants and Black Americans and the basis for the way in which each group had come to define itself. The combination of White America's understanding of Black immigrants as Black, Black immigrants' self-identification as distinct from Black Americans, and Black Americans' (sometimes) xenophobic reaction to Black immigrants caused tension between immigrant and non-immigrant Blacks. That tension was exacerbated as Black immigrants were positioned as belonging to the same group as Black Americans, a group that seemed to reject them, and a group of people with whom they did not readily identify.

These initial encounters between Black immigrants and Black Americans remained integral to the development of relationships between immigrant and native-born Blacks over time. Furthermore, immigrants' early experiences with Black Americans informed perceptions of racial and ethnic belonging. Some immigrants reported rejecting the term African American, and some rejected Black, despite acknowledging a similar African origin and phenotype. Mary Waters (1999) cited opposition to U.S. stereotypical notions of blackness as the basis for immigrants' distancing themselves from Black Americans. Her analysis of the tenuous relationship between the groups, however, did not account for the ways in which Black Americans' hostility toward incoming immigrants shaped immigrants' attitudes about Black Americans. Despite years of living in the United States, Mark and Marcia still harbored resentment and disdain toward Black Americans that dated back to their early immigration experiences.

Among my respondents, initial integration into low-income Black communities with scarce resources served as a catalyst for hostile relations with Black Americans. Black Americans often perceived Black immigrants as a threat and therefore treated them poorly within majority-Black communities. These experiences were also informed by structural barriers that placed Black immigrants and Black Americans in communities in which individuals feel they must compete for resources. These structurally induced circumstances allowed for friction between Black Ameri-

cans and Black immigrants as well as the internalization of negative stereotypes directed at the opposing group.

Socioeconomic status and mobility proved to be key elements in
determining the nature of encounters between Caribbean
immigrants and Black Americans. Craig, whose middle-class
status shielded him from extended experiences with lower-class
and working-class Blacks, described being well received by the
larger Black community. Middle-class Blacks, who generally
shared his value of upward mobility, did not perceive Craig as a
threat, nor was this group vying for scarce resources in the same
way that lower-income Blacks did. Craig described his opinion
about the relationship between Black Americans and Caribbean
immigrants.

> I, you know, there's a notion that ah Black Americans and Caribbean
> people don't get along and...when I, sometimes I hear it, I dismiss it be-
> cause it's nonsense. The point is that although there are differences, the
> similarities far outweigh the differences and how we view life going for-
> ward, is to me, largely the same, it's education, it's eventually developing
> your own economic resources, and building your own, so I just think the
> similarities far outweigh the differences.

Like Craig, Kerry Ann felt that there were many similarities
between Black Americans and Caribbean immigrants. However,
Kerry Ann also posited that there were key distinctions in the
ways in which racial discrimination affected the psychological realities of Caribbean immigrants as compared to their Black American counterparts. She argued:

> I'm very similar [to Black Americans] in the struggle for upward mobil-
> ity, but I'm different in a way that I don't, I didn't grow up believing that
> I can't achieve based on my color and that's what I think is the greatest
> difference. I think people who are born here grew up in this box that you
> can't get out of. Because I grew up in a different country where all my
> prime ministers is like [points to skin] and people in powerful positions
> look just like me...I am not limited to who I am so I don't need rein-
> forcement everyday to believe that, because I grew up in an environment
> where that was possible, it happened. P.J. Paterson look [points to skin],
> he's darker than me [chuckles]. You know, so I didn't need that addi-
> tional motivation to say I can do it. I know I can because I saw it.

Kerry Ann pointed out that all Blacks in America, despite immigrant status, must "struggle for upward mobility," but professed that for Black Americans, the relative absence of Blacks in positions of power in the United States compounds that struggle.

Caribbean immigrants maintain both insider and outsider status in terms of U.S. conventions of race. To some extent, Caribbean immigrant parents eventually come to understand the role of race and racism in the United States, but they remain relatively disentangled from the psychological impingement of racist beliefs and practices. It is this idea—the knowledge of racism without the encroachment of racial inferiority—that gives rise to Caribbean immigrant parents' distinctive racial and ethnic socialization practices.

For Caribbean immigrant parents, transnational experiences work to dispel U.S. myths of racial inferiority. This may sometimes result in parents being dismissive of racism and racist experiences or prompt attempts to counter negative stereotypes when they arise. However, psychological distance from a sense of racial inferiority does not exclude Black immigrants from racist experiences. Nor does it prevent racism—institutionalized and otherwise—from blocking Caribbean immigrants' efforts at upward mobility. Caribbean immigrant parents' ability to identify incidents or ideas as racialized and the extent to which they perceive racial encounters as legitimate threats play a crucial role in their decisions about racial and ethnic socialization.

Ethnic Socialization

Most of my respondents deemed ethnic socialization an intuitive process critical to rearing psychologically healthy and successful children. Parents preferred ethnic socialization because: (1) they experienced it in their own histories, (2) they perceived ethnic socialization as closely tied to upward mobility, and (3) they viewed ethnic socialization as a favorable means of responding to U.S. racism and avoiding the Americanization of Caribbean American youth.

The idea that parents could give their children the tools to circumvent the effects of racism by instilling a strong ethnic identity

served to diminish my respondents' belief in the need for racial socialization. They inadvertently addressed race through ethnic socialization practices. In essence, ethnic socialization served as
racial socialization by reinforcing strategies and messages that
countered messages fraught with negative racial stereotypes.

While Caribbean immigrant parents often made explicit attempts to socialize their children by promoting Caribbean ethnic
values, children many times experienced ethnic socialization simply through familial relationships and interactions and cultural
activities. Most of my younger-generation respondents experienced
ethnic socialization through membership in a variety of Caribbean
networks. In many instances, Caribbean American youth traveled
to the Caribbean one or two times per year. These travels exposed
Caribbean American youth firsthand to life in the Caribbean. As
Marcia explained, her daughter expected these travels would take
her to a resort, but they didn't.

> When I say, "You going to Jamaica, Missy." [She replies,] "I'm going to
> *Jamaaaaaica*, ooh, ooh" 'cause she see Jamaica on TV and she know that
> we always going so, she say, "I'm going to Jamaica." I say it's not what
> you thinking is where you going.

Marcia and Mark's youngest daughter, Missy, who was about 4
years old at the time, had never been to Jamaica, and for Mark
and Marcia it was imperative that she have the opportunity not
simply to experience Jamaica through television commercials but
instead to spend time in the rural communities in which both her
parents were raised. Despite the fact that Mark was raised in
Kingston, he wanted his children to spend time in the hills of Montego Bay. Particularly for parents who hailed from rural communities, it was vital that their children experience life without
American comforts. Caribbean American youth spend summer and
winter vacations with their grandparents, aunts, uncles, and cousins in their homes. These experiences gave students their own perceptions of the Caribbean.

Antoinette's description of her aunt's house in Jamaica where
she stayed during her visits illustrates this same form of ethnic
socialization.

> She lives in Spanish Town and she, well, it's a little shack. Well, it's a lit-
> tle ranch I would say.... It don't really have an upstairs and don't
> ranches [have] one [level]?... She has ackee trees and stuff like that and
> like you can go on top of the roof and stuff like, there's a ladder you can
> just stand up there or lay down up there and stuff....

Antoinette illustrates the clash of cultures when she refers to her aunt's shack as a "ranch" home. My parent respondents used international travel like Antoinette's to buttress messages implicit in life narratives and success stories. Through travel to the Carib-bean, young people learned about the poverty, scant infrastruc-ture, and the lack of modern amenities their parents had experienced. These experiences created opportunities for Carib-bean American youth to juxtapose their parents' humble begin-nings with a middle-class lifestyle and accept their narratives that hard work and ambition lead to upward mobility. Antoinette's ini-tial description of her aunt's home as a "shack" highlighted the ways in which Caribbean youth experienced and perceived the Caribbean context. She and her peers believed that their parents had overcome potentially insurmountable challenges as they pro-pelled themselves to middle-class status in the United States.

Ethnic socialization did not only hold up the Caribbean experi-ence as one of deprivation by comparison to middle-class American childhoods. Craig's son Jeffrey mentioned that his dad would often share experiences of what it was like growing up in Jamaica. These narratives often created a romanticized notion of life in the Caribbean in comparison to children's experiences growing up in the United States.

> My dad...usually tells me how he had to walk home and it was just a fun
> environment to be in and my mom usually tells me how, stories about
> when she was a child. She said that they would go down to the beach a
> lot and yeah, yeah. He usually played soccer and cricket and then walked
> home and he also went to the beach with his friends and walked home
> from there.

I asked Jeffrey whether he thought his parents were bragging about their childhoods and he said:

Yeah, my dad actually thinks that it was better to live back then...because there's a lot of, because the technology right now it, hurt, hurt people like, like predators on-line, that's why.

Narratives of the Caribbean as whimsical and buoyant helped to cement Caribbean American youth's adherence to the notion that the Caribbean is inherently special. Narratives of fun times at the river, hiking expeditions, and delectable fruit just waiting to be picked from the backyard further fueled 1.5- and second-generation youth's desire to remain connected to their parents' homeland. In part, these idealized narratives reflected that which Caribbean immigrant parents yearned for most and which was largely absent from the suburban locale in which they resided.

International travel solidified the messages conveyed in parental narratives and provided Caribbean American youth with first-hand opportunities to engage in or witness the activities to which parents alluded. For instance, when asked to describe his visits to Jamaica and Dominica, trips he took 2–3 times per year, Jeffrey explained, "We usually play outside and visit my dad's friends, mmm, yeah, and go to the beach...um, we, we can go to...the...field and play soccer." In Dominica he added that he would "usually...go on hikes and go...see the sights and stuff."

International travel is an essential element of ethnic socialization practices as it exposes youth to daily life in the Caribbean and provides firsthand experiences to buttress parental narratives. These experiences further tied youth to positive notions of the Caribbean and Caribbeanness, and these beliefs directly reflect lessons and personal investments that parents described to their children. The similarity between Jeffrey's reported experiences in the Caribbean and his father's stories reflect his father's decision to reconstruct experiences he believed to be useful in his own ethnic socialization, experiences that reinforced an informed knowledge of and pride in Caribbean heritage and identity.

Ethnic socialization by way of international travel also helped to inform Caribbean American children of distinctions between what it meant to be Caribbean and how that was distinctly different from what it meant to be American. For instance, Bryce, who often travelled to Jamaica twice a year, argued that people in Jamaica were "happy all the time" and "always smiling." In comparing Jamaicans to Americans, Bryce posited that even though many Jamaicans had not amassed a great amount of material possessions, they maintained joyful comportment and appeared satisfied with their lives. To Bryce, these characteristics were in stark contrast to Americans who were wealthier but "always frowning." These distinctions engendered ethnic pride and solidified ethnic affiliations. Comparisons between individuals in Caribbean and U.S. contexts also informed Caribbean American youth's perspectives of ethnic distinctions within the Black race as well as differences in how the groups experienced race.

International travel as a socialization strategy prompted appreciation for the opportunities afforded to Caribbean American youth in the United States and also provided opportunities for youth to experience Blacks across various socioeconomic strata. The ability to interact with poor, unemployed Blacks, those who work as farmers and marketwomen, and also experience middle-class Blacks who serve as business owners and politicians provided an image of Blacks as multidimensional—a message distinctly different from the mostly negative stereotypes of Blacks in the United States. Furthermore, these visits proved to Caribbean American youth that success or failure was not simply grounded in racial distinctions, but instead in other issues such as class background, education level, or work ethic.

Scholars of transnationalism speak to the ways in which the circulation of ideas through social networks transcends international borders and reproduces identities that represent particular places and spaces but are not necessarily enacted within those spaces (Abu El Haj, 2007; Horst, 2007). While trips to the Caribbean played a central role in forging transnational ties and remained a major component of Caribbean American youth's ethnic socialization, my respondents also forged ethnic connections by developing relationships within local immigrant networks. Caribbean immigrant parents intentionally sought to develop relationships with other Caribbean immigrants and create opportunities for their children to interact socially.

Both students and parents at Morristown sought to foster connections between Caribbean American students. For example, Kerry Ann and Craig knew each other prior to the beginning of the study, which explained their informal banter at the initial parent meeting. Kerry Ann and Craig planned engagements for Jeffrey and Bryce that extended beyond informal social interactions to include what they considered ethnically relevant activities. Soccer was rarely a sport of choice for Black students at Morristown Middle School or the Morristown community leagues; however, Jeffrey and Bryce played together on both soccer teams. The boys were encouraged to play soccer rather than other sports that attracted Black boys in droves. In part, this decision was made based on soccer's popularity in the Caribbean and their parents' love for the sport.

Antoinette and Elyse's parents were also friends and kept their children connected to one another and other Caribbean American friends in and outside of school. Most students whose parents didn't have the social access to foster these connections sought out other Caribbean American students themselves. According to Tamara, it was important to have friends from a Caribbean background. She explained:

> I guess we was just, we just got drawn to each other because we're from, like you know, like different, 'cause we...learn almost from the same values...'cause we know like the same, hmmm, like the same way we learn from each other, like the same way we act, like we act very much the same.

Although Tamara had a difficult time articulating why she and other Caribbean American students were "drawn to each other," somewhere along the line she had learned that it was important to develop friendships with people who shared similar values and experiences. Parents further reinforced these ideas by modeling their involvement in Caribbean networks. They also provided opportunities to engage Caribbean family and friends by taking frequent trips to New York City and Washington, D.C.

Beyond the intentional and unintentional means of ethnic socialization by way of endorsing Caribbean American peer networks, the parents I spoke with generally provided home spaces with Caribbean cultural items and markers. Almost every student in the study described visual representations of their respective islands situated at central places in their home. Families tended to recreate a sense of the Caribbean within their U.S. domestic space. When asked to describe her home environment, Elyse stated:

> Um, it's [cozy] you know when you walk in, the living room is to the left and...like the furniture and stuff is set up of like a, gives you like an island vibe, like bamboo looking um chairs and bamboo looking coffee table and um, we have two parrots and it gives you like an island vibe, you know, the colors and stuff....

Elyse saw her home as recreating an island feel. According to racial socialization scholars (Caughy et al., 2002), items placed in and around the home serve to socialize youth in accordance to particular values and interests. The associations Caribbean American students made between their physical homes in the United States and the sense of a Caribbean "home" further encouraged ethnic identities deeply tied to their Caribbean heritage.

Like Elyse, Tamara described elements of her home that reinforced her mother's connection to her Antiguan background as represented by visual displays of artwork and flags in the home. Tamara said:

> We have this one picture right above the TV and right before you walk inside and ah, it's ah, it's um, it's a picture of a sailboat in...Antigua going right into, into the harbor with like crab, with a net full of crabs after they got finished fishing in the morning and like it's like dawn coming up.

The central position of the painting articulated what Tamara's family valued and spoke to the centrality of the Antiguan experience and the family's connection to the place represented in the visual image. This painting also served as the cornerstone to other artifacts throughout the home such as the Antiguan flag that had once belonged to Tamara's great-grandfather, who served in the Antiguan military.

After residing in the United States for approximately 2 decades, Tamara's mother's ties to Antiguan heritage remained salient. Her commitment to the needs of Antiguan people showed that salience as much as her display of Antiguan artifacts. Tamara's mother organized and ran a national disaster relief organization for Antigua, a position that demanded a significant amount of her time. Similarly, Jeffrey mentioned that his dad demonstrated his pride in being Jamaican by way of involvement in organizations and social activities. Jeffrey said that his father would describe Jamaicans as "prideful"; in explaining this inference, he states: "'Cause my dad...shows that he is Jamaican through many activities."

In Jeffrey's analysis, his dad's involvement in Caribbean think tanks, Jamaican entrepreneurship and journalism organizations, and local soccer teams communicated his pride in being Jamaican. While parents may not have undertaken this kind of involvement in order to provide ethnic socialization to their kids, these actions communicated messages that invoked meaning related to ethnic pride and values. In particular, many of the parents in my study demonstrated community involvement and "giving back" as an ethnic value central to the Caribbean immigrant experience and value system.

Ethnic Socialization and the Caribbean Value System

In addition to instilling a strong sense of ethnic identity through intentional and unintentional strategies, ethnic identities were informed by several specific ethnic values. These fundamental values included: (1) hard work, (2) manners and respect (especially directed toward elders), (3) community involvement and interdependence, and (4) educational achievement. Craig's response to the question, "What were some of the values that you were taught by your family?" captured these values.

> I think, you know, the whole concept of working hard, um, you can get ahead in life by studying hard, working hard, getting an education, respecting people, respecting your elders. No matter what, one of the biggest lessons is, no matter what background somebody comes from, they're poor, rich, you treat them the same and that's, you know, carried me all through my life.

Hard Work

Of all the themes parents highlighted in discussing values, the one value that was most consistently articulated across families was hard work. Most often Caribbean immigrants deemed their propensity for "hard work" as essential to their ethnic identities. The ethos of hard work was central to the life narratives each parent shared with his or her children. According to Caribbean immigrants, a proclivity toward hard work was fundamental to lifelong success and widely representative of the Caribbean experience.

Immigrants who were reared in poor or rural communities spoke of hard work that began with the physicality of chores and daily routines. In other words, hard work as a necessary means of survival became integrated into ethnic scripts over time. Additionally, the absence of job opportunities in many small rural communities often forced Caribbean inhabitants to develop their own economic resources through entrepreneurship frequently tied to the availability of natural resources that required caretaking of crops and the rearing of animals, as Kerry Ann and Marcia described in their life narratives.

Mark, on the other hand, described his propensity for hard work as rooted in his desire to begin working at age 14. He reported:

> What happened is, my journey so long and I could sit here all day and tell you, and probably you have to put in a next tape, but, um, with me, always um, I'm one of those type that I'm a hard worker and always believe in working and having your own. I'm a Virgo and I love nice things and so forth. It's just that I been, when I tell someone that I start working when I was 14, I used to leave school and then I stop at the [grocery store], that's...the wholesale place, weigh the stuff, clean the bathroom....

Mark also spoke of holding multiple jobs after graduating from high school. He emphasized that "hard work" and *not* book smarts led to his socioeconomic advancement.

Craig, on the other hand, recognized that his upper-middle-class status shielded him from the need to engage in *hard work* as defined by physical labor or taking on multiple jobs. However, he noted that his family was able to achieve upper-middle-class status due to his father's commitment to working hard. Craig argued that although his family was upper middle class, "it didn't feel like it 'cause my father had to work hard." In essence, Craig implied that his parents' upper-middle-class status was not achieved on the basis of unearned privilege, but instead through his father's hard work, which afforded him the privileges of upper-middle-class status. This framing of his family's class position also reinforced the necessity of hard work in achieving success.

Students in the study showed an awareness of hard work as a deeply entrenched Caribbean value, too. Not only did Caribbean American youth gain exposure to parental value systems; many of them understood them as central to their lives. The first characteristic Geneva could name to describe how her mother would portray Trinidadian people was "hard workers, she always says that they are people that work really really hard." I asked what that meant, and she went on:

> Like, to like have a goal and to try to go for that goal.... [M]y aunt has a catering company and she caters to all the banks in Trinidad and she made that goal and she achieved that and now my grandma...she's a baker...but she like bakes for my aunt's catering company and she also bakes like wedding cakes and stuff like that so, if you wanna get something you have to work hard for it.

Geneva's description was rooted in several generations of experiences based in the Caribbean context. Examples like these demonstrated potential fissures in people's understanding of how and whether values promulgated throughout the Caribbean would transfer to life in the United States. Additionally, Caribbean perspectives regarding hard work were based on setting and attaining goals and not necessarily on educational achievement or securing a job. Instead, in the histories of my respondents' families, hard work functioned to enable people to establish autonomous means of income generation. Income generation through entrepreneurship might be the only viable option in countries with limited job opportunities.

Like Geneva's mother, Mark and Craig described sharing their perceptions and examples of the benefits of hard work with young people, including their own children. Craig used Barack Obama as an example. He argued: "Every Black child or every child in America can look and say that literally...anybody can become president, you know, working hard enough and believing in yourself." Mark also told his own story as an example of the benefits of hard work to high school students he hired to work in his catering business,

and hoped that his son, Charles, would also overhear these conversations. Mark recalled explaining to his employees that despite
hardships, he had been able to make strides in his development by
understanding that "nothing is easy...you gotta work hard and you
can achieve anything."

Parents' socialization efforts concentrated on the message of
hard work as a means to achievement in every family whose member participated in the study. Both professional and non-
professional families supported hard work within the context of
education and entrepreneurship as essential to attaining personal
and financial goals. Though "hard work" was pivotal to the Caribbean ethnic script, parents did not teach any one path to success,
but instead Caribbean American youth had the flexibility to tread
a variety of paths to success as long as they worked hard.

Good Manners

My respondents may not have emphasized good manners as
strongly as hard work, but they all regarded good manners highly.
More specifically, my respondents perceived behaviors around interpersonal interactions, such as acknowledging the presence of
others and demonstrating reverence toward elders, as essential
characteristics of a well-mannered individual. When I asked what
values Caribbean parents learned growing up, Kerry Ann stated,
"Education is the key to success and manners make a man. Those
are the things you always remember and be humble." In a similar
vein, Mark added:

> My mom, she always say, "manners carry you through the world" you
> know.... She always say even if you don't have any education, you can't
> read, you can't write, and you have manners, you never know who you
> pass in the hallway and say hi to 'cause that's probably the person who
> gonna interview you for a job.

My respondents perceived manners as supplemental to hard work,
as hard work alone would not bring success. For parents, "manners" were a set of culturally specific guidelines that ensured individuals' full participation in a social network in which mutual
respect and support bounded the parameters of participation.
Within a web of relationships, the display of good manners could

prove advantageous when opportunities arose or when an individual had unmet needs.

According to Caribbean parents, displaying manners can have profound implications for an individual's quality of life and propensity for upward mobility. As a result, parents felt strongly about conveying to their children this ethnic value. An individual's status within a network and ability to receive favors as a member of the network is tied to one's reputation among other participants. Likewise, one's ability to abide by cultural codes regarding manners and respect granted individuals greater access to resources. The ability to display good manners seemed to carry more weight for individuals to whom class status and educational attainment is restricted. This access is of particular importance in a context where resources are limited, and therefore one's livelihood may depend upon what can be garnered through relationships.

Like immigrants of other nationalities, Caribbean immigrants fear the Americanization of their children and the loss of cultural values and norms (Kao & Tienda, 1995; Zhou, 1997). Caribbean parents particularly express concern about preserving cultural perceptions of manners and respect. However, parents also found it difficult to reinforce rules that govern appropriate behavior in a context with different behavioral codes and in a generation that places less emphasis on the importance of good manners and respect.

Craig also argued that "things like respecting your parents, grandparents, and relatives...are part and parcel of growing up or being Jamaican." When asked to describe the practices that engendered respect toward elders, Craig explained that you must make eye contact with elders, come to them when they call you or ask you a question, as answering while in another room or at a distance was unacceptable, and always using a respectful tone when speaking to adults. Any tone of defiance or disdain when communicating with adults was deemed terribly inappropriate. Craig recalled having to reinforce these skills in his children, especially when their grandparents came to visit from Dominica and Jamaica.

Another specific way in which young people were to demonstrate good manners and respect was to verbally acknowledge passersby. Mark and Marcia expressed their frustration in trying to enforce this rule.

Mark: [The kids] get up in the morning and they walk by the room, even if the door is open, they walk by and then when they coming back that's when they choose to say good morning. I can't figure that out. I was like, okay, you passed and you saw me.... I get up, and they get up and go brush they teeth and do everything and that's when they say good morning, if they do say it. But we, we raise[d] [to believe that] as soon as you open your eye and you see the person, it's good morning and that's how I try to raise my kids.

Marcia: If you see adults, no matter who they are, we had to say good morning. Good morning, Mr. Whatever. Good afternoon, Mr. Whatever.

Mark: And [use] Mr. and Mrs.

Marcia: We could not pass them. Respect was, you know, a must. If you pass them um, they would say um, they go report us to our parents and they will say, how come you pass Ms. so and so and didn't say good evening and good morning blah, blah, blah, you know, so those were one of our expectations from my parents that you know, it was a must for us to have manners to our elders.

Mark and Marcia used examples of their upbringing to explain what they tried to instill in their children and why this was such a critical value. In some instances in which children did not adhere to Caribbean conventions of manners and respect, parents described them as becoming *Americanized* and therefore moving away from ethnic values, an infraction that often resulted in verbal tirades on the part of parents. While parents emphasized hard work as a Caribbean American value, they acknowledged that other groups of people might share that value. On the other hand, however, they understood *manners and respect* as specific to Caribbean people. Caribbean immigrants did not perceive that most Americans, regardless of race, embraced the same notions of manners and respect. As a result, they described manners as a particularly distinct ethnic marker.

Community and Family Engagement

In many instances, families also mentioned that a sense of community was central to the Caribbean experience and that, like manners, Americans lacked that sense. Many parents said the lack of community and absence of relationships with their neighbors bothered them more than almost anything else about transitioning to life in the United States. When asked if there was anything she was still adjusting to in the United States, Kerry Ann said:

> You know, the communal part of it. I think I should be able to go to my neighbor and say, "I cook dinner, you wanna come over?" Like I feel that you just closed in. You boxed in, you can't.... I go to Jamaica right now with my sister and she cooks and everybody comes over and eat. Like Mrs. Simpson what you have? Well, we cookin' suh and suh and suh. Okay, we comin' ova. No matter how poor people are, that's what they do and I just don't understand why we penny pinch, you look at how much money we have, oh we can't afford this. What is wrong with bringing friends and family together? I don't know my neighbors, neither does Bryce. They only want to know you to get in your business or where you work and I'm thinking, that's not life, that's not living.

A sense of togetherness, particularly as it related to family and the local community, was central to the identities and experiences of Caribbean immigrants. Immigrants' experiences in the Caribbean—living in rural communities and smaller cities where families had dwelled for generations—facilitated close relationships between family and the community at large. Close kinship bonds often include extended family and informal, yet equally significant, ties to individuals with no blood relation. The intimate ties between family, fictive kin, and friends brought deep meaning to the lives of individuals and were often the basis for contentment and joy. Like many recent immigrants, Caribbean immigrants go to great lengths to maintain these relations, and this further reinforces the centrality of family and community for Caribbean American youth (see Falicov, 2007)—another form of ethnic socialization.

Evidence of full membership in family and community networks also involved sharing resources. Monetary contributions and the sharing of food and other daily staples occurred regardless of individuals' economic status. While families most in need often received the most subsidies, these supports were often provided by family and community members with only a slight economic advantage. Marcia discussed how a sense of community, built around shared resources, was central to her experience as a child:

> Every Sunday a whole group of people used to come to our house, whoever didn't have food, come and eat. Even during the week, who didn't have food, oh come on over, we'll give you food, you understand. So, that's how my grand mom was. She was um...she was the main house in the community where people know um...if you don't have food to eat, you go to Ms. Mum's yard and she'll give you some food, you know, that's how it was and that's how she taught me and that's how my mom is too.

Not only did my respondents perceive giving as an ethnic value; they often described it as a family legacy. Several families in the study described the ways in which the concept of sharing and helping others, particularly those less fortunate, continued to be central to their lives even as they resided in the United States.

Sharing provides tangible resources such as food and shelter; it also manifests in the act of caring for and looking after others, whether kin or not. Seeing her grandmother feed and provide for the needs of others in their local community gave Marcia a sense of pride. Despite the lack of available space in Marcia's home, her grandmother would often take in people who had no place to stay. Marcia recalled:

> My grand mom went to town to sell, she sell like goods too and she met this lady, young girl, she was pregnant, and the young girl didn't have anywhere to go and she said, "Come on back with me." She took her off to...our one room house and the girl um, stayed with my grand mom until she had the baby. She give birth to the baby and then one day left the baby, I think it was like 10 months old, in front of the hot fire stove, and left and my grand mom had him ever since then and...that's...the only mom he knew and nobody can't tell her that's not her son. Sometimes my mom is jealous, my mom says, you love him more than you love me. You know, so you know, that's how it is.

Marcia's grandmother's act, though striking, is not so unusual in the Caribbean. Many families recalled having informally adopted individuals into their family. In Geneva's description of her family tree, she mentioned that her grandmother's best friend raised her mother because she was in a better position to care for a child. As a result, Geneva proclaimed, "I have two grandmothers!" Similarly, Elyse mentioned having an adopted sister who resided with Mark and Marcia, a teenager they had taken in and cared for. Through these stories and experiences, Caribbean American youth learned the values of community and interdependence and embedded them into their schematic understanding of the world. Because their parents taught these values through a framework of Caribbean heritage and legacy, they enabled Caribbean American youth to perceive themselves as potentially—if not actually—distinctly different from many Americans.

Education

The parents among my respondents taught education in a nuanced way in comparison to hard work, good manners, and valuing community cooperation and interdependence. On the one hand, parents argued, "I'm very proud that I was born [in Jamaica]. I was very proud that I grew up in a country where I see that the poorest of the poor can break the cycle of poverty by education, going to school and being ambitious." On the other hand, parents felt that formal schooling, and college attendance in particular, was not for everyone, nor was it the only means of achieving success. Respondents defined education and the value of education more broadly, as encompassing an array of educational structures. In some instances, "street smarts," informal learning from engagement with community elders, formal academic schooling, and learning a skill or trade were all embedded in the espoused value of education.

Although respondents cited educational attainment as a value endemic to Caribbean people, they differed about the ways in which education could be acquired. In a sense, Caribbean perspectives regarding the value of education as a means to upward mobility mirrored the famous debate between Booker T. Washington and W.E.B. Du Bois (Du Bois, 2007). Was it better to achieve socioeconomic mobility by way of formal education or by means of economic independence through skilled labor and entrepreneurship? Mark grappled with this question as he explained his perceptions of various educational trajectories. He started by explaining that his cousin, who lives in Jamaica, does not work as hard as he does and does not even have to wash his own car. Mark stated:

> He sitting there watching somebody wash his car for him and he never get up in the morning [to] go nowhere. Not saying that's how I want to be, but I'm saying working from 14 and you still seem like you can't get a grip on something. I don't believe in that, so I'm not gonna be used and abused by you know, by people.... That's why I try to pass it on to my kids, it's good to have an education, simple as I tell my daughter and all of them, college don't make for everyone, you know, it's nice to go, but...what happen is, you have a lot of people go there and they still come back and they, you know, waiter, and they back there cooking, but they go to college, so what go wrong, you know? So when you have a skill or a trade, you can't be hungry. My mom always say when you have a trade or a skill, if you hungry, [that means] you lazy, you understand, 'cause somebody gonna call you to build a bed for them, somebody gonna call you to go cook, somebody gonna call you for something pertaining to your skill or your trade so you can't go wrong with that. So, you know, that's my belief.

Not only does Mark believe in trades as viable options for upward mobility; he also believes that learning a trade may be an easier route to self-sufficiency and economic independence than earning a college degree. In other words, given the basic needs skilled labor and trades fulfill there are always opportunities for economic advancement, which is a safer alternative to having one's economic future determined by fickle markets and self-interested corporations.

For families in the study, current social class mediated their perspectives on whether formal academic training or skilled labor was the best route to upward mobility. Professional parents tended to support more traditional academic routes, and non-professional parents tended to highlight options such as skilled labor and entrepreneurship. I observed only one exception. Jade, whose mother was not a professional but was enrolled in a 4-year degree program at the time of the study, also endorsed a traditional educational trajectory. Professional parents who participated in the study worked as accountants, registered nurses, or in the corporate arena, while non-professional parents worked as nurse's aides, business owners, security guards, and chefs. Despite their respective career trajectories, however, one reality prevailed: many had achieved middle-class status.

Although families that were solidly middle class and those who were lower middle class differed from one another, I found evidence to prove that respondents had achieved middle-class status through varying degrees of educational attainment and hard work as supported by ethnic narratives. Additionally, many families engaged in some form of entrepreneurial venture. For some, these ventures were their main source of income, while others used entrepreneurship to supplement their income and amass wealth. To some degree, many families demonstrated a desire for economic independence through entrepreneurship.

Parents' educational and career backgrounds not only informed the messages they shared with their children regarding the best means to upward mobility, but also shaped their participation in their children's formal education. Non-professional parents, most of whom did not have significant formal education, expected their children to perform well in school but could offer little assistance. They had heavy work schedules, lack of experience with the material, and little awareness of their children's academic needs. However, professional parents engaged in their children's education by checking their grades regularly, perusing their notebooks to review information, and helping them to complete assignments and class projects. Coupled with messages regarding the value of and options for educational attainment, parents' educational background seemed to correlate with their children's educational achievement, as the children of professional parents were tracked into higher-level classes and those of non-professional parents into lower-level classes (as the next chapter will discuss further).

Conclusion

Ultimately, ethnic socialization was central to the experiences of Caribbean American youth. Caribbean immigrant parents engaged in ethnic socialization often without referencing race. They understood that the qualities and values they sought to instill as part of ethnic socialization were indicative of a Caribbean value system.

Whether ethnic socialization practices and messages held up in the U.S. context or not, parents transmitted to their children messages they had learned and taught what their own experience equipped them to teach.

Both professional and non-professional families among my respondents had attained some form of the "American Dream." They had amassed enough resources to purchase homes in a racially diverse and solidly middle-class community with exceptional public schools. Caribbean immigrant parents provided for their children what they thought were the best living situations and educational experiences they could afford. In an attempt to encourage their children to achieve at similar levels or higher ones, Caribbean immigrant parents relied heavily on ethnic socialization messages of hard work, family and community interdependence, manners, and an investment in educational attainment. However, Caribbean immigrant parents often failed to acknowledge the ways in which their racial and social class backgrounds might have constrained their mobility. An understanding of the costs of racism in the United States begs the question of how these families' lives would have been different had they been White immigrants or if all parents had integrated into middle-class communities and schools upon arrival in the United States. I would argue that in spite of their perceived successes, they paid an incalculable price because of their race, immigrant, and class status—a price that their life narratives of success and ethnic socialization practices failed to capture.

CHAPTER FOUR

Caribbean Immigrants, Racism, and Racial Socialization

As discussed in Chapter 3, ethnic socialization—as defined by the transmission of values, practices, and culture of people from the same region—is integral to the childrearing practices of Caribbean immigrants. Caribbean immigrants' parenting often focused on transmitting values specific to what is meant to be Antiguan, Guyanese, Jamaican, or Trinidadian. However, racial socialization—the means by which parents prepare their children to thrive in spite of the established racial hierarchy—was new to Caribbean American parents. For Caribbean immigrant parents, racial socialization was a different kind of socialization process, one that had to be learned and integrated into parenting practices over time. Consequently, racial socialization occurred to a lesser extent than ethnic socialization practices and with less certainty of the outcome. Unlike ethnic socialization, which was fairly consistent across parents, racial socialization varied tremendously and was informed by transnational notions of self and identity, which were devoid of strong racial underpinnings.

For Caribbean immigrants, racial socialization and the necessity of transmitting particular messages to one's children regarding not only ancestry but also race (as a notion tied to the social implications of one's ancestry and phenotype) was altogether new. Though Blacks in the Caribbean recognize themselves as Black people and descendants of Africa, these notions of race are not inextricably tied to social and economic expectations.

In particular, the concept of racial socialization and the impetus for parental racial socialization in the United States arose from the historical implications tied to the unique history of Blacks in the United States. Given the United States' legacy of the exclusion and oppressions of Blacks within the U.S. context over time, it has been imperative that Blacks in America rear their children to recognize, understand, and cope with American racism. While I would argue that racism is pervasive across the globe due to macro-structures designed to pillage nations and communities of color for resources used to support the capitalistic gains of mostly Whites in First World countries, micro-level racism, the kind that one deals with day to day, is relatively absent in the Caribbean context (Vickerman, 2001). As a result of this contextual distinction, the racial socialization practices of Caribbean migrants become of paramount importance.

When asked whether their parents ever talked to them about race growing up, each parent responded with a resounding "No!" However, their answers were often followed by descriptions of traumatizing experiences that propelled them toward a U.S. understanding of race. For Caribbean immigrants, integration into U.S. society included learning that *you are Black*, and learning *what it means to be Black*. Caribbean immigrants did not have the benefit of parental or communal guidance on navigating blackness specifically in highly racialized spaces like the ones in which they found themselves. Instead, Caribbean immigrants learned on their own, and in many instances rejected the imposition of U.S.-centric terms and beliefs regarding people of African descent.

Many U.S. scholars have argued that Caribbean immigrants hold to their ethnic identities mainly in an attempt to distance themselves from Black Americans and the marginalization to which that group is often subjected (Rogers, 2006; Waters, 1999). Others maintain that embracing national and ethnic identities in lieu of a dominant racial identity is evidence of an unhealthy racial identity in Black immigrants (Hall & Carter, 2006). However, these arguments do not account for the complexity of Caribbean immigrants' transnational position in relation to U.S. racial politics. Furthermore, scholars work from the supposition that Caribbean immigrants view Black Americans as their primary comparison group. In fact, this is an unfounded assumption informed by U.S. modes of categorization that are unfairly imposed upon Black immigrants. Caribbean immigrants in this study made distinctions not simply between themselves and Black Americans, but rather between themselves and *all* Americans. Camaraderie with other groups was rare except for relationships built with other immigrants from the Caribbean region and, in many cases, only the immigrant's native country.

With this in mind, it can be argued that any distancing from Black Americans does not readily imply a rejection of African ancestry or racial solidarity with Black Americans. What distinguished Caribbean immigrants from all Americans was their national origin and their perceived cultural distinctiveness. Furthermore, most Caribbean immigrants migrated to the United States with a profound consciousness of their history, one in which Blacks have been hailed as prominent leaders and visionaries. As eloquently stated by Kerry Ann in the epigraph to Chapter 3, Caribbean immigrants' resistance to American notions of blackness demonstrated their struggle to uphold the premise that they are in fact "human" first. However, Caribbean immigrants had not come to recognize this distinction as a privilege—a privilege that was not readily afforded to Black Americans, who have had to continually fight to prove their humanity to White America.

According to Hall and Carter (2006), a healthy racial identity is evidenced by an individual's ability to acknowledge the ways in which racism impacts the experiences of Blacks in the United States. However, such expectations place an unreasonable burden of responsibility onto Caribbean immigrants by insisting that they readily identify with and understand the struggles of native-born Blacks. In this case, a "healthy" identity was defined on the basis of having to acknowledge and combat unhealthy definitions of blackness—a definition that may not transcend psychological realities and geographical contexts.

As a result of these distinct experiences, parental racial socialization on the part of Caribbean immigrants often centered on *reactive* rather than *proactive* racial socialization measures. Without an intergenerational legacy of racial socialization experiences and parenting practices, Caribbean immigrants typically did not anticipate the need for proactive or protective measures of racial socialization in the way that Black American parents have. After living in the United States for several decades, Caribbean American parents still described racial discrimination as a strange and foreign concept. When asked whether her parents discuss things Black students are prone to experience in schools, Geneva responded:

> No, not really 'cause my mom said she didn't know about prejudice and
> stuff like that until she came here so I think it's just here, 'cause it's not
> a lot of that in Trinidad, like, you don't really like, talk about other peo-
> ple's races and stuff like that, so it's not like...my mom says as soon as
> she came here that's how...she started like knowing about prejudice and
> all that kind of stuff so, no not really.

In this example, Geneva cites her mother's lack of experience with racial prejudice as the reason her mother did not engage her in conversations around race. Just two parents in the study experienced K–12 education in the United States, one for only a short stint in high school. For the most part, immigrant parents were educated abroad in racially and ethnically homogeneous schools. The racial homogeneity of schools spanned the entire school population from administrators to staff to students. As a result, not only did parents have difficulty anticipating the presence of racism in their daily lives, but they also had little contextual understanding of the ways in which racism manifested in the educational experiences of youth. This distinction is central to understanding the racial socialization of Caribbean American youth, as many of their encounters with race and racism occurred at school. Unfortunately, parents did not anticipate, relate to, or validate their children's racialized experiences in schools, particularly in cases where racialized experiences were covert.

Most Caribbean American students in the study stated that their parents rarely made mention of personal experiences with racism. This pattern was all the more intriguing given racial socialization literature that argues that middle-class Blacks are more apt to identify incidents as racist than their lower-class counterparts (Williams, 1999, as cited in Hughes et al., 2006). However, findings from this study show that there might be a departure from the typical relationship between class and the acknowledgment of racism for Caribbean immigrants. Black Americans of higher socioeconomic status were more likely to view incidents as racist; however, the opposite was true for the Caribbean immigrants in this study. For Caribbean immigrants, the ability to recognize racism seemed to be mediated by their length of stay in the United States and whether they were integrated into the Black underclass.

An Unawareness of Race

Parents who were more recent immigrants were less likely to demonstrate an awareness of race. Nadette's family had only migrated to the United States about 3 years prior to the study. As a 1.5-generation American, Nadette could still recall her life in Jamaica and possessed a slight Caribbean accent as compared to other students in the study. Nadette shared that she had never had conversations about race with her mother, her primary guardian. In response to inquiries regarding racial socialization practices in her home, Nadette unequivocally stated that there was *no* mention of race. The following examples are excerpts from interviews with Nadette over the course of the study.

C: Do your parents talk to you about what it means to be Black?

N: No.

C: So your parents don't talk about race often?

N: No, not at all.

C: Okay, um, does your mom talk about things that Black children might experience in school?

N: No.

C: Do you talk to your mom about how you feel when you're in classes with mostly White students?

N: No.

Given Nadette's terse responses to my inquiries regarding race talk in her home, one might assume that she was a reticent adolescent. On the contrary, Nadette thoughtfully articulated responses to most interview questions except those related to explicit dialogue around issues of race. Although Nadette was in the process of formulating her opinion of U.S. racial conventions and politics through her experiences at Morristown, Nadette's mother showed few signs of attempting to grapple with what it meant to raise a Black child in America.

As the most recent immigrant of all the Caribbean parents in the study, Nadette's mother had not come to identify race as central to her experience in the United States and therefore did not recognize the need or possess the necessary skills to engage in racial socialization practices. For Nadette's family, explicit ethnic socialization was not necessitated, either. As relatively new immigrants to the country, Nadette's family mostly lived their lives as Jamaicans in the United States to the extent possible. Nadette's mother did not perceive the need to imbue in her daughter ethnic values, as she still possessed many of the qualities deemed appropriate for a Jamaican girl her age. According to Nadette's teachers, she struggled academically but worked hard and was well behaved, a combination of qualities they admired. Nadette's comportment reflected Caribbean ethnic values of manners and respect toward elders and value for education as displayed by her work ethic.

Pat & Craig: This Nonsense Called Racism

Nadette's family had been residing in the United States for only 3 years at the time of the study, and her mother's ability to recognize and therefore combat the potentially harmful effects of racism through the use of racial socialization practices created unrealistic expectations for this family. However, for parents such as Craig, Jeffrey's father, and Pat, Geneva's mother, who had lived in the United States for well over a decade and were integrated into the American middle class as adults, their perspective on race and racism was a bit different. Unlike Nadette's mother, who did not recognize the role of race in daily life, Pat and Craig recognized that racism did exist, but they were dismissive of its relevance. Despite their length of stay in the United States, Pat and Craig's perception of racial discrimination as unusual and absurd had not diminished. Pat regarded Americans who promoted racism and xenophobia as simple minded, specifically in their lack of knowledge of diverse people and places. Her dismissal of American "isms" as nonsensical further fueled the notion that these behaviors did not warrant serious engagement in the form of explicit racial socialization. As a result, Pat continued to embrace ethnic socialization practices as most central to her parenting strategies and underestimated the extent to which racial socialization might be useful in rearing her daughter. Although Pat urged Geneva to work harder than her peers because of the possibility of experiencing racial and gender discrimination, the topic was not addressed in any detail.

More extensive conversations regarding why Geneva would have to work harder and how to recognize racial and gender discrimination seldom took place between Geneva and Pat. Geneva received excellent grades and competed aggressively with her peers. She rarely noted experiences with racial or gender discrimination. However, she intuitively gauged that racial and gender distinctions might have a more indelible impact on her later in life, or once she experienced "the real world." Geneva did not view racial and gender discrimination as central to her experiences as a middle school student who resided at home with her parents. As she grappled with the idea of discrimination through our formal and semi-formal interviews, she also demonstrated a dismissive stance toward discrimination. In an effort to quell the dissonance brought about by the thoughts of impending racism and sexism, Geneva asserted, "No one is gonna tell me what I can and cannot do!" Geneva argued that, like Barack Obama, who had overcome racial constraints to win the 2008 U.S. presidential election, she, too, would overcome obstacles erected by race and gender discrimination.

According to Nakkula and Toshalis (2006), students like Geneva who embrace ties to a particular minority group but accommodate and engage successfully with the mainstream often face pressures to adhere to the perceived norms of one group over another. This tension is said to lead to psychological distress in many instances. Likewise, a lack of preparation for such issues enhances the likelihood that students will perceive and respond to racialized incidents as a threat rather than a manageable challenge, further feeding the cycle of anxiety around issues of race (Stevenson, Reed, Bodison, & Bishop, 1997).

Geneva's solid academic achievement and cheerful disposition often granted her favor with her peers and teachers alike; however, she was not being prepared for more challenging racial en-

counters. Even with the affordances of a highly competitive academic record and the likelihood that she would in fact achieve her
goal of becoming a medical doctor, Geneva's lack of exposure to explicit forms of protective racial socialization could eventually impede her ability to cope with discrimination-related stress in
subsequent years.

Like Geneva's mom, Craig also dismissed ideas of racism and
racial stratification as preposterous. He acknowledged that some
racial inequities exist, but he felt that they were based on false assumptions of inferiority and therefore lacked plausibility. He
thought extensive discussions of race to be unnecessary beyond
debunking myths of racial inferiority that feed the low expectations of Black youth. When asked whether his children's race
impacted their educational experiences in the Morristown community, Craig argued:

> I think it does, I will absolutely agree...and say that it does and I think
> we've tried to offset the uh, that issue by taking an active involvement in
> the schools, you know, starting with kindergarten, but you know...I
> think it does especially as they get older there is an expectations game I
> call it where sometimes the expectation is that they're not gonna do as
> well and what we want to do, what we have done is, you know, push him
> and say look, you know, forget that nonsense of people playing that ex-
> pectations game with you, you've got to be the best in the class, so we've
> tried to push them a lot right from kindergarten going right up and then
> the...other side of the coin is that we have to get involved in the schools,
> so we've tried to, you know, PTO, these kind of meetings, anything comes
> up, we contact the teachers or the uh principal so uh, I think it does, but
> we've tried to mitigate the effects of that by involvement.

Craig argued that the "expectations game" was, in fact, "non-
sense," and he worked to dismantle its effects by encouraging his
children to supersede teachers' expectations and outperform peers
of all races in the classroom. What Craig referred to as the "expectations game" is conceptually similar to notions of "stereotype
threat," a term coined by Claude Steele (1997). Steele explains
that the stereotype threat is "a socially premised psychological
threat that arises when one is in a situation or doing something for
which a negative stereotype about one's group applies" (p. 614). In
essence, Craig's awareness of the threat of education-related

stereotypes prompted him to reinforce to his children the idea that they were indeed capable of achieving high levels of academic success. When asked whether attempts to circumvent the potential risks of low expectations were well received by his children, Craig conceded that Jeffrey most often made the honor roll and that his youngest son had been identified as intellectually gifted and was receiving supplemental services at the local elementary school.

While racial discrimination was the impetus for Craig's actions and inadvertent racial socialization practices, there was still relatively little explicit racial socialization apparent in the Thompsons' home. When asked how often he explicitly engaged in transmitting racial socialization messages to his children, Craig explained:

> I would say, not as often as I should and certainly more so in the last year or so especially with Barack Obama running and becoming president so...when a news story comes up, I discuss the news story for example, you know, a lynching or a um, a cross on somebody's lawn you know, from that perspective, but I don't necessarily go out and say, sit down and discuss race, it has to be in the context of something, current event happening.

Craig's racial socialization practices were mostly limited to his increased vigilance as an active participant in his children's education, as he cited attending school events, assisting the boys with homework, supplementing their education by exposing them to international issues not presented in the curriculum, and encouraging them to do their academic best as racially motivated socialization strategies. However, he also recognized the need to expose his boys to Black role models and used the election of Barack Obama to drive home points he conveyed regularly to his children: through hard work, they are capable of being the best. More sporadically, however, Craig noted engaging Jeffrey on the subject of race-related media representations of Blacks and helped him to process current events that highlighted discrimination against Blacks. Inadvertently, these conversations also suggested the absence of such incidents in the Caribbean context.

Kerry Ann: Preparation for
Racial Bias and the U.S. Penal System

Kerry Ann, though similar to Craig in socioeconomic status during the time of the study, had had drastically different experiences with incorporation into the U.S. social milieu. Unlike Craig, Kerry Ann moved from Jamaica to a working-class community in New Kensington, where her experience with police harassment of her brothers colored her perspective regarding racial profiling and discrimination targeted at Black males. When asked if her father, whom she was reunited with upon migrating to the United States, ever discussed U.S. racial dynamics with her, Kerry Ann answered "No." Nevertheless, she did mention his emphasis on not getting "railroaded" by the U.S. penal system:

> [When] I came my dad tells us, "I'm going to work and that's where I'm going, you get in trouble that's on you, cause this is what gonna happen to you" [puts wrists together to signal wearing hand cuffs]. So they instilled that fear like very quickly. "What's gonna be your outcome if you choose that life?" he told my brother. He said, "Look, look at my arms, I have never had bars on me so if you choose that, that's what's gonna happen to you and I'm not coming [to bail you out]"...you know.

During that time, it was likely for Caribbean immigrants—Jamaicans in particular—to be targets of police harassment because of suspected gang and drug-trafficking affiliations (Headly, 1988; Huff, 1989). Kerry Ann also recalled the prevalence of Jamaican gangs during this time. Through the experiences of her brothers, Kerry Ann became quite aware of the potential dangers of being a Black male in New Kensington. Racial discrimination and profiling became all the more evident when Kerry Ann's brother experienced what she deemed an unnecessary run-in with the law. In an interview, Kerry Ann vividly explained:

> One day my dad, he was at work, [my brother] was 16 'cause I'm older so I probably was, if he's 16, I probably was hmm, 3 years older than him so I was what, 19. He driving his car, my dad bought him a car and he's coming up to get some food at the Chinese store up here on Merrick Ave. He get pulled over, he get locked up because he looks like a probable suspect. [laughs] Like how you just get locked up, he wasn't doing anything, he wasn't...he hasn't stopped yet to go buy what he's buying, noth-

ing.... My dad had to come home go get him from the 35th district, get a lawyer and my father had to spend legal fees, all this money...and it's so scary, the boy was 16 years old and it made him like fearful of people.

From these early experiences in New Kensington, Kerry Ann became acutely aware of the gross inequalities experienced by Black men in America. In particular, she saw run-ins with the law as instrumental in creating obstacles to the upward mobility and socioeconomic success of Black men in the United States.

Kerry Ann began to see how the intersection of race and gender distinctly influenced the experiences of Black youth. She believed she was insulated from the threat of police harassment because of her gender. To corroborate this point, Kerry Ann described an instance where she had been driving in one car while her husband followed behind her at an equal or lesser speed within the designated speed limit. Her husband, however, was stopped for speeding, although she was driving ahead of him. Kerry Ann argued that although they were not speeding, if they had been, she was ahead of her husband and therefore she should have been stopped. Experiences like this reaffirmed for Kerry Ann the danger of racial profiling to the livelihood of Black men in the United States.

As the mother of two Black boys, Kerry Ann's racial socialization practices were strongly influenced by the experiences of the Black men in her life. As a result, she expressed having regular conversations with her eldest son, Bryce, about race. She stated:

> I tell Bryce about touching girls. I said look, you touch them, you're supposed to be a liar, you're supposed to be aggressive.... I didn't learn that when I was growing up, but this is what [U.S.] culture does for you. Tells you what a Black man supposed to do, right. So I tell him, that's why I tell him don't walk through anybody's yard 'cause guess what, it's gonna be you because you are supposed to vandalize that's your whole thing, you're supposed to disrespect people's property and things. This is how we get into [trouble]. I'm like look, if you tear the stop sign down because you all [Bryce and White peers] were at the school bus stop swinging on it, it's going to be you [that's blamed] because you're the only one that looks like me [Black] there and that's what you're supposed to do so guess what don't lean on it, don't go close to it.

Kerry Ann's racial socialization practices were grounded in the fear that Bryce might get "railroaded" by run-ins with the law early on in life—not because his behaviors were more deviant than his White peers, but because his darker complexion visually marked him as a target for police and would warrant harsher consequences for infractions. Kerry Ann's concerns weren't simply grounded in her analyses of racial inequities. She recognized that the intersectionality of race and gender spawns distinct challenges. Kerry Ann understood that individuals in positions of power would more readily provoke her son because he was both Black *and* male. In particular, she was concerned that interactions with law enforcement officers might result in a tarnished record, which could later diminish opportunities for Bryce to receive financial aid to attend college or secure a well-paying job.

While many students in the study denied engaging in many explicit conversations about race with their parents, Bryce reported feeling overwhelmed by the racial socialization messages he received from his mother. The following interview excerpt confirmed that Kerry Ann regularly warned Bryce to monitor his behavior in public spaces out of concern for more severe consequences.

> C: ...Okay, um, do your parents tell you things that you should or should not do because you're Black?

> B: [eagerly answered before I finished asking the question] Yes!

> C: So what are things you should do and what are things that you should not do?

> B: I shouldn't like, ah, my parents tell me not to go out with my friends a lot 'cause if they're doing something bad they said that I'm gonna be the one that, like, ah [get in trouble]. They said like one time me and my friend was like throwing snowballs and ah, mom got angry 'cause she said if that...if a snowball breaks the window, they're gonna be coming to her door.

Kerry Ann's racial socialization practices centered on preparing Bryce for experiences related to racial bias. According to racial socialization scholars, preparation for bias is a strategy commonly used by Black parents in their rearing of Black boys in particular

(Hughes & Chen, 1999). Generally, preparation for bias is proactively used to raise awareness about potential dangers related to racism that might otherwise be overlooked by children and adolescents. Kerry Ann often engaged in preparation for bias socialization strategies by warning Bryce of potentially daunting consequences for behaviors that might lead to trouble with White adults such as neighbors, teachers, and—most important—law enforcement officials.

Although Kerry Ann's racial socialization practices seemed overbearing to Bryce, especially given his desire to enjoy the company of his mostly White peer group, her racial socialization practices were limited in scope and directly related to early migration experiences in which her brothers were targets of racial profiling. Kerry Ann's sense of the dangers Bryce might face as a Black male was heightened by her family's integration into the predominantly White Morristown community where Bryce would be made a more visible target. Proactive preparation for bias related to the criminalization of Black boys and men was the basis for racial socialization practices endorsed by Kerry Ann. As a CPA in corporate America, Kerry Ann recognized that Blacks were not expected to advance and were not given many opportunities for promotions; however, she was unaware of the extent to which Bryce might have been experiencing similar discrimination at school. Hence, the racial socialization messages shared with Bryce remained narrow in focus.

Kerry Ann encouraged Bryce to work hard to outperform his White peers as a general means for achieving success in the United States, but she was unaware of the ways in which his attempts to work hard might be subverted by negative racial experiences or stereotypes that pervaded the school, community, and society at large. Bryce embraced a racially diverse peer group, which fed Kerry Ann's assumption that classes at Morristown were integrated and that most students maintained a diverse peer group. However, Bryce was tracked into higher-level classes as compared to many of his Black peers, who were relegated to low-level, racially homogeneous classes. Institutionalized practices that sorted students into high- and low-level classes determined the peer group to which students were exposed and engaged. Kerry

Ann was unaware of these distinctions or that they posed a potential threat to the quality of education Bryce received in this middle-class community. Her racial socialization messages insisted that run-ins with the law and other authorities were the solitary obstacle Bryce would face as a Black male. She maintained:

> If they can fight, if they [Black boys] can overcome...issues [with the law], they can do as well as anybody else. Like most of the times, the reason why they can't is because they got bogged down with the system and it totally railroads them because every time you go, they say look at your record, this is it.

This realistic yet myopic view of American racism had profoundly influenced Kerry Ann's racial socialization practices. She was capable of recognizing and contesting more explicit forms of racial aggression linked to early experiences with racism in the form of racial profiling. However, the extent to which she identified incidents as racist and worth discussing with her children was limited to events that were unequivocally racist in nature and informed by her early migration experiences. Her narrow experience in assessing more subtle forms of racism that might have been equally crippling to her son's development went unnoticed. Kerry Ann's background as an immigrant from a majority-Black country posed limitations to her ability to assess and address her son's more comprehensive racial socialization needs.

It is argued that in more racially diverse spaces, Black children are more likely to experience racial conflict (Stevenson, McNeil, Herrero-Taylor, & Davis, 2005). The implications for such experiences, particularly in the school context, are vast and can lead to social and academic withdrawal, psychological distress, and an internalized sense of worthlessness. Opportunities to prepare Bryce for those experiences were largely missed by his mother. As highlighted in Chapter 1, there are many types of racial socialization messages parents can share, and while some of them have positive effects in youth, others do not. Despite the noble intentions of parents, racial socialization messages do not always give rise to positive outcomes; however, parental racial socialization provides a lens through which we can understand how and why Caribbean American youth take up particular racial and ethnic identities.

Mark and Marcia: Intraracial Conflicts

Mark and Marcia were also integrated into low-income and work-ing-class communities upon migrating to the United States. How-ever, unlike Kerry Ann, Mark and Marcia had prolonged, conflict-ridden relationships with Black Americans in those communities. Kerry Ann promptly went on to the military and college after high school and was integrated into a more diverse and upwardly mo-bile group of peers. In contrast, Mark and Marcia remained in lower-income communities for much of their young adult life.

Contentious relationships between native-born Blacks and Black immigrants were sparked, in part, by Black Americans' own internalized racism, lack of experience with Black immigrants, and the perceived threat of Black immigrants taking jobs from U.S.-born Blacks. In turn, these experiences contributed to the dis-tancing of Black immigrants from Black Americans and their sup-port of stereotypical perceptions of Black Americans as true. Both Mark and Marcia's early relationships with Black Americans thrust them into a state of foreclosure,[1] whereby they did not ex-plore other alternatives to initial perceptions of Black Americans that were reinforced by early experiences with and negative stereotypes of them. Those experiences led to an inflexible disposi-tion toward Black Americans that persisted over time and further promoted distrust and separation between the two groups.

While several students in the study noted some cultural dis-tinctions between themselves and Black Americans, few students reported being explicitly socialized to believe negative stereotypes describing Black Americans. However, Mark and Marcia's chil-dren, Charles and Elyse, reported receiving messages that many Black Americans were averse to working and did not take advan-tage of resources available to them. Elyse recalled being troubled by her parents' negative depictions of Black Americans. When asked how she felt about her parents' attitude toward Black Americans, Elyse shared this:

> I feel offended 'cause I am a Black American. Well, I'm African Ameri-can, you know how I am, but I'm living in America, I was born in Amer-ica, I feel offended cause is it my fault? If you wanted...to have me, why

didn't you have me in Jamaica so you won't have to harass me about how
I am as a Black American?

Here, Elyse struggled with her parents' notions of what it meant to
be a Black American and their projection of Black Americanness
onto her, despite her own means of self-identification. Elyse was
consistently left to grapple with what it meant to be of Caribbean
descent, although she had been born and raised in the United
States. The communication of socialization messages related to
interethnic bias was twofold: (1) socialization messages conveyed
adherence to negative stereotypes about Black Americans as a
group, and (2) parents communicated dissatisfaction with the
overall Americanization of their children and their growing adherence to U.S. norms and a privileged lifestyle. In part, Mark and
Marcia's description of their children as "lazy" and "messy" was
grounded in comparisons between their responsibilities as children
growing up in Jamaica and the carefree lifestyle they believed
their children had as Americans.

Despite consistent messages related to interethnic bias, Mark
especially engaged in reinforcement of racial pride messages and
the historical legacy of Blacks through what could be considered
environmental socialization. According to Caughy, Randolph, and
O'Campo (2002), racial socialization occurs not only through explicit means of communication but also through overall experiences as well as environmental conditions and exposure to a
variety of artifacts. Magazines, music, books, carvings, paintings,
and the like are often cited as dominant means for communicating
messages regarding race. In the home of Mark and Marcia Young,
several images were mounted near the main entrance. These pictures included images of Barack Obama, Marcus Garvey, Bob Mar-
ley, Martin Luther King, Jr., and Nelson Mandela. In interviews
with Mark, Marcia, Charles, and Elyse, they each mentioned these
pictures as significant to their home environment. Not only were
the pictures framed and mounted in a central location; the children were required to name each individual and his contributions
to eliminating racial inequities.

While on the one hand Mark and Marcia reinforced stereotypical notions of Black Americans, they also acknowledged the consis-

tent marginalization of Blacks across the globe and the legacies of those who have worked to eradicate inequity. By acknowledging the work of historical figures, Mark and Marcia also communicated to their children pride in their African ancestry. To Mark, the legacy of historical figures reinforced the notion "that no matter how far you go down, you still can come out and be somebody." Depictions of historical figures also worked to buttress the themes presented in the life narratives of Mark and Marcia as they argued that with hard work, sacrifice, and ambitious goals, individuals could defy seemingly insurmountable odds.

In addition to these two distinctly different racial socialization messages explicitly communicated to Elyse and Charles, a great deal of what they learned about American racism was derived from the family's experiences with "racist neighbors" upon moving to the Morristown community. It was through this experience that Charles and Elyse were regularly exposed to racial socialization messages that helped to hone their ability to identify racism, process the basis for racist behaviors, and experience strategies for coping with and defending oneself in the face of racist encounters. When asked about the incidents that ensued with her neighbors, Elyse explained:

> We have these neighbors...and it's like him and his mom are always watching us. It's like they have nothing else to do, [but] watch us and...call the police every second. Last time, you know when you have the cookouts and stuff, we had...a little party for my brother...out back...we was playing music, they called the police like three times saying the music was loud. We turned it down the second time and then there was no further we could turn it down; we turned it down so it won't disturb them and then they kept calling the police. They called the police so much the police said, ignore them, just ignore them and then on top of that...as soon as we put gates up and stuff, 'cause you know how you want your privacy.... We put our fence up and then he went and measured our fence and had the nerve to come knock on the door and say our fence is too high. My parents were like why are you measuring our fence saying it's too high what you want it to be low so you want to look in our yard? Come on!

Elyse went on to add that "there was another lady across the street, she's always looking at us weird and stuff." When asked why she believed her family was the target of such disturbing scrutiny, Elyse proclaimed: "[In] my opinion, I think because we're Black because my mom told me the lady across the street…kept asking her what did she do for a living, how did she get her car and all that stuff and why you asking us that? Why don't you ask the other neighbors that?" Elyse observed that the heightened degree of surveillance experienced by her family differed considerably from that of their White neighbors. It was through this comparison—the irrational behaviors of her neighbors and Elyse's awareness of stereotypes that Blacks were expected to live in poor communities and "work for White people"—that informed her conclusion that these situations were provoked by racial bias.

Although Mark and Marcia might not have generally engaged their children in racial socialization relative to awareness of racism or methods for coping with racial stress, the family's experience with its neighbors provided examples of how to identify individuals and behaviors as racist, as well as how one might cope with and address such issues as they arose. Mark mentioned to his children that he did not move to Morristown because he was particularly interested in living in an integrated community where he would have to endure what he perceived as racist attacks against his family; instead, he moved to Morristown because he and Marcia wanted their children to have access to a better education. Mark and Marcia's decision to endure racism at the hands of their neighbors for the sake of their children's education communicated an important message to their children: a good education is imperative, even when one has to struggle to attain it.

Despite claims that their children were not required to attend college and that tertiary education was not for everyone, Mark and Marcia expressed the desire for their children to have a firm educational foundation and, at the very least, graduate from high school. Marcia dropped out of high school in the eleventh grade, but she maintained that her children would have to leave their home if they chose not to complete high school. By establishing this guideline, Marcia expressed the seriousness of her expectation. Mark and Marcia set an example for attaining middle-class status with little formal schooling and promoted entrepreneurship as a viable option for their children, but their lived experiences and sacrifices to pay an exorbitant amount of taxes for the sake of their children's education spoke volumes about the degree to which they valued formal education.

It was through these implicit connections between experiences with racism in a White, middle-class community that Elyse and Charles were socialized to acknowledge and combat racism. The ongoing dispute with their "racist" neighbor continued until the Young family was taken to court, where Elyse was called to the stand to testify in defense of her dad. According to Elyse, the experience was quite harrowing and completely unnecessary. However, when asked whether she preferred living in Morristown as compared to the New Kensington neighborhood they had moved from several years ago, Elyse explained:

> Ever since I moved [from New Kensington] um, they have a new principal and the academic scores with the children went down so low, lowest probably out of the whole [State] and I don't want that, I want a good education, this is the place for good education...so that's one of the reasons why we came here. I'm glad.

In addition to challenges Elyse's family faced with racism, Elyse also mentioned that she spent less time outside in her suburban neighborhood as compared to New Kensington. She noted that there weren't many children in her new neighborhood with whom she could socialize. Despite many of these challenges, however, the Young family was determined to stay in Morristown. According to Elyse, they were not going to allow their neighbors to run them out of the neighborhood. She explained: "We came from...a noisy neighborhood to a quiet neighborhood...my parents wouldn't give up that opportunity...we don't wanna be around that anymore...."

In a similar vein, Mark and Marcia encouraged their children to stand up and fight in the face of racism, as they did in addressing the issue with their neighbor. Moreover, these parents also encouraged and supported their children when they chose to take action in racist situations, as this excerpt from an interview with Marcia illustrates.

> It was horrible like the other day Charles was on the school bus and um, I think he um, the bus driver reported him for calling this boy a name, but he said, "Mom," I said, "What happen Charles?" He said "Mom, listen, he called me a nigger" and...I say, "What did you call him back?" He

said, "The MF [mother fucker]" you know, I said, "Okay, good for you
son" you understand because don't let people push you around 'cause he
had no right calling you what he called you so if he didn't bother you, you
wouldn't have bothered him. If he didn't call you a name, you wouldn't
have called him a name. I'm not saying go pick a fight, never taught him
that, but don't let people boss you around and push you around, you understand, fight for your right, defend yourself, you know.

Charles, who was most often a quiet yet upbeat child, had resorted
to the use of inappropriate language after being called a nigger on
the school bus by one of his White peers. However, racial incidents
were dealt with on a case-by-case basis as situations arose and
therefore did not call for consistent efforts to engage in proactive
racial socialization.

When asked about the racial climate of Morristown Middle
School and whether all the students at Morristown were afforded
the same education, Mark and Marcia assumed all was well. Like
other Caribbean parents in the study, they were unaware of racial
divisions and variations in class levels and academic expectations.
At one point, Marcia mentioned that Elyse had been contemplat-
ing becoming an actress. Marcia scoffed at the idea but was willing
to support her daughter's interest. However, Marcia was unaware
of opportunities for Elyse to explore this passion through participation in the school musical, a major production at Morristown
Middle School. Unfortunately, like most extracurricular activities
at Morristown, the cast and orchestra for the musical were overwhelmingly White. There were many incredible opportunities open
to Morristown students; however, Black students were not encouraged to take advantage of these opportunities and did not see
much representation from other Black students, staff, or faculty.
As a result, students believed that these activities were not for
them or open to them.

Conclusion

In Chapter 3 I discussed Caribbean immigrant parents' reliance on
ethnic socialization strategies as a means of preparing their children for success in the United States. Parents were quite proactive
in their implementation of ethnic socialization practices. Antithetically, explicit forms of racial socialization were limited to re-

active measures. Parents who did acknowledge race-related issues referred mostly to overtly racist and often traumatizing experiences that occurred shortly after their migration, present experiences with explicit forms of racism, or current events displayed in the media to prompt explicit engagement in racial socialization. However, support around interracial conflict, preparation for discrimination, and ways to identify and address aversive and institutionalized forms of racism were relatively absent.

Parents' inclination toward racial socialization was determined by their length of stay in the United States and the characteristics of the community they were integrated into. Caribbean immigrants who lived in the United States for fewer years were less likely to engage in conversations around race than those who had been in the country longer. More recent immigrants did not consider race as central to their experiences and had a difficult time identifying incidents and institutional systems as racist. However, Caribbean parents who experienced the jarring reality of the intersections of race and low social class as they struggled toward upward mobility were more likely to identify various forms of racism over time. Parents who were initially incorporated into low-income communities with schools whose resources were scarce witnessed disparities between them and other middle-class and mostly White Americans. Those who assimilated into the middle class had a more difficult time acknowledging the seriousness of race and racism in the United States.

This chapter has focused on racial socialization tendencies of Caribbean immigrant parents. The next chapter explores the myriad racial socialization messages that Caribbean American youth received in the school context, which ultimately complicated—and sometimes contradicted—the racial and ethnic socialization messages they received at home. Messages youth received at school projected onto them hegemonic notions of being a Black American.

Note

1.   For more on identity foreclosure, see Nakkula & Toshalis (2006).

Racial Socialization at Morristown Middle School: What Caribbean American Students Learn About Race and Racism by Way of the "Not So Hidden" Curriculum

> Jeffrey
> Child of Craig and Miriam
> Happy as a clam, smart as Einstein
> Who loves Chinese food and sports
> Who needs the air of hope
> Who gives 100 percent effort and more
> Who fears World War III
> Who would like to see Spain and China
> Child of Jamaica
> Thompson

This poem was written by Jeffrey Thompson, a Caribbean American student at Morristown, and displayed on the wall of his science classroom. In its simplicity, the poem illustrates some of the ways in which schools offer up opportunities for students to celebrate and explore their histories, realities, and hopes—their identities. Despite the assignment's uniformity of format, this template allowed Jeffrey to carve out a space for himself that highlighted his uniqueness and made him distinguishable from his peers.

In this particular moment, Jeffrey shared a piece of himself that subtly challenged essentialist notions of Black male students that permeated the Morristown context. In his poetic self-depiction, Jeffrey was "happy" and "smart," not aggressive and academically challenged, as many Black males were often pegged by school officials. He described himself as giving "100 percent effort and more." He was hard working, not lazy, and instead of being just Black, he asserted the centrality of Jamaica to his self-definition. Despite the ethnic identities nurtured in the homes of

Caribbean American students, these identities often became invisible at Morristown in lieu of more homogeneous and essentializing racial categorizations embedded in institutionalized practices and enacted through politics around the Black-White achievement gap.

Arising from the contention that race plays "a significant part in children's socialization and in their academic pursuits" (Rong & Brown, 2002, p. 251), this chapter explores the ways in which Caribbean American students' school experiences were colored by their race regardless of students' personal and familial perspectives or the centrality of their ethnic identities. Evidence of the school as a key agent of racial socialization was present in the following findings.

- White privilege pervaded the social and academic milieu of the school, reinforcing a deficit framework for Black student achievement and engagement.
- Formal and informal rules governing participation in academic processes helped to situate Caribbean American youth in their prescribed location in the U.S. racial hierarchy.
- 1.5- and second-generation youth received messages about race and racism through their observations of disciplinary sanctions that frequently led to the hyper-surveillance of Black youth and the rationing of harsher consequences for infractions, as compared to their White counterparts.
- Low academic expectations along lines of race and social class were communicated through youth's experiences with and observations of student-teacher relationships.

White Privilege and the Real Wages of Blackness for Caribbean American Students

As highlighted in Chapter 4, the migration of Caribbean immigrants to the United States often prompted the development of political orientations that incorporated understandings of U.S. racism and to some degree solidarity with Black Americans in the struggle against racial inequity and oppression. Despite this ideological stance, Caribbean immigrants were less adept at identifying the true costs of racism and embraced life narratives and parental socialization practices that reinforced ethnic values they believed to be universally applicable across international borders.

While instructive, these ethnic socialization messages were often incapable of holistically addressing the racist structures and experiences Caribbean American youth faced in the K–12 public school system. This essentially left them with little assistance in negotiating the racial politics of school and the larger society. Parents did not expect teachers and administrators to inflict psychological damage on Caribbean American youth by way of racial stigmatization, and in most instances teachers were not purposely invested in racial discrimination. However, White teachers lacked the knowledge and skills necessary to pierce the veil of White privilege, and their investment in White privilege recreated school-wide systems of marginalization for Black youth. White privilege can be defined as the right to exclude those who do not possess "whiteness" while reserving certain privileges for those who do.[1] According to McIntosh (1998), White privilege is "an invisible package of unearned assets" that Whites can redeem each day yet remain oblivious to their benefits. McIntosh likens White privilege to "an invisible weightless knapsack of special provisions, maps, passports, codebooks, visas, clothes, tools, and blank checks" (p. 188). White privilege can take many forms, from taking for granted the ability to find bandages that match one's skin tone, to assumptions that Whites are morally upright (and non-Whites deviant), or the ability to buy books and toys featuring Whites (McIntosh, 1998).

Recurrent subject matter documented through interviews and school-wide observations suggested that (1) White privilege enacted by teachers and students often wielded the power to relegate the academic and social participation of Caribbean American students to the periphery, and (2) institutionally embedded messages of White superiority incited conflict between Caribbean immigrant values and the racial socialization messages embedded in the fabric of the Morristown school experience.

Examining the Embeddedness of White Privilege Through Achievement Gap Discourse

Despite the good intentions of many White teachers and administrators at Morristown, White privilege was intricately woven into the ideology and practices of the institution. School-wide dialogue around the Black-White achievement gap played a significant role in capturing the institutionalization of White privilege. Such problematic dialogues were enhanced by the implicit and explicit ways in which White teachers and administrators secured their interests and the academic and social welfare of the White students while effectively disenfranchising Black students at Morristown, including those of Caribbean descent.

Initial encounters with Morristown administrators, teachers, and support staff were central to examining the experiences of Black students overall. In particular, these encounters helped to situate Caribbean American students within a context that had been inundated by racial politics. Through the implementation of the CWT ("Can We Talk?") program, which prompted discussions with Black students and Morristown teachers about race at their school, views on issues of race and educational disparities at Morristown were uncovered. As long as inadequacies attributed to students and their families were believed to fuel the achievement gap problem, teachers and administrators were eager for our team to work with students. In particular, teachers' and administrators' anxieties regarding student performance were assuaged only if the school's complicity in achievement disparities were left unchallenged. However, attempts to destabilize assumptions about students and student achievement grounded in racist ideology aroused intense opposition from teachers who had initially supported the CWT program.

The widespread currency of whiteness led to the enactment of White privilege, which was furthered through achievement gap discourses that (1) promoted deficit theories, (2) allowed teacher fear to dictate the cessation of critical discussion regarding race, (3) reframed racial issues to focus on the interests of White teachers and students, and (4) selectively endorsed a color-blind stance that rendered invisible the experiences of racial and ethnic minorities.

These forms of resistance arose during the second phase of the CWT project, during which teachers were made privy to students' perceptions of teacher bias that led to overall feelings of academic and social inadequacy for Black students. CWT participants posited that Black students experienced greater scrutiny as compared to their White peers, withstood harsher disciplinary sanctions, and were not expected to engage in rigorous academic pursuits. Students also highlighted the absence of a consistent means of addressing racially insensitive epithets that their White peers invoked without reservation.

The presentation of these findings had a profoundly polarizing impact on the staff and destabilized efforts to maintain idealized notions of the school as pluralistic and progressive. The enactment of White privilege, on the one hand, enabled White teachers to dominate racial discourse by discussing race and racial minorities on their terms and granted them authority to evade racial discourse and dismiss evidence of discriminatory practices within the school system. Staff-only follow-up meetings to the CWT program presentation were facilitated by the school principal and provided an open forum for backlash against findings derived from the CWT project, thus silencing the few teachers who sought to further interrogate and respond to students' feelings of marginalization at Morristown.

Deficiency-centered responses to the achievement gap that tracked lower-class students of color into lower-level classes and required participation in remedial after-school and in-school programming were not challenged. Teachers refused to consider disparities in student treatment and the provision of remedial instruction to students who performed at the lower end of the Black-White achievement gap scale. Instead, teachers insisted on maintaining a deficiency-centered approach to addressing student achievement, which absolved them of responsibility for the qualitative distinctions between the academic and ecological experiences of White and Black students.

This deficiency-centered stance pervaded the school and was deeply ingrained in instructional practices geared toward Black youth from working-class, lower-middle-class, and non-professional families. Subversive tracking policies, which will be discussed in more detail later in this chapter, further substantiated the nearly school-wide investment in the deficiency approach. Teachers' power to reinforce a deficiency stance and failure to interrogate students' claims further demonstrated the power of White privilege to delegitimize the voices of Black students. The achievement gap, which was in part maintained by the circulation of White privilege, had a profound impact on the educational experiences of Caribbean American students in the study. Similar to other Black children in mid- to lower-level classes, Caribbean American Students primarily came from working-class, lower-middle class, and non-professional homes and were relegated to mid- to lower-level academic tracks. Six out of ten Caribbean American students in this study were represented in this demographic.

The institutional deficiency orientation reflected an implied acquiescence by teachers to stereotypical notions of Black children as incapable of the rigors of Morristown's academic program and essentially incompatible with the expectations of full participation, membership, and access to benefits generally garnered from enrollment in a middle-class suburban school district. This dynamic illustrated the very essence of White privilege that enables Whites to "think of their lives as morally neutral, normative...average, and also ideal" (McIntosh, 1989, para. 10).

In effect, this setting caused Black students to experience Morristown as second-class citizens whose schooling was expected to make them more like their White peers, albeit by way of unequal exposure and access to resources. Black students were not offered the academic benefits of rigorous academic instruction representative of higher-level classes, nor did they enjoy equal access to extracurricular programming and resources. Well-resourced extracurricular activities like the drama club, band, and orchestra were designated as White spaces, and so were sports such as tennis, soccer, and lacrosse, to name a few. The extracurricular engagement of Black students was relegated to Black boys' participation in sports such as football, basketball, and track and field, with few non-sports-related options and even fewer options that piqued the interest of and extended invitations to Black girls.

Many of the typical efforts to address the achievement gap at Morristown centered on remedial academic support structures set in place to address the academic shortcomings of students. Deficiency-centered instruction took the form of after-school programming, compulsory computer-based test preparation using specialized software, and remedial and lower-level academic classes.

Assumptions of student deficiencies devoid of the acknowledgment of the ways in which racial disparities played out and impacted student engagement and participation in multiple facets of the school community limited the ability of Morristown teachers and administrators to meet the needs of Black students successfully. There was little work done to shift the focus of curricular content, encourage the participation of Black students in a wider array of extracurricular activities, or provide comparable resources for activities that engaged the interests of Black students. Of even greater importance than the school-wide deficiency stance directed toward Black students was the teachers' inability to reflect critically on institutionalized practices that alienated Black students. In fact, the very fundamental nature of White privilege makes it possible for White teachers to own and control the "cultural turf" of the school in ways that made them and White students "confident, comfortable, and oblivious," and other groups "inconfident, uncomfortable, and alienated" (McIntosh, 1989, para. 65).

As both racial and ethnic minorities in the Morristown milieu, Caribbean American students' outsider status was amplified as their place in the Black-White binary was complicated by their more nebulous constructions of identity. However, their very existence and experiences with transnational Black identity politics challenged polarized and essentialistic notions of race that marked the attributes of Whites as neutral and good and those of Blacks as heavily marked by pathologies and paralyzing challenges. Nonetheless, Caribbean American students learned that White skin garnered privilege and Black skin disadvantage, a reality that troubled their parents' idealism regarding the currency of their espoused ethnic values.

Socialization Conflicts

Despite the presence of parental socialization and media socialization at the forefront of socialization research, the politics and ideologies embedded in the institutionalized practices of schools serve as strong forces for socializing members of their communities. The power of institutions to engage in socialization through hegemonic structures and practices has received little attention. The role of individuals in the socialization of youth is clear, but the synergistic impact of the institution as a socializing agent warrants additional consideration. In his book *Lenin and Philosophy and Other Essays*, Louis Althusser (2006) recognized the institution as a primary agent in replicating and supporting certain ideologies. He theorizes that

> what we normally think of as ideological positions—thoughts, opinions, world-views, with all their political implication and consequences—never exist only in the mind or in individual experience and consciousness; they are always supported and reinforced, indeed reproduced, by social institution and apparatuses, whether those are state based, like the army or the judicial instance, or seemingly as private as the family and the school, the art museum and the institutions of media, the church and the small-claims court. Ideology is institutional first and foremost and only later on to be considered a matter of consciousness. (p. xiii)

This demonstrates the power of the institution and the potential impact on its members. In this case, it reiterates the role of schools in reifying the marginalized status of Blacks regardless of immigrant origin.

It is frequently argued that teachers play a prominent role in shaping the values, perspectives, and identities of youth (Delpit, 1995). However, when teachers, administrators, staff, and students as members of particular institutions reflect and reinforce particular values throughout their institution, the impact is magnified, and *institutional socialization* occurs. Institutional socialization not only works to shape the values of individuals within institutions, but it also reflects and maintains the hierarchical assignment of roles and related expectations of individuals who occupy space within particular institutions. Morristown Middle School as an institution served to socialize children around issues of race and racism and conveyed to them specific messages regarding their place in the school as well as in society at large. While discourse around race and racism was seldom explicit, students learned a great deal about their place in the U.S. social structure from school experiences.

All too often school spaces restrict identity examination and expression by sorting students into predetermined roles and categories on the basis of race and class background (Feagin & McKinney, 2003). Although some theorists have argued that Caribbean immigrants and their children skillfully employ ethnic identities as a means of circumventing the consequences of racism (Waters, 1994, 1999; Ogbu, 1991a), at Morristown, Caribbean American students' ethnic identities were often concealed and precluded from the larger discourses around identity. Unlike research regarding the experiences of Caribbean immigrants in long-established immigrant gateways, data from this study highlight the ways in which contextual factors such as the relative saturation of immigrants in a particular demographic and the absence of model-minority stereotypes mitigate the potential benefits of displaying Caribbean ethnic characteristics as well as possibilities for escaping the brunt of race and social class inequities.

School experiences were central to the racial socialization of Caribbean American youth and worked to disrupt the racial and ethnic socialization messages that 1.5- and second-generation youth received at home. At school, Caribbean American students were subject to institutionalized practices that sorted students on the basis of race and social class regardless of espoused family values and efforts at upward mobility commonly attributed to immigrants and their children. Caribbean American students learned about and lived U.S. racism and racial hierarchies in ways that were distinct from their parents' experiences, and even the students' own beliefs regarding the role of race and racism as an impediment to the social and economic success of Blacks in the United States were challenged by racialized school experiences. The school context played a vital role in socializing Caribbean American students around the privilege that whiteness afforded their peers and, antithetically, the disadvantage and stigma wrought by blackness. These distinct experiences created ruptures between the espoused values of Afro-Caribbean families and the expectations of and characteristics ascribed to Black students at Morristown.

The Role of Caribbean American Students in School Participation Structures

Participation structures—defined as the ways in which racialized groups of students were permitted to engage in the school community through their involvement in classroom dialogue and extracurricular activities—overwhelmingly included White students and either excluded or demoralized students of color. The majority-White teaching staff wielded White privilege that critically informed the academic and social priorities of the school, thereby maintaining the school's adherence to White, middle-class norms. White students dominated classroom space and displayed *de facto* ownership of highly regarded academic and extracurricular resources. Black students, on the other hand, were often located at the periphery of the school's priorities and were rarely represented in higher-level courses and select extracurricular activities. Morristown students also came to internalize and perform their respective roles as dictated by racial stereotypes and academic and social expectations.

These binary distinctions were further complicated by structures that situated Caribbean American students of higher social class on the periphery of the White, middle-class center, and Caribbean American students of lower social class closer to the center of the mostly Black and lower-middle-class periphery. The respective positionality of Caribbean American students from non-professional and professional homes also informed whether students were afforded opportunities to engage in academic and extracurricular spaces and how such participation was expected to unfold.

Ethnographic observations revealed several distinct features of student participation: (1) intersections between race and social class influenced the academic tracks in which Caribbean American students were placed; (2) Caribbean American students in majority-White, high-level classes experienced marginalization through their inability to participate fully in intellectual spaces dominated by Whites; and (3) Caribbean American students in majority-Black, lower-level classes experienced stratification that reinforced stereotypical notions of Black intellectual, social, and cultural inferiority.

In higher-level academic classes, Caribbean American students learned they were inferior to Whites given their inability to embody and display the privileges afforded to their White counterparts, while Caribbean American students in lower-level classes learned they were inferior to Whites as a result of pathologized characteristics perceived as inherent to Blacks—both experiences having distinct influences on the students' psyches and their perceived position in the racial hierarchy. Regardless of the level of the course, students of Caribbean descent were exposed to messages that reinforced feelings of racial inferiority.

Figure 1. Classroom and extracurricular participation structures at Morristown Middle School

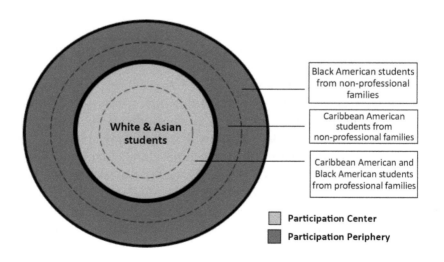

Intersections of Social Class and Race: Locating Caribbean American Students in the Racialized Tracking System

As students poured out of their respective classrooms into the hallways, the diverse racial composition of Morristown quickly became evident. The student body was split almost equally between Black and White students, who together comprised approximately 85% of the total student population. (The remaining 15% of the student body was comprised mostly of Asian students and, to a lesser extent, Latino students.) Although biracial and multiracial students were present at Morristown, there was no systematic means of documenting their racial background.

The diversity apparent when students changed classes became less visible once the halls cleared and students settled into their respective classrooms. Although classrooms at Morristown boasted representation from a wide array of racial and ethnic groups, demographic representation within classrooms was skewed. In higher-level academic classes, one found mostly White and Asian students, with modest Black representation; in lower-level classes, there was often a higher representation of Blacks and few White or Asian students.

While school administrators asserted that classes at Morristown were not "tracked," observations and informal conversations with teachers revealed underground tracking practices. In one math class, the demographics were as follows:[2] twelve Black boys, one Black girl, one White girl, and one girl who appeared to be Latina. Similarly, a class called Reading Workshop, designed to assist students through the use of remedial reading strategies, was comprised of nine Black boys, nine Black girls, four White boys, and one White girl. The demographic makeup of these classes did not reflect the nearly 1:1 ratio of Black and White students represented in the school. Lower-level academic classes were skewed toward Black students, and White students were most predominant in higher-level classes. There was also evidence of intersectional disparities when accounting for both race and gender. White male students were disproportionately placed in high-level and advanced classes, White females in mid-level classes, and Black

evenings and nights as a security guard. Neither parent was home after school to ensure that Antoinette fulfilled her academic responsibilities. In fact, Antoinette was charged with the additional responsibility of caring for her niece and nephew when she returned home from school, further diminishing opportunities to focus on academic endeavors. The following dialogue reflects Antoinette's analysis of her poor academic performance.

C: Do you feel you do well in school?

A: No.

C: Why?

A: Because the computer and the phone is very distracting...

C: ...from doing your...

A: ...homework.

C: Which is the main thing that is bringing your grades down?

A: Um hm! [yes]

C: Okay, and um, and you also [mentioned] watching your nephews.

A: ...and they are very distracting, very...

C: And what do you do with your nephews?

A: I just sit down and talk on the phone and they run around the house and then I yell at them...and sometimes my brother will have them and I'll have my niece.

C: Okay, so [there are]...three kids?
A: [nods yes] One is 6 and one is 4 and one is 1.

Academic profiles of students were deeply intertwined with the affordances and limitations wrought by their parents' social class. Social class held grave implications for whether students were tracked into high- or low-level classes, which generally determined whether students were exposed to participation structures that either reinforced Black students' exemption from privilege or exposed them to stereotype-enhancing messages. While it has been argued that Caribbean American students generally outperform their native Black American counterparts (Kao & Tienda, 1995; Massey, Mooney, Torres, & Charles, 2007; Waters, 1999), the prevalence of such model-minority depictions render invisible the extent to which Caribbean immigrant youth are vulnerable to woes of low socioeconomic status and how these experiences in turn impact identity formation, academic achievement, and perceived boundaries for participation in the larger society that they learn from in-school tracking systems and racial socialization.

High-Achieving Caribbean American Students and Ownership Over Classroom Space

For Caribbean American students, social class often dictated their placement in high- and low-level classes, but, more importantly, their experiences within particular classes held profound implications for their racial socialization experiences and ability to participate in the school community. Students whose parents had earned college degrees and worked as professionals were generally tracked into higher-level classes. The remaining two-thirds of Caribbean American participants in the study, who were from nonprofessional families, were tracked into majority-Black, middle- and lower-level courses.

In majority-White classes, Caribbean American students' classroom experiences socialized them around what I refer to as *exemption from privilege*. Caribbean American youth were not given the same latitude as Whites to address the teacher informally and call out in class. In comparison, Caribbean American students in lower-level classes more commonly experienced *stereotype enhancing* racial socialization. In these classes, Black youth were pegged as deviant and low achieving as reflected by low academic expectations and performance of students in these classes, as well as their tendency toward disruptive behaviors.

Observations of participation structures in majority-White, high-level classrooms brought to the foreground a common set of themes central to the experiences of some Caribbean American students. In particular, Bryce, Geneva, Jade, and Jeffrey were rewarded for their academic prowess by their placement in high-level courses; however, their assignment to such classes also exposed them to racial socialization messages that defined academic space as belonging to White students. In such spaces, the demonstration of White privilege was amplified, as was the Caribbean American students' exemption from such privilege.

Despite consistent denial of institutional tracking by administrators, classroom teachers were often more forthright about the pervasiveness of tracking throughout the school. Katie Ackerman, a science teacher, noted that although the district required that students be heterogeneously grouped, certain classes were skewed toward high and low achievers, with a few good and average students interspersed. Dispensation of tracking guidelines led to the overrepresentation of White students in Ms. Ackerman's class, which was further complicated by the presence of several "gifted" White boys and one biracial boy. Ms. Ackerman reported consistent challenges with this group of gifted students, whose placement into mainstream classes was requested by their parents.

In Mrs. Ackerman's classroom, these students consistently dominated class discussion, disregarded class rules, and criticized the intellectual capacity of their peers in the presence of Caribbean American students Jeffrey and Bryce. The following vignette from Ms. Ackerman's classroom demonstrates the ways in which White privilege played out in highly stratified intellectual spaces at Morristown.

Two girls from Ms. Ackerman's classroom, one Black and one White, shared information with the class about muscles in the human body and their functions in the form of a PowerPoint presentation. Once the girls finished presenting and began entertaining questions, the "gifted" boys began to interrupt the presenters as they attempted to answer their peers' questions. These interruptions, however, were completely out of the purview of the question-and-answer format. Instead of asking questions about the topic at hand, the boys began by criticizing the students for not providing enough information during their presentation. Next, they paraded their intelligence by asking questions presenters were unable to answer.

The presenters were then verbally assaulted by the boys because of their inability to answer their questions. As the boys continued with their verbal tirade, the White female presenters asserted, "Can we move on to some real questions please?" Next, the boys began to ask questions that were outside the scope of the girls' presentation. Immediately, another one of the boys asked, "How do muscles grow when you exercise?" The White female began her explanation by saying, "Well, it's kind of self explanatory...." " Before she was able to finish her statement, however, one of the boys yelled, "Uh, no it's not, it's not, how is it self-explanatory?"

After the class settled a bit, the presenter began to explain that muscles are like a rubber band that stretches once it is manipulated. Then, another one of the boys yelled, "Yeah, but after you stretch them, they go back." During the entire debacle, the Black female presenter stood by her White partner watching as the events played out, but did not engage in the debate. Instead, she was silent, and her White comrade was left to fight the battle against the "smart boys" alone.

This example illustrates not only the ways in which tracking was endorsed by the school, but it also describes the ways in which the White males were given leeway to dominate class discussions and behave in disruptive and inappropriate ways in the classroom with relatively few consequences. Although Black students were present in this mostly White science class, they were generally forced to the margins of the classroom discourse. In allowing this situation to occur in the classroom, the students—Black and White—were learning a great deal about White privilege. They learned that White students—particularly males—were intellectually superior and, given their superiority, they were in a sense "above the law." In other words, these boys were able to create their own rules for classroom participation, negotiate the rules that had been established, and determine whose knowledge was deemed a valuable contribution to academic discourse.

The same set of boys were also enrolled in Mr. Murphy's social studies class, where their conduct was similar to the behaviors they displayed in Katie Ackerman's science classroom. According to Mr. Murphy, one of the boys regularly denigrated his peers and questioned his teacher's curricular choices and academic expertise. Mr. Murphy explained that during one class session, Owen asked why the class had been studying the Great Migration in lieu of other large migrations that have occurred throughout history. Mr. Murphy said that in the past, Owen would have simply yelled, "Why are we studying this?" Certain students believed they were entitled to openly critique their peers' academic ability and could determine what academic content was most worthwhile. The Great Migration focused on the migration of Blacks from the South to many Northern cities in search of work in industrial plants. During the study of the Great Migration, Mr. Murphy also traced the current socioeconomic status of Blacks to the mass exodus of industrial plants from urban communities that left many Blacks with few job opportunities and fueled the cycle of poverty. Although it was generally rare for such content to be integrated across the curriculum at Morristown, when these conversations occurred, their value was openly contested by students who marked the content as unimportant relative to other areas of study.

Not only were racial dynamics at play in these scenarios, but elements of class and gender politics were also being enacted. Each of the gifted boys—or "intellectual bullies," as Mr. Murphy called them—were the children of high-level professionals such as scientists and medical doctors. Not only were they given extreme latitude to dictate the flow of class instruction because of their perceived ability, but the parents of these boys also formally created a group focused on advocating for the needs of academically gifted students. According to Ms. Ackerman, the principal's responsiveness to middle-class professional parents' concerns often worked to the detriment of other students in the school, since these students' needs were often met at the expense of less privileged students. Ms. Ackerman explained that the boys' parents requested that their children receive individualized instruction in mainstream classrooms as opposed to the one-on-one instruction they had been accustomed to being pulled from mainstream classrooms to receive. Ackerman argued that one of the results of providing the boys mainstream instruction was their piousness and constant degradation of teachers and peers.

In addition to dominating class discussion, many White male students were deeply invested in being perceived by their teachers and peers as intellectually superior. On several occasions, I witnessed White male students overtly naming the hierarchical academic structures that existed in the school, specifically when they

were labeled advanced. During observations in an English class at
tended by one of the academically advanced Caribbean American
students in the study, a White student asked the teacher aloud
"Ms. Kelley, is this enriched English? People say this is the stupic
class. People say this is on grade [level], they're just jealous." Ms
Kelley replied by telling the students that they were "superb," but
did not confirm whether the class was enriched or on grade level
This student's playful banter demonstrated that despite adminis
trators' attempts to conceal evidence of tracking and its resulting *de
facto* racial segregation, both teachers and students were aware o:
academic distinctions among students. Additionally, White males
seemed to be particularly invested in making these distinctions
known, reinforcing broader trends of racial and gender privilege.

The small number of Black students assigned to majority-
White, advanced-level classes were sent clear messages that
marked the intellectual space of the classroom as the property of
White students more generally, and White males in particular. As
a result of White male dominance in Ms. Ackerman's science class,
other students were silenced and discouraged from speaking up
and fully engaging in the learning community. The silencing of
Black girls' voices was especially evident in Ms. Ackerman's class,
as White girls seemed to be the only ones who challenged the dis-
respect of their White male counterparts. During the encounter
described in the aforementioned vignette, Jeffrey, one of the Caribbean American students, and one of few Black males in the class,
sat in silence, neither contributing to the deprecation of his peers
nor acting in defense of them.

Despite the often-inappropriate behavior exhibited by White
students as they dominated classroom discourse, few attempts
were made to curb students' behaviors through the use of disciplinary sanctions. In addition, the impact of White students' behavior
on the learning of their peers was not seriously taken into account.
Teachers' dismissal of these incidents helped to reinforce the idea
that they were acceptable, thereby normalizing White privilege.
Although teachers spoke to me about the challenges of dealing
with the attitudes and behaviors of these children, they did not
openly show their disapproval of, or challenge these behaviors in
the presence of the other students. These incidents reflected clear

disparities in behavioral expectations and consequences in the classroom and served to further socialize students around racialized expectations.

The unequal distribution of students in certain classrooms along both racial and gendered lines further fueled students' ability to monopolize classroom discourse. With a disproportionate number of White males in high- and advanced-level classes, it became easier for students who were in the majority to sway the direction of the class. White females, who were overrepresented in mid-level classes, had the opportunity to dominate classroom discourse with little competition from their male counterparts. Even though the behaviors indulged in by White males in the classroom were essential in outlining racially disparate rules for participation at Morristown, White girls often demonstrated ownership over classroom space as well. Similar to White males, White females were at liberty to dominate classroom dialogue but were less apt to denigrate their peers in the process. As opposed to raising their hands to answer questions, reportedly an expectation of all students, White girls would often speak out in class, sharing their thought processes as they attempted to solve problems or stating whether they agreed with or understood academic content. In this way, White girls were free to draw teachers' and students' attention to their academic interests and needs, albeit in ways that were less abrasive than their White male counterparts.

During Ms. Carter's math class, several White girls sat close together near the front of the room. Throughout instructional time, the girls were extremely vocal and dictated the direction of most of the dialogue in the classroom. In fact, as I watched for most of the class session, there were very few instances where students outside of this group voluntarily participated in the class discussion. In this instance, the group of White girls did not raise their hands to ask questions or answer questions, but instead spoke loudly and without acknowledgment from the teacher, as White boys often did.

As the class reviewed answers to math problems, one of the White girls in the class asserted that she knew how to complete the problem and, without being asked by the teacher, volunteered to go to the board to solve the problem. She wrote the problem on the board and explained each of her steps. At one point, she miscalculated a step involving simple multiplication, which was brought to her attention by another White student. She responded to the error in jest, corrected her mistake, finished the problem, and went back to her seat.

As students continued to work on practice problems, Vivian, another White girl in the class, explained that she was unsure of how to complete a particular problem, but asked if she could go to the board to solve the problem. Despite the assertion that she was unsure of how to complete the problem, Vivian confidently walked to the board, acknowledging that her attempt at solving the problem "might not work out."

The remainder of the class session continued in a similar vein. White female students demonstrated ownership of classroom space by determining when and how they would participate, with little interruption from the teacher or their peers. Although the teacher circled the room often to check on individual students, the White girls dictated the flow of the lesson and determined who had opportunities to participate in whole-group learning activities. Not only were the girls allowed to establish the guidelines for how they would conduct themselves, but they also determined the flow of the classroom and which problems were difficult and should be reviewed. Situations like these often led to the invisibility and disengagement of students of color in the classroom, since few attempts were made on the part of the teacher to elicit the participation of other students. Furthermore, these behaviors on the part of Black students would have been deemed inappropriate and worthy of disciplinary sanctions.

Classroom teachers allowed and encouraged participation structures that overwhelmingly included some students and excluded others. Somewhere along the line, White students—both boys and girls—learned that they were entitled to ownership over classroom space. On the other hand, Caribbean American students and other Black students watched as White students freely engaged their teachers with idle banter, called out in class, and drew attention to their academic needs and interests often at the expense of other students' participation. While a sense of investment and engagement in one's education is not inherently problematic, the lack of responsibility taken by teachers to ensure the full incorporation and participation of all students reinforced institutionally racist practices. Teachers' failures to address classroom racial dynamics further encouraged students to engage in behaviors that reinforced the entitlement of White students and the subsequent marginalization of Black students and other students of color.

In Morristown classrooms, White students learned and displayed behaviors typically deemed appropriate for their racial group. Caribbean American students, on the other hand, learned that teachers' academic and behavioral expectations of them differed significantly from those of White students. While White students were given flexibility to manipulate school rules and routines as they saw fit, non-White students were either held to extremely rigid standards that precluded their full participation in the classroom or were subject to such low expectations and levels of accountability that they did not approach academic matters with seriousness. Further evidence of these claims will be presented in the next section of this chapter.

Learning and Living the Stereotypes: Experiences of Caribbean American Students in Lower-Level Classes

Black students' perceptions of "unfair" expectations in the classroom led them to either disengage from or disrupt the learning environment. These themes were most evident in classes that were either demographically representative of the school's diverse population, or in classes that were overrepresented by Black students, as opposed to majority-White classes.

At Morristown there was a variety of race and gender concentration of high-, middle-, and low-academic-level classes that often determined the extent to which students participated in their respective classes on the basis of race and gender. High-level classes were densely populated by White boys first, then White girls, then Black girls, and last by Black boys; likewise, the participation of these students was often stratified along race and class lines. In lower-level classes mostly occupied by Black students, those students had greater opportunities to participate, but for Black boys class participation often occurred through disruptive behavior rather than academic engagement.

Lower-level classes at Morristown were characterized by their own participation structures and represented the experiences of the majority of Caribbean American youth in the study. Themes captured by way of observations in the Reading Workshop class offered at Morristown were typical of themes observed in many lower- or mid-level classes. Here is one such observation:

> Reading workshop was designed to offer remedial reading instruction to students and mirrored the demographic layout of many such low-level classes at Morristown. Both Antoinette and Elyse attended the Reading Workshop class together, along with what appeared to be mostly Black students and several White students. On an average day, White students in the class would quickly get settled and begin reading their books; however, Black students typically took longer to start working and were consistently dissatisfied with their choice of text. Early on in the class period, a Black male student reported to the teacher, Mrs. Klein, that one of his Black female counterparts had an "attitude." Although the boy did not elaborate on the issue or confirm why the girl had an attitude, the classroom teacher immediately asserted, "If she doesn't like it, she can find a new book from the class library and then go to the library and find a new book to read on her own time." Ms. Klein's comment was then followed by remarks from Antoinette, who stated, "There are no good books in the library." In response, an older Black woman, the teacher's assistant, replied, "Don't judge a book by its cover. You must be a speed reader to have read all the books over there."

As I looked over at the shelf of books from which students were expected to choose, I noticed that very few books were written by Black authors or depicted Blacks as central to the storyline. The students appeared to be uninterested in the books, and there was little evidence of a concerted effort on the part of the school administration and teachers to provide books that spoke to the interests and experiences of students of color. As the class session continued, several students—all Black—expressed their desire to find a different text or expressed no interest in the text they were reading. And, in each instance, the teacher's response was the same—the students needed to find a new book during homeroom or activity period. However, finding a new book did not appear to be a solution to the problem. Students regularly changed their books and complained about them. This class, in a well-resourced school district and mostly attended by Black students, did not provide reading materials that matched the interests of students and would keep them engaged in reading.

In contrast to Black students, White students in this classroom seemed to experience the texts quite differently. None of the White students complained about their books during the class session. Instead, they engaged the teacher about the characters in their books. At one point during the class session, Mrs. Klein held an extended conversation with one of the White girls in the class. As the White student excitedly described one of the characters in the story, Mrs. Klein expressed how much the character's disposition was similar to that of her own daughter. Mrs. Klein explained that her daughter never wavered in her beliefs despite adversity. This interaction between the teacher and the student was indicative of a unique relationship between the White student, her teacher, and the character in the book. It was also reflective of a type of class participation to which Black students were not often privy. This situation demonstrated the White teacher's and student's ability not only to relate to one another, but also to the literature that students were made to read. It was through these types of connections that learning often took place; however, such opportunities were rarely available to Black students. Instead of enjoying the literature, Black students repeatedly stumbled through disappointing iterations of mainstream literature.

In over a year of observations at Morristown, it was evident that White students generally engaged their teachers in informal conversations and often made connections to teachers' life experiences unrelated to academic content. This was true regardless of the teachers' race. In Ms. Carter's math class, White students would often ask questions like, "Ms. Carter, do you like Ms. Lee? She's mean." In other instances, they would also engage informally in dialogue around academic content, demonstrating a holistic integration of their personal and academic selves.

There were additional differences in how students were able to relate to teachers and class content. When Black students raised questions in class, they were perceived as coming from a place of deficit and irresponsibility rather than curiosity and inquiry. In the aforementioned description of the White girls in math class, several students admitted that they had not completed particular math problems and were unsure of the steps needed to complete the problems. Nonetheless, these proclamations were treated with respect, and students were given the opportunity to work through the problems in front of the class, encouraging their participation, voice, and academic risk-taking. However, when Black students posed questions in class, they were often met with disgruntled and disparaging commentary. During the same Reading Workshop class, Antoinette called her teacher over to ask a question pertaining to her book. Mrs. Klein read a portion of the book and stated, "If you were to read the story you will realize that they call him boy because he doesn't have enough self-respect to…, but right now you can refer to him as the main character in the story." Instead of welcoming Antoinette's momentary interest in the story and her desire to complete the task assigned by the teacher, Antoinette was disparaged for not reading the text closely enough.

These types of distinctions in participation structures clearly reflected the values of wider society and reproduced systems of racial and social class hierarchies within the school. Although the mere existence of such hierarchies are in fact important, students' internalization of and reflection on these hierarchies brought to the fore the painful realities of the costs of being Black in America—costs their parents had not fully understood or prepared them to handle. As a result, Morristown was not always perceived as a safe space for racial and ethnic minorities such as the Caribbean American students.

Disciplinary Disparities:
The Surveillance and Punishment of Black Bodies

Caribbean American students in the study were rarely subject to disciplinary sanctions at school. Despite the academic challenges some of the students faced, most teachers described Caribbean American students as "well behaved" or "nice" kids. However, the perception of Caribbean American youth as well behaved did not preclude them from observing, analyzing, and internalizing institutionally racist practices in the form of disciplinary disparities between Black and White students. Even when students could not identify personal experiences with racism at school, they still felt implicated in racial dynamics by virtue of being Black.

Disciplinary discrepancies between Black and White students demonstrated: (1) a lack of consequences for White students who did not adhere to school guidelines as described in the previous section; (2) harsher and more frequent punishment for Black students; and (3) in the case of Black boys, extreme leniency on the part of White teachers in ways that negatively affected their academic achievement. This section will focus on the latter two themes. Although these two themes appear paradoxical, teacher treatment of students fell consistently into one of these categories, leaving little middle ground for Black students. Either teachers reprimanded Black students more harshly for infractions their White peers were absolved of, or their fear of Black boys prevented them from disciplining them when sanctions were most appropriate and, more importantly, when their behaviors negatively affected their academic performance.

Excessive and Frequent Discipline of Black Students

As the students were arriving at school one morning in May, there was a young White counselor in a fitted green wrap dress and wedge sandals supervising students as they came through the doors of the school's main entrance. Nearby, there was also another older White woman who was seated at a desk right in the middle of the entrance also assisting with the morning routine. As students flooded through the doors, a Black girl stood alongside the counselor and identified students one by one as they entered, commenting on which students had not adhered to the school's dress code. She specifically identified several White students. As one White girl entered the school in shorts that obviously had not met the length requirement, the Black student remarked, "Put your hands down, your shorts are not arm's length." As this process continued, it became obvious that this Black girl's goal was to draw the counselor's attention to the obvious infractions of her White peers. However, none of these infractions were addressed. After unsuccessfully pointing out White students who had broken school policy, the girl then began pointing out Black students. It was as if the student was testing school authority to see whether they would choose to discipline Blacks after ignoring the obvious infractions of White students. After all her attempts "to see who would get in trouble" failed, she left for class.

Shortly thereafter, I entered the front office of the school building and no-
ticed a Black girl sitting in the office pouting. I did not recognize her, but
she was holding an envelope in her hand that I had asked another stu-
dent to give to her, since she had not attended the Caribbean American
Student meeting I held just moments earlier. As I listened, I realized she
was in the process of being reprimanded by a teacher for wearing flip-
flops to school. I asked the teacher if I could talk to the student for a mo-
ment because she should have been in the meeting I just held. I sat down,
introduced myself, and explained that I was the person who asked that
she receive the letter in her hand. I asked her what was wrong given her
despondence. She said the teacher told her she had to put on her gym
shoes because she could not wear flip-flops. I proceeded to ask her why she
had a problem adhering to the teacher's request and she replied, "Teach-
ers wear flip-flops."

This vignette is one example of the ways in which racial inequities played out in the form of student discipline. Furthermore, it
reflected Black students' perceptions and protests of those inequities. After several White students—who clearly were not in dress
code—entered the school building and were not reprimanded, a
Black girl sat in the office, missing class time, because she wore
flip-flops. The Caribbean American student mentioned in the vignette did not participate in the study. It leaves me to wonder how
her day might have been different or whether she would have participated in the study if she were given the same leniency as White
students and if she were able to attend the meeting rather than
being relegated to the office for breaking the dress code.

This Caribbean American student was aware that she had disregarded school policy, but she was also aware that there was a
double standard. The mostly White teaching staff was entitled to
wear flip-flops, but students—in particular, Black students—could
not. In many instances, Black students' "behavior problems" and
non-compliance with school rules were acts of resistance toward
the racist practices that became a part of the daily experiences of
students in school. It is this type of resistance that Ogbu (1991a)
described as oppositional to mainstream structures and therefore
an impediment to academic success. However, these acts of resistance often help students to feel empowered and cope with the racial discrimination they experience each day.

Teachers' and administrators' inconsistencies in who was required to adhere to school rules and whether and to what extent

consequences were rationed sent clear messages to Black American and Caribbean American students about the effects of blackness on one's life. In an interview, Elyse Young mentioned that, "If [White] kids were doing something, I see that Black kids are mainly getting blamed for it.... For example like, not blamed, but like...you get in trouble easier than White kids, that's what I mean...if a Black kid did something, they would suspend them." Nadette, another study participant, confirmed her discomfort with trends in disciplinary disparities.

C: Do you believe that Black students are treated differently in [school]?

N: Some, 'cause the teacher, like it depends on the teacher because the teacher will get down on your case like really start yelling at you, like going nuts, but like if it's another student, she probably talk calm and stuff, which is so not fair. Sometime I be looking at it, I'm like this is so wrong. Yeah.... Like when somebody else do something, like she talk[s] in a kinda calm, kinda different voice, which, I don't like that.
C: Okay, and you think that's because of [the students'] race?
N: Yeah.

Nadette rarely reported personal experiences with racism, but she still had some sense that Black students were treated unfairly. As she saw it, teachers did not respond similarly when Black students and White students were disciplined. She used examples of Tyriq to make her case. Tyriq was biracial (Black and White), but positioned very differently from the gifted biracial student in Ms. Ackerman's science class whose father was a prominent scientist. Unlike the other student, Tyriq came from a lower socioeconomic background, and his style of dress and body language emulated what some deem "hip-hop style." Nadette viewed Tyriq as Black and believed that the slightest embodiment of blackness left students susceptible to unfair discipline. This was especially true for Black and biracial students whose cultural style least resembled that of White, middle-class students.

Nadette was often praised by her teachers for being a "hardworking" and well-behaved student. Throughout my entire time at Morristown, there was only one instance I can recall where she had to be redirected by her teacher. In this particular case, Nadette was asked to lower her voice as she talked with another student during art class. Despite the relative dearth of examples of Nadette and other Caribbean American students being subject to reprimands by their teachers, their perspectives about racial discrimination were not drawn from their personal experiences, but rather from observations of how other Black students were treated at Morristown. Institutionalized racist practices at Morristown Middle School taught Caribbean American students a great deal about racism and discrimination, ideas they believed to be a reflection of the larger U.S. society.

Self-Fulfilling Prophecies and Classroom Disruptions in Majority-Black Classes

While students cited harsher and more consistent punishment for infractions as evidence of racial discrimination, my observations of classrooms throughout the school documented another trend. On the one hand, Black students were subject to harsher consequences; on the other hand, there were also innumerable instances where Black boys were free to disrupt the classroom without there being *any* consequences. Both trends—harsher discipline and a lack of discipline—were problematic, and both reinforced similar negative stereotypes of Black students.

In one language-arts class, the teacher and co-teacher failed to discipline several Black male students even when their unruly behavior warranted disciplinary sanctions and interfered with their learning and the learning of their peers. During one class period, several Black male athletes (on the school's football team) engaged in a raucous debate regarding their athletic prowess. This dialogue continued throughout instructional time as the boys, who were situated in different areas of the classroom, yelled things like, "[You suck], I gotta help you block!" Then Khalif, one of the boys, arose and walked around the classroom. After being asked to return to his seat, Khalif slowly sauntered to his seat, pausing to talk to other students along the way. While all this chaos ensued, the teacher, still attempting to conduct a lesson, asked the class to explain what the theme tells you about a story. Without taking a moment to consider the question, Khalif raised his hand and answered, "The moral message [of the story]."

Similar occurrences continued throughout the class session. However, whenever teachers posed questions regarding academic content, the boys responded effortlessly. The boys' ability to simultaneously disrupt the classroom *and* participate in class discussions was an indication that they were capable of handling more rigorous academic content than they were given credit for in this lower-level class. These observations indicated that, in some cases, Black boys were assigned to classes that did not reflect fully their capabilities or challenge their intellect. Such misplacement and expression of lower expectations, both behaviorally and academically, encouraged students' "acting out."

As the same class session continued, D'mir, another Black male student, yelled across the room to Khalif, "Who you talkin' to? Who you fuckin' with young boy!?" At this point, I was sure that one of the two teachers in the room would address D'mir's grossly inappropriate comment. To my disbelief, however, the teacher continued with the question being posed, asking students to volunteer to identify themes in the story. Alicia, a Black girl in the classroom, described the theme of the story as "Try your best and you can accomplish anything." Alicia was then criticized by the boys for offering a "soft" and "corny" response to the question. In response to the boys' criticisms, Alicia remarked sassily, "I don't see *you* coming up with anything else!" In an attempt to find examples from the story to support Alicia's theme, D'mir yelled, "Squeaky practices all the time." The teacher acknowledged D'mir's answer to the question as an acceptable response, but never addressed his consistently inappropriate behavior.

Like the White male students in advanced and high-level classes, Black male students were also given the latitude to dominate class discussions and taunt their female counterparts. However, Black male ownership of classroom space was restricted to majority-Black, low-level classes. Both the behaviors displayed in Ms. Ackerman's science class and in this English class were grossly inappropriate. However, the behavior of the White male students positioned them as academically astute and superior to their peers, whereas the Black male students' display of similar behaviors marked them as unruly and deviant, thereby justifying their placement in remedial classes.

While it could be argued that the teachers' reluctance to address the negative behavior of the Black boys in the classroom might have been a strategic attempt to mitigate their attention-seeking behaviors, the cost of allowing such behaviors had far-reaching consequences for the boys and the other students in the classroom. As a result of the teachers' inability to curb student behavior, the entire class lost time that could have been devoted to academic and intellectual growth. Additionally, the lack of disapproval on the part of teachers reinforced the idea that their behavior was acceptable—or, in fact, that Black boys were wild and unmanageable. By ignoring these behaviors, the teachers actually helped reinforce stereotypes that depict Black men and boys as angry, aggressive, and erratic.

Teachers either worked excessively to control Black students through harsher discipline or, as I have indicated, allowed them to behave in ways that supported stereotypical notions of Black students as uncontrollable and inherently drawn to misconduct. Teachers' decisions to allow inappropriate behaviors to escalate worked to further disadvantage Black students, given that students would continue to push boundaries. The result was suspensions and other extreme forms of punishment.

Despite White teachers' inability to manage the behavior of Black boys in the classroom, the boys' role in the classroom shifted from that of deviance to responsible students in classrooms where teachers challenged their misdeeds and held them to high academic and social standards. Several of the boys from the aforementioned literacy class also attended math class together. However, their math teacher, a young Black woman named Ms. Carter, took a completely different approach with the boys. In contrast to the negative behaviors displayed in the literacy class, the boys mostly sat quietly and attentively in Ms. Carter's algebra class. This counterexample demonstrates that there were teachers in the building who had developed useful strategies for working with many of the same boys whose behavior seemed out of control. The following vignette highlights the shift in students' behavior and their role in the participation structures of the classroom given appropriate levels of accountability.

In Ms. Carter's math classroom the students were asked to work in groups to solve problems on a handout. After allotting several minutes to attempt the problem, Ms. Carter gave the students rulers and said to them, "Now, how would you figure...out [the problem]!" As time elapsed, Ms. Carter informed the class that another group was near completion of the assignment. D'mir became upset and requested additional time to complete the problem before the steps were explained to the entire class. Per D'mir's request, Ms. Carter granted the class several additional minutes to decipher the answer to the problem, and after several minutes she checked with D'mir to find out if he had yet to solve the problem. D'mir responded, yelling, "I don't even know how to do it!" Ms. Carter responded, "Okay" and moved toward the board to solve the problem. At that point a White female student seated next to D'mir asked Ms. Carter, "Can D'mir move over there?" Ms. Carter responded, "No, you need to learn to work with anyone." After first explaining the problem, Ms. Carter mentioned to D'mir that she was going over to the phone to call his parents. Immediately, D'mir walked over to her desk to find out if Ms. Carter was serious about calling his parents. As Ms. Carter awaited an answer on the phone, she explained to D'mir that he needed to demonstrate more patience in the classroom and that his tendency to yell out in class was disruptive. As they engaged in dialogue, Ms. Carter also pulled up D'mir's test scores on her computer and showed him his grades. Once D'mir caught a glimpse of his last test score he shouted, "Oh no, I'm retaking the test! Isn't that an E or something?"

Although D'mir made attempts to disrupt Ms. Carter's classroom, Ms. Carter was unrelenting in addressing his negative behaviors, and she helped him to make explicit connections between his behavior and its impact on his academic outcomes. By making these connections, Ms. Carter reinforced her expectation that D'mir was to do well academically and socially. She held him accountable for his behavior in ways that were fair and addressed the specific behaviors he displayed. Additionally, by holding D'mir accountable for demonstrating appropriate behaviors and meeting academic requirements, Ms. Carter's disciplinary strategies signaled to other students that D'mir was capable of and expected to make good choices.

Of the five boys who acted out in the literacy classroom—led by not one teacher but two White teachers—only D'mir's behavior had to be addressed in Ms. Carter's classroom. Ms. Carter's classroom served as a valuable counterpoint to the previous teachers' literacy classroom. The contrast between the ways in which the boys behaved in both contexts informs the notion that perceived student deficiencies were, in part, linked to the enactment of racist ideology that allowed for performance of stereotype-enhancing behaviors in the classroom. Examples from Ms. Carter's classroom illuminated the pervasive and unchallenged assumption of White teachers that depicted many Black students as averse to and incapable of meeting rigorous academic expectations, and reinforced the idea that students lacked the skills and decorum necessary for appropriate classroom engagement.

In the previous description of the two literacy teachers' inability to address the behaviors of Khalif and D'mir and to hold them to high behavioral and academic standards, it also became apparent that the boys were not being challenged academically. Their ability to simultaneously disrupt the class and to participate in class dialogue by answering questions correctly indicated a mismatch between the boys' skill level and their class placement. While this academic mismatch had neither been identified nor aggressively challenged by the White literacy teachers, Ms. Carter advocated for several of the previously disruptive boys to be moved to her advanced math class. Although D'mir continued to push boundaries in Ms. Carter's class through the display of inappropriate behaviors, Ms. Carter was able to distinguish his improper behavior from his academic ability and moved him to a class that appropriately suited his academic skill level. While attempting to make this switch, Ms. Carter recalled being faced with much resistance from school counselors. After successfully fighting to have D'mir placed in a more advanced math class, Ms. Carter noted that he went from receiving A's to C's, but there was also marked improvement in his behavior. In the higher-level math class, D'mir could not disrupt the class and perform well academically. The more challenging content required D'mir to focus on his academics and forgo clowning around. He had to put forth more effort to solve problems in class and prepare for exams. His preoccupation with the advanced math content detracted from his ability to simultaneously disrupt the class and maintain decent grades.

Caribbean American students in the study were placed in mostly mid- to low-level classes. In some cases students appeared well suited to their placements, but not so much in others. Tamara, for instance, was an extremely articulate and thoughtful girl. I had worked with her the previous year through CWT, and she often raised thought-provoking questions in class. However, it was not until the following school year that her counselor informed me that she had been identified as a special education student. It was unclear how a student with whom I had worked closely and perceived as intellectually astute was designated a special education student. As I delved further into Tamara's academic profile, I noticed that she had consistently poor math grades. However, consistently poor math grades did not explain why she had not been placed in advanced classes in other content areas. It was discrepancies like this one that often cemented an institutionalized stance on the academic expectations of Black students from a variety of backgrounds.

In an interview with another White female teacher who also struggled to manage the behavior of some of the Black boys in her classes, the teacher posited that many of her colleagues feared Black boys and, as a result, were reluctant to discipline them as necessary. In her assessment, such fear led to the proliferation of negative behaviors as Black boys pushed boundaries with an increasing number of teachers by performing the stereotypical roles pre-established for them. This conversation occurred after an incident in which Brian, a Black boy in one of her classes, boasted to one of his counterparts, "My grades is legit. I got teachers on my side." Brian went on to explain that he was able to maintain good grades by coercing and tormenting teachers rather than earning them. This student's assertions demonstrate his awareness that teachers were malleable and that their fear of Black males gave him the leeway to shirk his academic and social responsibilities. Because of what he perceived as teachers' fear of Black students, Brian was able to go through the process of schooling on his terms. Those terms played into stereotypical notions that vilified Black males and marked them as dangerous and threatening but, more importantly, allowed them to move through the school system without acquiring the requisite skills.

Ms. Lewis and her teaching assistant, Mr. Kim, reported that Brian often attempted to negotiate the terms of his class participation and engagement. She said she often explained to Brian, "I am not going to do something for you just to get you to do what you are supposed to do." The teachers also cited D'mir as another Black boy who used teachers' fear of him to navigate the process of schooling on his terms. Mr. Kim explained that he asked D'mir to do something, and D'mir said that he would if Mr. Kim allowed him to listen to his iPod, a request that Mr. Kim denied.

Such instances support the notion that Black boys were aware of the fear they engendered in teachers, and, as a result, they used that fear to negotiate with and control teachers. In her book *Other People's Children: Cultural Conflict in the Classroom*, Lisa Delpit (1995) shared the following assessment of teacher fear shared with her by a Black student:

> There are three kinds of teachers in middle school: the Black teachers, none of whom are afraid of Black kids; the White teachers, a few of whom are not afraid of Black kids; and the largest group of White teachers, *all* of whom are afraid of Black kids. (pp. 167–168)

This quotation gives evidence to students' perception of teacher fear. While the power to negotiate and dominate the process of schooling was handed over to White students by virtue of their race, gender, and class privilege, Black boys who similarly desired to dominate the classroom context often resorted to the use of aggressive behaviors, since other means of participation were often restricted.

Students' knowledge of teachers' fear of them also has potentially far-reaching consequences on student behavior, identities, and self-esteem. According to Ms. Lewis and Mr. Kim, Brian often "personalize[d]" and "internalize[d]" their responses to his behavior and did not understand that he was also complicit in the destructive cycle of performing the stereotypical role of the Black male. Brian attributed teachers' dispositions toward him as linked to his inherent qualities.

Black boys often experienced a tension between the benefits of White teachers' malleability and the negativity aroused by their perceived ability to leverage teacher fear as a means of gaining visibility and respect. Black boys used teachers' perceived fear of them as collateral for negotiations, but were simultaneously hurt by their inability to develop fulfilling relationships with teachers that were based on trust, admiration, and mutual respect. While teacher fear allowed for momentary satisfaction on the part of Black boys by allowing them power to manipulate individuals and situations, temporary and unstable bouts of power also destabilized boys' sense of self, which made them feel that they were often unfairly attacked by teachers and disliked overall—a sentiment frequently expressed by students in informal circles.

The aforementioned examples give evidence to the distinct ways in which Black and White students were allowed to participate in academic aspects of the Morristown community. Through these disparate structures of participation, students were able to identify with and fulfill their expected roles in U.S. racial hierarchies. The training for complicity in hierarchical structures that served to marginalize Black students of Caribbean and native U.S. backgrounds was provided through schooling experiences at Morristown.

Academic Expectations and the Engagement of Caribbean American Students

Like racial disparities reflected in discipline, observations and student interviews also revealed discrepancies in academic expectations between White and Black students. These disparities played out in several ways. The racially skewed composition of classes and their correlation to students' perceived ability levels was one way in which expectations were communicated. However, this section highlights additional ways in which teachers communicated academic expectations to students by (1) regulating students' ability to participate in class discussion and (2) excessively scrutinizing students' performance on assignments and assessments. Teachers also communicated expectations that impacted student engagement and made possible Caribbean American students' internalization of other Black students' acts of resistance as deviance. Caribbean American students tracked into mid- and lower-level classes experienced subtly communicated expectations that affected perceptions of their own ability and caused them to internalize and project onto their Black peers negative racial stereotypes.

Difficulties Participating in Classroom Dialogue

While some Caribbean American students in the study expressed having limited personal experience with racism at school, when asked directly, they clearly articulated the ways in which racial inequities played out in the school. The basis of such assertions was often Caribbean American students' observations of teacher-student interactions. Although students were not always aware of the more nebulous ways in which race and racism impacted their experiences at Morristown, they knew that overall academic expectations, discipline, and participation structures were marked by racial disparities.

While I discussed class participation in great detail earlier in this chapter, I revisit the topic to highlight the ways in which patterns in classroom participation—namely, teachers' tendencies to call on certain students and ignore others during class discussions—also reflected teachers' academic expectations of students. In an interview, Tamara shared the following.

> A teacher sometimes will like, what she will do is like...you'll know the answer and she'll just...purposely pick on somebody else that...doesn't really know the answer, but if a Black person raises their hand and says oh, I would like to answer this question or something, she would wait and see if anybody else wants to answer that question and then she'll pick on them. I mean, it's not, I don't...think it's the fact that you raise your hand too much in class [and she wants to] give someone else a chance, I think it's the fact that that's the way teachers are. I mean not all teachers, but some teachers I have. They look at you and then they wait for somebody else to raise their hand...and it may not even [be] the fact that you are like raising your hand so often...but, like you can tell, like wow that's a little wrong. Like, I just don't understand that.

Tamara's account of her teachers' reluctance to call on Black students in the classroom spoke to the messages communicated to students about academic expectations on the part of teachers. In this example, Tamara was given cause to question whether she was not expected to participate in the classroom and the degree to which she had ownership over classroom space or whether she was not perceived as "smart enough" to answer particular questions and contribute to classroom learning. It was in moments like these that students were encouraged to reflect on racial dynamics and question their inherent qualities and capabilities, given the implicit messages they received from teachers.

During a classroom observation, one teacher's communication of lower expectations was not so subtle. In the following vignette, Elyse was left angered and frustrated by her teacher's attempt to have her White peers "help" her.

I entered the classroom to find students divided into groups of 3–4 students. Elyse was partnered with two White girls. Immediately, I noticed that Elyse showed an excitement about the work she was doing in the group and displayed a rare, passionate disposition as she explained her answers to the questions. At one point, Elyse asserted, "I think [the answer] is eight! I think it's eight!" Shortly thereafter, her teacher, Mr. Pollock, began circulating through the classroom and headed over to Elyse's table. Mr. Pollock looked over at the two White girls in the group and exclaimed, "You guys have to help her alright! Explain why she's wrong, you wanna make sure she [understands]." As Mr. Pollock explained to the two White girls why they should help Elyse, she stared intently at him in disbelief. Once he walked away, Elyse turned to the girls and asked, "What does he mean, that I'm stupid?" Her peers dismissed her concerns, stating she was being overly sensitive about Mr. Pollock's comment, but Elyse was not convinced that was the case. The stress and anxiety raised by this experience was captured by changes in Elyse. She immediately became preoccupied with Mr. Pollock's remark and sat massaging the back of her neck and shaking her leg, showing visible signs of distress. The previously excited student, who was interested and engaged in the learning process, had shut down based on what she perceived as her teacher's lower expectations of her.

Teachers often make decisions about whether to place students in heterogeneous or homogeneous ability groups. A heterogeneous group can improve the learning of stronger students by reinforcing what they know and gives lower-level students an opportunity to learn from their peers rather than the teacher. However, teachers must always be aware of how student groups lead to perceptions of who is capable and who is not. In this example, Mr. Pollock specifically instructed the White students to help the Black student in the group. Despite the teacher's good intentions, his request implied to Elyse that she was less capable than the other students in the group and that they, in fact, knew why her answer was incorrect.

After class, Elyse approached Mr. Pollock to ask him what he meant by his comment—a very courageous move on her part. During their conversation, Mr. Pollock attempted to retract his statement, but Elyse's perception of his comment as insensitive and belittling had not changed. He did not assuage her concerns, and, to Elyse, his explanation seemed both insincere and illogical.

Although teachers' communication of academic expectations is not always this explicit, students are adept at deciphering underlying messages and teachers' attitudes toward them. Teachers' comments and behaviors were consistently scrutinized and analyzed by students in the study. It was through students' analyses of these experiences that they came to understand the role of race in their lives.

Teacher Scrutiny and Assumptions of Students' Attitudes and Dispositions Toward Learning

It was assumed that White students from upper-middle-class backgrounds would perform well academically; however, for Black students—both Caribbean and American—high academic expectations were rare. Most teachers at Morristown would argue that the majority-White teaching staff did not perceive Black students as less capable than their White counterparts. However, students' accounts of school experiences tell another story. In several instances, students reported that teachers had accused them of cheating on assignments or exams when they did perform well. Inadvertently, students learned that teachers did not expect them to perform well academically because when they did, they were subject to intense scrutiny. Students felt their teachers doubted their investment in academic achievement and questioned whether they would expend the time and energy needed to achieve academic success.

In Geneva's enriched literacy class, I watched as one student pleaded to her teacher that her group did not copy another student's work. During this particular class, the students were asked to work in pairs or groups of three to answer questions on a worksheet. Two groups, made up mostly of Black students, challenged one another to see which group would complete the assignment first. As Geneva's group moved ahead quickly, a Black girl from the opposing group grabbed Geneva's paper, placed it face down, and continued to answer questions with her group. Ms. Kelley then went over to the group and interrogated the students, asking whether they were copying from Geneva's paper. One of the students in the group explained that they took Geneva's paper so that Geneva's group couldn't work on their questions, which would give their group a chance to catch up to them. However, this student's explanation did not suffice. Several times the student explained, "I took her paper from her because she is farther than us. No, I wasn't copying. I took her paper so that we could catch up." While my observation confirmed that the students were not cheating, this scenario demonstrated Ms. Kelley's assumption that the students *were* cheating. Ms. Kelley's continued interrogation of the student despite her plea of innocence implied that the student's word could not be trusted and that perhaps the student lacked academic integrity.

Shortly after this incident occurred, however, a White boy yelled across the room, "She's cheating!" in an attempt to call Ms. Kelley's attention to the behavior of a White girl in the class. However, Ms. Kelley barely looked over in the direction of the two students and did not go over to assess whether the boy's claim was legitimate. In contrast to the lengthy process of interrogation the Black student endured, the accusation that the White student was cheating was dismissed.

The microaggression committed by this teacher buttresses assumptions that people of color are "presumed to be dangerous, criminal, or deviant on the basis of their race" (Sue et al., 2007). In subtle ways, students of all races were made to learn racism in schools. White students learned that Black people could not be trusted, while Black students internalized these racist stereotypes. White students learned to play the role of privilege, while Black students learned to internalize and reinforce their marginalized status. Black students also learned that they could not trust all White people.

Teacher Expectations, Student Disengagement, and Perceptions of Resistance

Regular exposure to low academic expectations prompted some students to assume a resistant stance in schools or disengage from the academic environment to the extent that they could. While resistance demonstrated by Black students in the study was mostly disruptive to the learning environment, Caribbean American students who participated in the study were often limited to resistance in the form of mild disengagement, as opposed to outright academic disengagement and resistance through classroom disruption. Caribbean American students' families strictly reinforced ethnic values around respect for one's elders and held tenaciously to expectations that students bring home good grades, or at the very least passing grades. Caribbean American students, particularly those enrolled in low- to mid-level classes, had to maintain a tenuous balance between acknowledging racial inequities and meeting the academic and behavioral expectations of their parents.

Observations of widespread student disengagement on the part Black students at Morristown served to socialize Caribbean American students around the academic identities of Blacks. In particular, exposure to Black students who were disengaged from the learning process, and school overall, influenced Caribbean American students' stance on the importance of education to the larger Black community. Consequently, some Caribbean American students internalized negative perceptions of Blacks in regard to academic engagement. These unchallenged assumptions often stemmed from institutionalized forms of racial socialization. Caribbean American students viewed their Black peers' resistance to and disengagement from learning as inherently related to race rather than students' means of coping with school-wide disenfranchisement.

The following interview with Antoinette demonstrated the ways in which she internalized negative perspectives of Black students based on their acts of resistance toward racial inequities at school.

C: Okay, so do you think Blacks perform differently than other races in schools?

A: Yes.

C: Okay....

A: Because I don't think they, like most Black kids some of them do like to learn...the little [unpopular] people, the people who pay more attention to their work, [but] most of...the [Black] people at this school...pay more attention to like their friends and stuff and White students they just get to work.

C: Okay, so you're saying Black students are more into like, socializing?

A: Um hm [yes].

C: ...and the White students are more focused on their schoolwork?

A: Yup.

This exchange indicates several things: (1) Antoinette observed the consequences of institutionalized racism without fully understanding why students chose to disengage from the learning process, and (2) she lacked exposure to Black students who were committed to doing well academically because she was tracked into majority-Black, lower-level classes. As a result of tracking, lower-level students had few opportunities to interact with other Black students who did well academically *and* were socially accepted by their peers. As a result, tracking helped to further solidify entrenched notions of inadequacy on the part of Black students.

While students noticed disparities in the way Black students were treated, they were not conscious of how these students learned to cope with these inequities. For example, Tamara was able to describe experiences where teachers called on White students to answer questions even after Black students had raised their hands. What students did not recognize was that after several unsuccessful attempts to engage in class discussion, students would stop participating altogether.

On another occasion, Antoinette explained that she felt the parents of Black students were summoned to school more often to deal with the disciplinary transgressions of their children. The following quotation reflects Antoinette's summation of the matter.

> I think [White and Asian parents] come to school less than most Black parents because White[s], Asian[s], they're more...humble and stuff and us Black children are very, well, disruptive in a way. Like, most of us are distracting and class clowns and stuff and that makes our parents have to come up because the...the principal might want to talk to them about us....

Essentially, the ways in which race and racism played out in the school served to perpetuate a cycle whereby Black students were treated unfairly and responded to inequitable treatment in ways that reinforced negative stereotypes about their group. Moreover, as Antoinette's comment indicates, students began to see these responses to unfair treatment as inherent characteristics of Black students. Teachers and administrators doled out harsh disciplinary sanctions to Black students whose behaviors were often responses to racial microaggressions. However, students did not recognize the cyclical nature of teachers' actions and their peers' responses. Instead, teachers were deemed unfair in their treatment of Black students, and Black students internalized notions of their group as not valuing education.

Tracking and Interracial Student Relationships

Not only did *de facto* tracking sort students into first- and second-class learning experiences, it also affected the social relationships and networks of students throughout the school. The Morristown school district was regarded as one of the best not only because of its solid academic reputation, but also because of the rich ethnic and racial diversity of the student body. Few local suburban districts could compare. However, parents failed to realize that while diverse groups of students were housed in the same school building, students' interactions with and opportunities to learn from other groups were limited by the racially distinct outcomes of academic tracking.

Students often became friends with students they met in their classes or with whom they participated in extracurricular activities. Unfortunately, classes and extracurricular activities were segregated by default, which limited interracial interactions. Some sports teams (e.g., basketball, football, and track) consisted mostly of Black students, while other teams (e.g., tennis, lacrosse, and soccer) attracted White students. White students almost exclusively attended activities like band, orchestra, and theater.

Instead of recruiting Black students to participate in the school's long-standing activities and including the ideas and interests of Black students, the school created additional clubs that lacked adequate resources and institutional support and were run by the few overtaxed Black teachers at the school. One of those activities—the step team—was developed only during the final year of this project as an add-on, and was described by administrators and teachers as an activity that would give "troublemakers" something to do. Unsurprisingly, this and similar activities were comprised mostly of Black students.

Despite ethnic and national distinctions that Caribbean American students made between themselves and their peers—both Black and White—they were well aware that they shared the racial background and hence the racial "baggage" of their Black American peers. In no way were Caribbean American students exempt from the racial politics of Morristown. However, the racial and ethnic socialization received by Caribbean American students in their homes shaped the ways in which they analyzed and responded to racial incidents that occurred in the school building. (This will be discussed at length in the next chapter.)

This work indicates that current researched-based assertions that Caribbean immigrants "have done well in terms of adjustment, employment, and community life" negate the many challenges faced by this population (Rong & Brown 2002, p. 251). Evidence from the experiences of Caribbean American youth at Morristown supports the claim that Caribbean immigrants are not protected from negative stereotypes that Americans associate with Black skin (Model, 2008). These notions of blackness often conflicted with parents' perceived experiences and understandings of U.S. racism and contradicted the ethnic socialization messages students received about what it meant to be Black from the standpoint of their Caribbean parents.

Despite the racial and ethnic socialization that Caribbean American youth experienced at home, aspects of their racial and ethnic identities were implicitly challenged by their daily experiences within the Morristown context—experiences that reinforced hegemonic and stereotypical conceptions of blackness. While parental socialization reinforced ethnic identities grounded in values relating to hard work, educational achievement, the display of good manners, and community camaraderie, Caribbean American students experienced in school racial divisions by way of academic and extracurricular tracking, lower academic expectations, and biases reflected in the discipline of students and implicit rules that governed the participation of some students in the learning environment to the exclusion of others. These disjunctures in racial and ethnic socialization messages had profound implications for the identity development of Caribbean American youth.

Notes

1. See Harris (1993) for more on White privilege.
2. Racial categories are based on observations of students' phenotype

Converging Identities and Realities: Finding One's Place in the Home, School, and World

During the very beginning of the study, I went from classroom to classroom describing my research project to determine which students were first-, 1.5-, or second-generation Americans at Morristown. While in Mr. Asafa's class, I rattled off the usual pitch explaining to the class that my parents were from the Caribbean and that I was interested in learning more about the thoughts and experiences of Caribbean American youth. Thereafter, I sat at a table on the periphery of the classroom and asked students to sign their names and provide contact information if they were interested in learning more about the project. As I waited for students to sign their names, Charles sauntered over to me, maintaining a distinctly cool posture and explaining confidently that his family was also from Jamaica. He proceeded to ask whether I was familiar with traditional Jamaican foods like ackee and salt fish and fried dumplings. Charles shared that his grandmother cooked a Jamaican breakfast for his family most weekends—a meal he enjoyed. As I welcomed his serious yet childlike banter, I began to wonder how often Charles had opportunities to share his ethnic background at school. I also surmised that Charles was deeply tied to his ethnic heritage. After interviewing his parents, however, they shared another side to the story. According to Charles's parents, he was not deeply tied to his Caribbean roots at all. Instead, he balked at his parents' attempts to have him eat Jamaican foods and engage in various cultural activities. In their assessment, Charles had "played" me; he had presented an inauthentic self.

According to Nakkula and Toshalis (2006), adolescence marks the beginning of youth's theoretical thinking; it is a time when youth test their assumptions of the world through real-world experimentation and begin to interpret their world in new and interesting ways. For the adolescents in this study, the task of identity development was an intricate process. Varying identities competed for dominance and were often manipulated by the realities of students' lived experiences as well as the sociocultural politics surrounding definitions of race, ethnicity, and nationality. Within their families, Caribbean American students were sometimes accused of not being Caribbean, as asserted by one father at the initial parent meeting. To most parents, their children's birth or extended stay in the United States precluded them from being Caribbean on nationalistic terms. Though they were not perceived as fully Caribbean in the home, however, students asserted and often privileged their Caribbean identity in the school space and among their peers. Despite their desire to reach their own sense of self and identity constructions, asserting an ethnic identity proved difficult in a school context where teachers, staff, and administrators privileged the Black-White racial binary and de-emphasized other forms of identification.

The children of immigrants were caught in a psychic middle ground between imposed and self-proclaimed identities that often gave rise to identity conflicts. As students sought to determine their place in the world, they were faced with imposing definitions of what it meant to be both Black and Caribbean American. Students' identities were greatly affected by both the home and school environments, which ultimately left youth to resist, embrace, or redefine the identities imposed by educators, peers, parents, and the larger society.

This chapter highlights several recurrent themes relative to the racial and ethnic identities of Caribbean American students at Morristown Middle School: (1) larger politics and experiences around race, ethnicity, and nationality shaped the complex racial and ethnic identities of students and posed challenges for the development of cohesive hybrid identities; (2) a Black racial identity was central to students' identity constructions and shaped largely by socialization experiences in the school context; (3) the types of race talk that occurred in homes were reflected in students' understandings and interpretations of U.S. racism; and (4) ethnic socialization created an alternative to essentialist discourses on blackness in the United States.

Complicating Identity Constraints: The Role of Ethnicity and Nationality in Shaping "Racial" Identity

Students in the study sought to carve out their own unique identities that neither privileged nor downplayed race over ethnicity, but instead allowed for both identities to coexist. Despite their internalization of hybrid identities, students' identities were challenged by political discourses that circulated throughout their homes, schools, and the larger society. This section illuminates two key points: (1) students' hybrid identities challenged dominant discourses on race and ethnicity, and (2) students understood that challenges to essentialist discourses often did not disrupt others' race-centric assumptions of who they were.

Despite an understanding of the distinctions between race and ethnicity, study participants often expressed the degree to which these identities were deeply intertwined. During initial interviews, each participant was asked, "What race do you consider yourself?" Students consistently sought clarification regarding the question. In several instances, my question was followed by a question from students rather than an answer. When Antoinette was asked to define her race, she replied, "You mean Black or White...[or] Jamaican or American?" After some probing about why she raised the question, Antoinette explained that although racial and ethnic categories are distinct, her personal sense of identity was not defined by one category over the other, but both categories together. Antoinette further asserted that she self-identifies as *both* Black *and* Jamaican.

When asked the same question, Tamara did not seek clarification. She simply privileged her *both-and* stance, stating that she is both African American and Caribbean, with little concern for whether my question called for a response grounded in U.S. conventions of race. When asked to tell me her race, Elyse explained that she was Caribbean American, but perceived by others as being African American *because* she is Black. Elyse also used a *both-*

and stance, identifying herself as both Caribbean American and Black.

Although it was clear that participants were aware of the dissimilarity between race and ethnicity, their responses to questions about race often prompted them to reference their ethnicity or seek clarification regarding whether my questions necessitated making a distinction between the two categories. In cases where I reiterated that I was specifically interested in having them identify the racial group to which they belonged, I was often given two answers—first their race and then their ethnic group. In cases where I asked questions without making a distinction between race and ethnicity, students would often identify both their race and ethnicity separately, solely their ethnicity, or a hyphenated hybrid of both.

Students' responses to questions regarding race demonstrated their resistance to prevailing notions of race and ethnicity that foreground racial distinctions and render invisible the multiple salient identities students embodied. This privileging of ethnic identities was particularly apparent within a school context deluged by politics concerning the Black-White binary that often reduced students to stereotypical characteristics frequently associated with race. Caribbean American students' ethnic identities complicated unchallenged assumptions grounded in U.S. racial discourse, and despite few formal opportunities to openly assert their ethnic identities in school, students created their own informal networks of Caribbean peers and took advantage of open-ended school assignments that created space for them to share their Caribbean selves. An example is the assignment highlighted in the epigraph to Chapter 5, wherein Jeffrey described himself as a "Child of Jamaica."

While students often answered "the race question" with multi-layered descriptions of race and ethnicity, nationality also surfaced as a means of self-identification. In essence, race, ethnicity, and nationality—whether the students' or their parents'—were used by students as a primary means of self-identification. As mentioned earlier, when asked to define the racial group to which she belonged, Antoinette mentioned that she was both Black and Jamaican. For her, being Jamaican served as both a specific ethnic group and also as her nationality, despite the fact that she was born and raised in the United States.

A similar phenomenon was noted by Thea Abu El-Haj (2007) in an article entitled "'I was born here, but my home is not here': Educating for Democratic Citizenship in an Era of Transnational Migration and Global Conflict." Like the Palestinian students in Abu El-Haj's study, Caribbean American students also expressed varying degrees of belonging to the United States. Youth in Abu El-Haj's study held conflicting notions about their connections to the United States because of the treatment they received from teachers in schools after the 9-11 attacks and U.S. responses to global conflict. Similarly, Caribbean American students were critical of the ways in which Americans regarded Blacks as second-class citizens. This dynamic shaped their notions of nationality and citizenship, further pushing them toward a Caribbean identity. However, students also realized that they were not completely Caribbean. Some students viewed themselves as American relative to their parents, but also used "'American' to refer to the native Whites they encountered...those 'Americans' [who were] part of a different world that would never include them because of their race/ethnicity" (Kasinitz, Mollenkopf, & Waters, 2002, p. 1034).

Several Caribbean American students who described themselves as belonging to some other place—a place not defined by the location of their birth—took up a transnational lens. This phenomenon is effectively captured by a quotation from Jamaican religious philosopher Mutabaruka. On the syndicated Jamaican television show *Religious Hard Talk*, Mutabaruka stated that if a goat is born in a pigpen, it doesn't make it a pig. In an attempt to highlight Jamaican diasporic connections to Africa, Mutabaruka poignantly argued that the long history of Blacks residing in various countries throughout the world does not make them any less African.

Although the term Caribbean American was most often used to emphasize ethnicity and/or nationality rather than race, there were several instances where Caribbean American students used their hyphenated nationalities in place of race. For students it seemed perfectly logical that if a *country/region + American* connotes race, as in the case of the term "African American," then the term Caribbean American could also legitimately imply race.

Geneva, one of two study participants born in the Caribbean, identified as Trinidadian, since Trinidad was her place of birth. When asked whether she considered herself Trinidadian or American, Geneva responded, "Well, I usually say I'm Trinidadian. Like, [if people ask] where are you from? I'm from Trinidad, that's what I say." At the age of 2, Geneva migrated to the United States, where she had spent most of her life; she felt that identifying as American would be dishonest, given her birth abroad. In an attempt to clarify why she could not fully assume an American identity, she stated that she considered herself "Americanized, but not American." Geneva recognized that being an American citizen and having American "qualities" did not alter the fact that she "feel[s] like [she's] Trinidadian."

On the part of second-generation students, transnational encounters such as frequent trips to the Caribbean and extensive contact with family in the Caribbean played a key role in shaping ethnic identities. As described by Bryce, his hybrid identity was in part solidified by his frequent trips to Jamaica and ongoing relationships with a network of Caribbean family and key peers. Transnational ties, which often included frequent travel to the Caribbean, helped most students feel connected to their parents' homeland.

Bryce reported traveling to Jamaica to spend summer and winter vacations with his aunt and cousins each year. This vacation ritual was so much an enjoyable part of Bryce's routine that his parents decided to forfeit Bryce's semi-annual trip as a penalty for bringing home mediocre grades. For students who did not experience the Caribbean by means of frequent travel, their homes were wrought with ethnic activities and symbols, which also resulted in transnational experiences. They also had consistent access and exposure to networks of people, whether locally or internationally, who served to reinforce ethnic socialization messages and further cement students' connections to the Caribbean and subsequent formations of deeply embedded Caribbean ethnic identities.

These phenomena reflect the salience of transnational, ethnic, and cultural ties for students. For Bryce and Charles, their ethnicity was oftentimes defined as their "race" or primary mode of self-identification, while the other participants (eight out of ten) used U.S. racial conventions to define their race—a definition that was also supplemented by their Caribbean ethnic identities.

Students generally defined race on the basis of phenotype and linkages to African ancestry and ethnicity to the cultural conventions they adhered to on the basis of familial connections to the Caribbean. They were quite aware that they were Black, and, in rare cases, they considered themselves African American. Here I make the distinction between being Black and African American because only a few students used the term African American to describe their race. By definition, students felt that the term Black often encompassed a wider array of people from the African Diaspora, while the term African American related to people of African descent whose ancestors had been brought to the United States as slaves.

Limitations to Self-Identification

Throughout the study, students were clear about limitations to their self-identification given normative U.S. conventions of race that relied on the "one-drop" rule. Students posited that in the United States blackness was demonized, and little could be done to avert dominant assumptions about Blacks that were grounded in racist ideology.

When students used the term African American to describe themselves, they did so knowing that this phrase was interchangeable with Black or that they were considered African American by virtue of being Black. Although students primarily identified their race as Black, they also used the term African American in instances where they felt the term was politically correct. Elyse made the distinction between the appropriateness of the terms Black and African American by first stating that her race is Caribbean American, but that she is perceived by others as African American, and follows that assertion by stating: "I'm as you say in I guess slang, I'm Black, a Black person." In this case, more general societal politics surrounding racial identity informed her choice of words used for self-identification, regardless of whether they reflected her personal sense of identity.

Elyse's younger brother Charles also recognized constraints on how he was able to define his identity. When asked to define his race, Charles resisted the use of the terms Black or African American. After several failed attempts at prompting him to state his race as defined by phenotype and ancestry, I asked Charles what he used to identify himself on official forms that did not include Jamaican American as an option. Charles then explained that he would normally choose "Black" as his race. He further explained that he often chose Black "Because, um, there's like no other way to, um, write it. There's like, like basically, I only choose the one that's more of an option to me." Charles implies that Black as a racial category did not fully capture his identity; he was forced to choose "Black" because it was the only option available to him. The following exchange between Geneva and me similarly illustrated the tensions between the identities ascribed to students and the identities students embrace.

C: Okay, what race do you consider yourself?

G: Black, yeah um, African [correction] not African American but like um Trinidadian. That's how I really consider myself.

C: You consider yourself Trinidadian so you don't necessarily consider yourself Black, but mostly Trinidadian, is [that] how you identify?

G: Like Black Trinidadian.

C: What race do other people consider you?

G: Um, my like family, like my real family um Indian and...Venezuelan and Black, yeah.

C: Okay, why do you think...that's different from how you define yourself?

G: I think it's because like that's the way that they were raised. They were raised a certain way. Like my mom, I think she was the first one...to actually raise a kid here [in the United States] so like our perspectives are different. Like, I consider myself to be Trinidadian Black and I consider myself like everything that I am.

C: Okay, so your family in Trinidad considers you to be multiracial, but in America they would just consider you Black so that's what you consider yourself?

G: Yeah.

Geneva, whose phenotype marked her as multiracial in my eyes, felt she had to adhere to U.S. conventions of race. Geneva noted that she was in fact multiracial and that her multiracial identity was recognized within the Trinidadian context and within her family. However, she also explained that the label she has adopted as a Black Trinidadian was a byproduct of being one of the first children in her family to be raised in the United States. Geneva's racial identity transitioned from multiracial to Black by virtue of contextual racial politics of the U.S. geographical space. These two dimensions led Geneva to a hybrid identity—Black Trinidadian.

As previously mentioned, students whose parents hailed from two different islands or countries in the Caribbean relied on the term "Caribbean American" in referring to their ethnicities. For example, Elyse—whose mother was Jamaican and biological father Guyanese—was referred to by her mother as "Guyjamerican." In an attempt to simplify the term constructed by her mother, Elyse chose to describe herself as Caribbean American, often noting that her parents were from two different places within the Caribbean region. Likewise, Jeffrey mentioned that he identified as Caribbean American because his parents are from the Caribbean and he was born in the United States. In most cases, students specified that they were Jamaican American or Trinidadian but used more general terms such as Caribbean in instances where multiple nationalities/ethnicities were included in their self-identification.

Jeffrey also explained that he considers himself Caribbean American because both his parents were from different countries in the Caribbean region and he was born in the United States. In Jeffrey's case his mother was born in Dominica and his father in Jamaica. While other students' hyphenated descriptions of their identities referred to specific islands and countries in which their parents were born, Jeffrey would sometimes identify as Jamaican and in other instances use the term "Caribbean," since it encompassed the birth countries of both his parents.

Understanding the Black Experience

Although students' identities consisted of several amalgamations of ethnic, racial, and national markers, students held clear ideas about what it meant to be Black in America despite their ethnic affiliation or birthplace. While students' perceptions of the degree to which they were personally affected by race varied, they all acknowledge the history of American slavery and the ways in which the institution of slavery fueled the disenfranchisement of all Blacks in the United States. Students argued unanimously that the racial experiences of Blacks in the Caribbean varied drastically from those of U.S. Blacks because of the relative absence of Whites in the English-speaking Caribbean.

Caribbean American students generally considered themselves Black, and in some cases African American, despite modes of racial classification in the Caribbean. The students used U.S. racial standards as a primary means of defining race, even in instances where students reported being of mixed ancestry. Although students defined race in rather uncontested and simplistic terms, they expressed their personal connection to their identities as Black people and their knowledge of the social implications of blackness in more complex ways.

When students were specifically asked to explain what being Black meant to them, they most often began by expressing that being Black was of great importance to them. Students emphasized the legacy of slavery as key to defining this importance. Instead of viewing slavery as a source of shame, students expressed pride that Blacks had survived the hardships of slavery and continue to thrive and serve as notable members of society. During a one-on-one interview, Elyse stated, "I'm very honored [to be Black] because we have so much history...like we had a history of slavery and I'm glad we made it through slavery and we actually have a month to call our [own]." Antoinette also expressed the importance of a slave past and its role in defining the importance she placed on being Black. Antoinette expressed that she was proud to be

Black. In her description of why being Black "mean[t] so much to [her]," she explained:

> Well, in a way it's sad and fun, but because you look back to...slavery, how cruel they was to Black people and sometimes some people might wish they was White, [because] they get more respect, but then when you're Black you can like have more pride, pride in yourself and stuff. So like, you can stand up...based on what you know from slavery and stuff.

It was evident to many students that there were consequences associated with being Black. These consequences included being on the receiving end of discriminatory practices both historically and at present. However, for many students a source of pride was derived from withstanding adversity and maintaining a Black identity in instances where blackness was expected to bring about feelings of powerlessness and shame. In essence, it was through withstanding the struggles of blackness that students found pride in the accomplishments of Blacks.

For students, being Black was about more than just African ancestry. More importantly, it was about a long legacy. To them, being Black was not about one particular point in history but rather concerned significant connections between the past and the present. Students readily recognized disparities between the socioeconomic statuses of Whites and Blacks, but they also felt that the accomplishments of Blacks were particularly noteworthy in light of the resistance they faced in their quest for upward mobility and equality.

According to Natalia, being Black meant she was tied to a meaningful history as the descendant of slaves, but she also recognized that "there's like new stuff happening, like Obama becoming president." Oftentimes, the connections between the legacy of slavery and modern-day accomplishments served to affirm Black racial identity for Caribbean American students. A longitudinal lens was used to assess the status of Blacks in America, a perspective that often took into consideration the difficulties Blacks have faced. Caribbean American students maintained a connection to the history of Blacks in the United States despite their ancestral connection to the Caribbean. This is one line of distinction between first and subsequent generations of Caribbean immigrants.

While students cited numerous reasons for being proud of their racial heritage, they also took into account common stereotypes of Blacks. There were instances when merely asking students to describe what it meant to them to be Black led to vocalized resistance against stereotypical notions of blackness. In contrast to the findings of Mary Waters (1994, 1999), students in this study did not demonstrate opposition to Black Americans; instead, they resisted the pervasive negative stereotypes about Blacks in the United States. After being asked what it meant to be Black, Tamara stated:

> I don't really think that [being Black] really means anything, I mean 'cause I can succeed just as much as any other race if I just put my mind to it. So I mean...to be Black, I'm proud of that, that I'm African American and like...my ancestors before me have paved the way for me to [be] here now so...I feel as though I have no other choice but to be proud of who I am.

The question of what it means to be Black struck a cord with some students, which led to their resistance against hegemonic ideology, but for others this question prompted visible signs of discomfort. Students actively pushed back against negative racial stereotypes. Bryce, whose peers were primarily White and who expressed never having experienced a racist incident, first pretended that he did not understand the question. Then he emphasized that the stereotypes he was about to mention were strictly observations from television and had nothing to do with his personal experiences. In describing perspectives of Blacks, Bryce reported:

> I have no idea, probably, uh, they probably think about their families like coming from, I watch a lot of TV, alright I'm a talk about what I see on TV [okay]. Poor families, a lot of poor families, um, let me see, really, live in hoods, live in hoods, yeah, ah, let's see...something bad, huh, well, they steal, no, no, no, no, no, what you call it, since they live in the hoods they like kill people, yeah um, let's see, ah they do...I think they did, I don't know, that's it, that's it, that's all I could think of.

As Bryce rattled off his observations from television, he laughed and spoke in a playful tone of voice, a style that was unconventional for this student who usually appeared poised and mature. After further inquiry, Bryce also added "abusive fathers," "angry," and "drug addicts" to his list of stereotypical perceptions of Blacks. Bryce also argued that these representations are applied to "African Americans, Jamaican Americans, whatever American, if you're colored, just like Black." Bryce asserted that stereotypical representations of Blacks in America were not relegated simply to native-born Blacks. Instead, these representations served to portray all people of African ancestry, including Blacks of Caribbean origin.

Reading Racism: Lessons from Parents, Teachers, and Peers

Exploring Race Talk with Parents and Peers

Given the disparities in Caribbean parents' experiences and analyses of race and racism, explicit attempts to engage in racial socialization varied in terms of the types of messages that were conveyed and the frequency with which parents explicitly engaged their children in race talk. Race talk is defined as the explicit engagement of children and their parents in conversation about race and racism as a form of racial socialization.

While some parents were deeply invested in creating opportunities for race talk and exposing their children to stories of race and racism tied to their personal experiences, others relied on sources that were removed from their personal lives. In these instances, parents drew heavily from media representations of Blacks and other individuals' narrative retellings of racially charged experiences as opportunities to engage in race talk. These disparate racial socialization practices as representative of distinct forms of race talk reinforced analyses of micro-level racial interactions, macro-level racial dynamics, or a blend of both. However, some parents neglected to engage in race talk at all. Evidence from variations in race talk suggest that (1) students were more apt to identify racial discrimination when exposed to race talk grounded in the experiences of parents and close relatives, (2) narratives focused on systemic racism led to fewer reports of personal experiences with racism, and (3) peer groups were able to mediate students' perceptions of racism.

Parents' Personal Examples
of Experiences with Racism

Students in the study unanimously agreed that racism existed; however, distinctions were evident in their assessments of having had personal experience with racism. Oftentimes, students' perceptions of those experiences were aligned with the socialization messages shared by their parents through race talk. Race talk concerning micro-level racial experiences provided concrete descriptions of the manifestation of interpersonal racism and offered examples of how to deal with racist experiences. However, students who were mostly exposed to race talk grounded in macro-level analyses of racial incidents and devoid of personal connections to the lives and experiences of family and friends neglected to identify racist incidents in their personal experiences, despite the belief that racism continued to exist on a macro level. Overall, participants who were primarily exposed to micro-level examples of racism or a combination of macro- and micro-level racism were more likely to admit having experienced racism. On the other hand, participants who encountered or discussed macro-level socialization or received little to no explicit socialization were less likely to identify racist incidents in their personal interactions with peers of other races. Students' exposure to experiences and dialogues that reflect race conflict help to shape their perspectives regarding what it means to be Black in the United States and the extent to which racism is a modern-day issue with which they must contend.

While the degree to which parents explicitly socialized their children around issues of race varied, it was clear that parents' affirmation of personal stories regarding racism influenced whether students perceived and articulated particular incidents as being racist. Personal stories included examples from the lives of parents themselves or parents' sharing and affirming the experiences of other close family members or friends. Tamara's mother, Patricia, consistently engaged in race talk as she helped her daughters—one in high school and one in graduate school— navigate the racially charged contexts of their respective educational institutions. Patricia seldom spoke of her personal challenges with racism in the United States; however, she often acknowledged the experiences of her two older daughters and actively worked to assuage their anxiety and distress over racially charged encounters.

Tamara's exposure to race talk between her mother and sisters helped her to acknowledge the potential for experiencing racism and demonstrated the usefulness of parental support as a means of coping with racist incidents and learning strategies for addressing racist encounters. The experiences of Tamara's sisters served as an avenue for racial socialization, as these conversations were increasingly embedded in the larger family milieu. Though many participants were hesitant to identify incidents as racist and therefore inappropriate, Tamara responded strongly to incidents with racial undertones.

When asked to describe a personal experience with racism, Tamara shared her experience of being called the N-word by a White classmate. What follows is her retelling of the event:

> We had to write an essay on...us, from A to Z and...what each [letter] stands for.... Like A I had for...I forgot what it was but like I had for "B" I'm beautiful, "C" I'm casual and then you had to write an essay on each one of the words and...I was writing my rough draft for the [letter] N and a young boy next to me—he was White—he was like, "You know what [word] the [letter] 'N' stands for?" And then he, he whispered in my ear.... He was like..."Isn't that what you are?" and I nearly smacked him, like what is wrong with you and I just got really upset and I actually, I left class and I didn't come back until the rest of the period [until I knew] that he was out of the classroom 'cause I was really upset.

After Tamara informed the teacher of the incident, the White male student was removed from class and forced to apologize. His explanation of this derogatory remark as "just a joke" further enraged Tamara. Although she mentioned making amends with the student formally, Tamara said that she kept her distance from him because she felt that she needed time to recover emotionally from the incident. Her response to this racial epithet also demonstrated Tamara's disapproval of racially charged "jokes." Her response differed from that of students whose parents did not engage in microlevel racial socialization. Participants whose parents did not share personal stories about racism did not approach such racially insensitive insults with the same degree of indignation.

Charles and Elyse's parents (Marcia and Mark), however, shared with their children both personal stories regarding race and racism and accounts of systemic racism. While Marcia and Mark often crafted personal narratives, their children were consistently drawn into the family's experiences with a "racist neighbor," thereby making the narrative a shared family story. The Kim family's struggles with a "racist neighbor" helped them to examine not just how they were being treated, but whether their treatment reflected larger stereotypes about Black families, and whether there were racial disparities in how such treatment was rationed. After many seemingly illogical and unwarranted attacks from a White neighbor, the Kim family cited racism as a determining factor in the ill treatment they had received. When asked to describe a personal experience with racism, Elyse recalled her family's experience with that White neighbor. After I prompted Elyse to explain why racism seemed to be a plausible explanation for these experiences, she stated:

> White people think that all Black people should be like the stereotypes of races...like all Black people are supposed to...either work for White people or we're not supposed to have nice jobs and stuff and we're supposed to be living in [a poor neighborhood] or something like that. That's the stereotype, I believe. I really can't stand [that]. That's how I feel my neighbors act.

Elyse connected the larger societal stereotype about Blacks to her family's experiences with neighbors who continually harassed them in their middle-class residence. In describing one of several issues that had surfaced, Elyse recalled that her neighbors called the police on her family several times, saying their music was too loud, although the music had been turned down and even the police thought it was ridiculous for the White family to continue to call them. Elyse cited her neighbors' behavior as irrational, and therefore racism seemed to be a plausible explanation for their behavior. The recommendation of the police to ignore the neighbors after the music had been lowered to minimal levels confirmed for Elyse that their neighbors did not have legitimate cause for harassing their family and that something else was at play.

In generalizing such personal experiences with her White neighbor, Elyse explained that particular signs helped her determine whether an incident was inherently racist. Elyse did note that determining whether someone was racist was difficult and required ongoing observation of a person's actions. According to her, someone could "secretly discriminate against Black people, 'cause that's how some people are, sometimes it's hard to find them, but sometimes they're standing right in your face." She continued to assert, however, "I can't just say that...one person from their race is racist so I'm gonna think all of them are. I'm not like that. I'll get to know a person, but if I've been sensing some fishy things, then I'll think something...." After being asked to explain how she senses "fishy" behavior, Elyse elaborated:

> If like...they're mainly nice and stuff to a lot of people, but to Black people they're looked at with [an] attitude and all [of] that. Then, I would think, okay [pause]...yeah, I think...they're racist.... If I just see it, I see the way they act. I'm not gonna do it...on only one thing, I mean if I only see one little suspicious thing, but if I see more things happen, then I'll suspect that person's probably racist.

Elyse intelligently articulated the steps she used to identify racist behavior and classify people as safe, unsafe, or suspicious. Her clear and concise explanation demonstrated her ability not only to recognize potentially racist incidents; it also revealed that she had developed a system for determining whether one's behavior was regular enough to warrant distancing herself from that individual. Elyse demonstrated a level of judiciousness that had not been demonstrated by most participants. In part, her adeptness with identifying racism could be explained by her having learned about racism through her family experiences and subsequent conversations regarding what they perceived as discrimination from their White neighbor.

Narratives of Systemic Racism

Students whose parents engaged in racial socialization by way of race talk centered around systemic issues reported never having experienced racism. Although students who claimed that they never had a personal experience with racism tended to come from professional families and were in more racially heterogeneous classes, they also attended the same school, lived in the same community, and had access to the same teachers as the students who reported that they did have personal experiences with racism. One is forced to ask how this discrepancy arose. My research indicates that one difference that existed between students who reported experience with racism and those who did not was whether or not their parents engaged in race talk related to such experiences. What was missing from some students' repertoires was an account of how racism played out in the lives of the parents and other close family members or friends. Without these personal examples, students seemed to have a difficult time identifying what racism might look like in interpersonal relationships, especially in instances where racism seemed covert and therefore difficult to detect.

In Jeffrey's case, his parents did engage him in race talk. However, household conversations regarding race were prompted mainly by media reports and representations of Blacks. Given that Craig, Jeffrey's father, admitted to having very few encounters with racism, there were rarely opportunities to move beyond broad discussions about race and racism. As a result, Jeffrey could articulate that racism existed in theory but had difficulty identifying the ways in which racism might have been a part of his daily, lived experience. Similarly, students whose parents rarely took up race dialogue overall—or racism in particular—also neglected to identify experiences with racism. Natalia, Geneva, and Tory each had a difficult time identifying instances where they conversed with their parents about race, whether regarding personal experiences or systemic examples of racism. Noticeably, the absence of conversations about personal connections to race and racial experiences influenced these students' analyses of their experiences.

Peer Groups: Mediating Parental Racial Socialization

Despite these trends, there were several instances where students' reports of experiences with racism were not aligned with parents' tendencies toward discussing micro-level and macro-level racial encounters. In these cases, students' relationships with peer groups seemed to weigh heavily on their perspectives regarding racism, and in both cases peer perspectives were reflected in students' responses regarding their experiences with racism. In instances where parents did not engage in race dialogue or engaged solely in macro-level interpretations, it would be expected that their children would lack a racial lens through which they could interpret interactions with teachers, peers, and community members. However, students who had older siblings or close friends who shared with them personal stories regarding experiences with racism—experiences that were not necessarily taken up by parents—were still likely to report such experiences.

In essence, students' peers served to influence their determinations about race and racism. Peers' mediation of parental racial socialization practices also applied to students whose parents did engage in dialogue regarding personal experiences with racism. Bryce did not have any older siblings or cousins who lived locally and maintained a mostly White peer group, and he insisted that he had never experienced racism despite his mother's attempts to alert him to the potential of experiencing negative racial encounters. Bryce, unlike Tamara, viewed racial epithets as "jokes," not serious offenses. The following exchange illuminates Bryce's carefree approach to derogatory jokes regarding racial, cultural, and religious difference.

B: ...everybody gets made fun of at school.

C: Okay, who gets made fun of?

B: The White Christians, the Jews, the Blacks, Asians, and the Mexicans, I mean, I mean the Spanish.

C: Okay, so you said everyone gets made fun of equally because of their...

B: I don't know...'cause of their um, what you call it, just how they are.

C: Okay, so what are some things that you would say to make fun of a White Jewish person or things that you've heard?

B: Probably their hops and like money.

C: What are hops?

B: Jumping abilities.

C: Oh, you mean their ability to play basketball?

B: No, not to play basketball, just their jumping abilities [laughs].

C: They can jump?

B: No, they can't.

C: They can't jump?

B: It was funny.

C: And, they like money, you said?

B: Yeah, a lot. Some kid dropped a nickel and ah, this is funny, [laughs].

C: And what happened?

B: Sorry, nothing [apologizes for laughing].

C: Why are you being silly, Bryce?

B: Sorry.

C: The kid dropped a nickel and what happened?

B: He pounced on it like a tiger [still laughing]. It was funny. You should have saw it, it was at lunch.

Despite Bryce's mother's attempts to engage him in conversation about race on personal and systemic levels, Bryce's mostly White peer group normalized derogatory epithets regarding racial, ethnic, cultural, and religious groups. Bryce's peer group did not view the "jokes" they endorsed as problematic, nor did they acknowledge connections between their behaviors and systemic and historical inequities. The boys were invested in maintaining friendships that transcended racial (and other forms of) difference and were therefore reluctant to identify individuals or incidents as racist or problematic as doing so could have potentially threatened the solidarity of the group. This elusive stance toward race exposed Bryce to a type of socialization that discouraged students from critical dialogue about race and difference and did not view racial, ethnic, and religious epithets as serious offenses. Bryce outwardly embraced the idea that he was "clueless" when it came to identifying and understanding how race operated in the U.S. context. According to him, race was "irrelevant," an assertion he would often make whenever his mother pushed him to consider race as a valuable aspect of his relationships with his teachers and peers. Bryce's perception of race as inconsequential was further illustrated in the following dialogue.

> *C:* Um, do you believe that racism still exists?
>
> *B:* Yes.
>
> *C:* Okay, can you give me some examples or explain why you think that's the case?
>
> *B:* Ah, let's see, ah [takes a while]...hmmm, I, have no idea.
>
> *C:* So why did you say yes?
>
> *B:* 'Cause my parents keep on talking about stuff. They say you have to have really good grades, wait, wait, wait.... I know what they said, I just forgot a little, huh, ah, if you're like, since I live in a White neighborhood, they tell me not to like throw snowballs because if something is broken, they're gonna be knockin' down her door first I mean knockin' on her door first, something like that. On TV they talk about people getting pulled over and more Black people get pulled over, uh, yeah, that's about it, 'cause I am clueless.... I'm not good at [noticing] the bad things, just, ah, I have the eye of an optimist.

Here, Bryce boasts of being told about the vicissitudes of racism but asserts his choice to remain "clueless" and optimistic about racial issues. Rather than heeding the warnings of his mother, Bryce instead chose to downplay the possibility that his blackness could place him at a disadvantage relative to his White peers. He conceded that all students have similar encounters with negative racial and ethnic stereotypes but does not recognize that all stereotypes or racial and ethnically charged "jokes"—as he calls them—are not equally damaging. Bryce does not perceive distinctions in the types of negative portrayals attributed to certain groups. His example of a Jewish student being cast as a miser is inherently different from being typified as violent, lazy, or unintelligent—traits generally ascribed to Blacks.

The dissonance that race talk—and specifically discussions about racism—created for Bryce was substantial. When asked to pinpoint racial stereotypes or describe messages shared by his mother, Bryce engaged in a performance of sorts—pretending he could not identify racist incidents or messages about race, but later offering very detailed accounts. Despite what appeared to be resistance to internalizing messages of racial inequity, Bryce seemed to maintain an account of racial socialization messages he received from his mother and the larger society.

Course Levels, Peer Groups, and Personal Racism Experiences

Whether students were members of heterogeneous of homogeneous peer groups was most often dictated by their placement in high- or low-level classes. While the make-up of peer groups informed students' overall views of racism, it also influenced their perceptions of *personal* racism experiences. Students identified instances of racism throughout history, by way of contemporary stereotypes, and sometimes through the school experiences of their Black peers. However, they struggled to identify their own personal experiences with racism. This trend was evident across all students, but most apparent among students who were enrolled in majority-White, high-level classes and whose parents were professionals. During interviews, Jeffrey, Bryce, and Geneva—all high-achieving students—each expressed unequivocally that they had never had personal experiences with racism. In comparison to their Caribbean American counterparts in low-level classes, their classes were overwhelmingly White, as was their peer group.

According to racial socialization scholars, racial incidents are most likely to occur across diverse racial groups (Stevenson, McNeil, Herrero-Taylor, & Davis, 2005; Thornton, Chatters, Taylor, & Allen, 1990). However, Caribbean American students whose classes were predominantly White reported never having personally experienced racism. There are several plausible explanations for these divergent findings in addition to peer group-mediated attitudes and exposure to macro- and micro-level examples of racism. First, students in this study were limited in their ability to identify more elusive forms of racism. Second, students desired to maintain relationships with their mostly White peer groups, so they overlooked racist incidents and adhered to the cultural norms of their White peers, which created less dissonance and consequently less fodder for racial conflict. Lastly, the "good Blacks"—students who were assigned to high-level courses and whose parents were professionals—received more equitable treatment from teachers and other school personnel than their peers in low-level classes.

During an informal conversation, Bryce and Jeffrey's math teacher shared glowing remarks about the boys and pegged them as among the brightest in the class. She also expressed her delight in working with them. However, a follow-up conversation with Bryce's mother revealed a different story. Bryce's math grades were poor and did not accurately reflect his academic ability. He had not been submitting homework assignments regularly, which brought down his grades, even though he performed well on assessments and demonstrated his understanding of math content through active class participation. The contradiction between Bryce's poor grades and his teacher's expressed satisfaction with his performance subtly revealed the way in which expectations differed for high-achieving students across race. The teacher's simultaneous praise of Bryce's performance despite subpar grades sent the message to him that just getting by was okay. This also undermined his mother's efforts to help Bryce improve his grades and hold him to high academic standards.

In spite of students' perceived equitable treatment, there was evidence that high-achieving students were also experiencing what Craig called "the expectations game." The teacher regularly praised Caribbean American youth for academic performance that was less than stellar in comparison to their White counterparts. These experiences further advanced notions of lower academic expectations for Black students, even though they possessed the skills necessary to meet rigorous academic standards. In essence, being better than most Black students, but not as good as Whites, was good enough.

Ladson-Billings maintains that a critical component of being a good teacher to Black children is to expect and ensure academic excellence (1994). Ladson-Billings argued that teachers must "attend to students' academic needs, not merely make them "feel good" (p. 160). This teacher failed to maintain an expectation of excellence in all aspects of Bryce's performance. Such inconsistencies in reports of student success also demonstrated high-achieving Caribbean American students' exposure to more nebulous forms of racism. These elusive racial encounters often went unnoticed by Caribbean immigrant parents and Caribbean American students.

Elusive forms of racism experiences contradicted students' assessment of their classroom experiences as race-neutral. When asked if he had ever experienced racially charged social interactions or heard his peers make derogatory remarks toward Blacks, Bryce implied that he had, but mitigated the seriousness of such remarks, stating that all groups were made fun of at Morristown. Such assertions excused racially charged remarks and negated the potential for Caribbean American youth to identify racial dynamics in their peer relationships. By overlooking racist remarks, Bryce and other high-achieving students were able to maintain friendships with White peers as well as idealized notions of life at Morristown.

Additionally, students like Geneva, Bryce, and Jeffrey did not fit the stereotypical perspectives of Blacks at Morristown. Their behaviors and appearances often mirrored those of their White peers. Their speech patterns, ways of dress, and outward display of academic prowess were closely aligned with the profiles of their White and Asian counterparts. Given such similarities to their White counterparts and dissimilarities between these students and the stereotypes of Blacks that often circulated in the Morristown community, Bryce, Jeffrey, and Geneva were deemed acceptable in the eyes of their White peers and teachers, and they were therefore less likely to be outwardly ostracized in ways that other Black students had been. In some ways, these students' inability to see their experiences as racist reflected their privileged treatment compared to other Black students and the differences inherent in their more elusive experiences with racism.

Students in majority-Black, lower-level courses, however, compared their school experiences to Whites in higher-tracked classes and the few Whites who were assigned to their classes. These comparisons led students to identify more experiences of racism involving teachers and their White peers who mocked the cultural styles of students who more readily adhered to what they deemed Black cultural norms.

Ethnic Difference and an Alternative Black Experience

Despite students' limited ability to identify the manifestation of racism in their own lives, they still viewed racism as inextricably linked to the overall experience of Blacks in the United States. However, they held firmly to the belief that Blacks in the Caribbean did not experience racism. This perspective—whether entirely true or not—provided students with an alternative view of life—life without racism.

This section of this chapter supports the following notions: (1) ethnic identities grounded in transnational accounts of blackness provided an alternative to the U.S. Black experience, even if only psychologically; and (2) given the ways in which ethnic socialization challenged essentialist notions of blackness, ethnic socialization served as a form of racial socialization for Caribbean American youth, buffering them from the ill effects of U.S. racism and the threat posed by racial stereotypes.

Transnational Accounts of Blackness

When asked whether the experiences of Blacks in the Caribbean were different from the experiences of Blacks in the United States, Tamara and Bryce had this to say:

> T: Well...I mean it's different yes, but I guess...in Antigua we are a predominantly Black...nation or culture, whatever. We...basically...can't discriminate against each other 'cause we're almost all alike and whatever, but I mean when you come here, it changes a little 'cause you feel more self-conscious about yourself, but at the same time you don't be-

cause you know, you still have that pride in yourself, but I guess there you can't really discriminate against anyone 'cause you're all...the same, you know.

B: 'Cause in the Caribbean like, the majority of people living there are Black so there's not, there can't be a lot of discrimination.

C: Okay, so what has your experience been like being there in Jamaica? Do you feel like that's the case, that there isn't a lot of discrimination?

B: There's not any discrimination. They're all nice. They're all nice people. They're always happy and joyful.

Students asserted that the sheer lack of racial diversity in the English-speaking Caribbean significantly diminished the potential for racist encounters. Even students who seldom travelled outside of the United States argued that the experiences of Blacks in the Caribbean differed greatly from the experiences of Blacks in the United States. Students who had not travelled to the Caribbean still had an imagined sense of an alternative reality.

In many instances, students tied the well-being of Blacks in the Caribbean to the types of relationships fostered in Caribbean communities. Students explained that people in the Caribbean looked out for one another, were kind to one another, and helped to provide resources for those less fortunate as supported by ethnic socialization narratives. Similar to Bryce's description of Jamaicans as "happy," students perceived Caribbean Blacks to be in a state of contentment relative to their Black American counterparts. Students viewed U.S. communities as divisive, given the fissiparous impact of racism on social relationships in America, particularly in racially diverse communities.

The Internalization of Ethnic Socialization as a Form of Racial Socialization

For Caribbean American students, ethnic socialization served as a form of racial socialization. By virtue of buying into ethnic distinctions that were tied to majority-Black or majority-minority countries (in the case of Trinidad and Tobago), students were positioned to resist stereotypical notions of blackness that often pervaded the U.S. social milieu.

Ethnic socialization provided an alternative to U.S. notions of blackness as evidenced by students' shifting "racial" identities. The inextricable ties between students' Caribbeanness and their race defined an alternative blackness—a blackness that was different from the stereotypical views of Blacks that pervaded Morristown Middle School and the de-racialized notions of identity embraced by their parents. According to Kasinitz and colleagues (2002), Caribbean American youth "are creating a vibrant youth culture that is neither 'immigrant' nor 'middle American,' but something new...they are forging identities that differ strongly from that of their parents' country of origin, but also differ from those of mainstream White or Black Americans" (p. 1022).

Parental ethnic socialization messages often focused on ethnic pride, historical legacy, egalitarianism, and one's ability to achieve despite obstacles, messages that mirror the racial socialization of Black American families. These ideas, though ethnic in nature, were also transferable to students' understanding of their racial selves and taken up by students as such despite their parents' intentions.

While some students demonstrated resistance toward the inequitable treatment of Black students at Morristown by disengaging from the school environment or disrupting the school environment, Caribbean American students relied on their alternative identities as a means of resisting claims of Black inferiority. Unlike other forms of resistance, the employment of alternative identities did not engage them in disputes with teachers and administrators or negatively impact their academic performance. Instead, Caribbean American students resisted through a psychological reality that diverged from the contextual experiences and expectations of students within the Morristown community. While I argue that Caribbean American youth possessed a distinct psychological reality, I do acknowledge that such a reality is neither exclusive to Caribbean American youth nor does it preclude students from the ill effects of racism. Instead, I contend that an alternative psychological reality derived from ethnic socialization served as a buffer for Caribbean American youth, similar to the ways in which various forms of racial socialization protect Black American youth.

Ethnic socialization served as a protective mechanism for Caribbean American youth. This idea of embracing ethnic ties as protective rather than as a source of distancing from Black Americans or opposition toward Black Americans, contrasts greatly with the findings of other researchers (Rogers, 2006; Waters, 1999).

Additionally, Caribbean ethnic values, grounded in manners and respect for elders and adult authority, limited the extent to which Caribbean American youth felt they could be assertive in their resistance to adult perpetrators. Despite their acknowledgment of injustices, teachers' reports of Caribbean American students as "well behaved," "nice," and "hard working" demonstrated the extent to which these students adhered to school rules despite their acknowledgment of inequities. For students who readily acknowledged experiences with racism, they dealt with the infractions of their peers far differently from the ways in which they addressed negative racial encounters with teachers.

As mentioned earlier, Charles, a relatively quiet student, called a White peer a "mother fucker" on the school bus after being called a nigger. Charles was reprimanded by the bus driver for his behavior and ultimately reported to school administrators. However, his mother was in support of his response. As she shared the details of the incident, she insisted that Charles should not let anyone push him around. She felt that in this situation, his use of inappropriate language was justified. Although racist incidents on the part of teachers were far less direct, racial slights directed at students by teachers typically went unaddressed even when noted.

In sum, Caribbean American students' status as 1.5- and second-generation Americans forced them into a third space that was neither fully American nor Caribbean, a space that students were able to generate and negotiate in tandem with the forces of contextual and transnational politics around race and identity. Although Caribbean American parents failed to engage students explicitly in a great deal of racial socialization, distinctions between ethnic socialization in the home and racial socialization in the school created enough dissonance for students that they were able to rethink and reposition themselves within dual realities. While this third space did not altogether safeguard Caribbean American youth from experiences with racism, it did give them an alternative lens through which to analyze their experiences and create their own alternative identities.

The (Re-)Making of a Black American: Findings, Implications, and Recommendations

Countless studies have documented the insidiousness of U.S. racism. Racism in the United States has been cited as one of the most significant factors affecting the physical and mental health of Blacks, their chances for upward mobility through education and enterprise, and their overall quality of life. Although some question the extent to which racism is still relevant, as seen in media debates that took place during the early stages of President Barack Obama's presidency, the aftermath of his first election and re-election tell a very different story. Racism in the United States is alive, well, and thriving.

For some time, scholars have sought to define and theorize racism, highlight its pernicious effects across different stages of the life cycle and in different contexts, and call for a more just society. Still others focus on ways to mitigate the influences of racism. Although Black immigrants stand at a confounding yet provocative intersection of all of this, that group has not been made a priority in research agendas surrounding race.

The experiences of Black immigrants have great potential to inform what we know about the nature and impact of U.S. racism. Several insightful studies document the correlation between Black women's birth abroad (in the Caribbean or Africa) and rates of producing babies of low birth weight. These studies have found that when controlling for risk factors, Black women born abroad had higher percentages of babies of high birth weight and lower percentages of babies of low birth weight (David & Collins, 1997; Pallotto, Collins, & David, 2000). Fang, Madhavan, and Alderman (1999) reported that "Infants of foreign-born black mothers had significantly higher birth weight...and a lower proportion of low birth weight (10.0% vs. 16.7%) than did infants of all US-born black mothers" (p. 2). Additionally, Fang, Madhavan, and Alderman (1999) reported that "in poor communities, the risk of low birth weight for Caribbean- and African-born black mothers actually was less than that for white mothers" (p. 1). Similar findings have been consistent across several studies (Fang, Madhavan, & Alderman, 1999). There is also evidence to suggest that the age at which one migrates to the United States and length of stay in the United States also have an effect on birth weight (Bates & Teitler, 2008; Dominiguez et al., 2009). The longer Black immigrants are in the U.S., the more likely they are to experience outcomes similar to their U.S.-born counterparts.

One might ask, why do these studies matter? How are they relevant to the issues of racial and ethnic socialization of Caribbean immigrants? Or perhaps we should be asking: Why are foreign-born Blacks from developing countries ravaged by colonial exploits more likely to have healthier babies? What is it about being in America over time and being made into a Black American that gives rise to such deleterious conditions—conditions that affect even newborn babies' ability to live and thrive? What does this mean for all Blacks in America? Most relevant to this study is this question: How are Black immigrants who migrate to this country in search of opportunities and a better future for their children implicated by these findings?

In the case of education and socioeconomic mobility, there is evidence to suggest that by the third generation, the benefit of being an immigrant diminishes (Rong & Brown, 2001). All these things imply that being made into a Black American is a costly endeavor for Black immigrants. *The (Re-)Making of a Black American* connotes the process of racialization and Americanization Black immigrants undergo that is ultimately tied to their marginalization and oppression. In this study, Caribbean American students' encounters with the hegemony of U.S. racism, in the face of parental attempts to reinforce a positive self-image through ethnic socialization, have shown just how difficult it is to protect Black children from racism. However, the ability to identify socialization messages students receive at home *and* at school help us to understand how these processes occur and what kinds of messages students receive, which can ultimately inform changes in how parents and schools engage our youth in support of healthy identities and positive social and economic outcomes.

This work has attempted to add nuance to previous research on Caribbean immigrants and their children by examining the ways in which Caribbean American youth's identities manifest through a matrix of transnational discourses that defy space, place, and time, while simultaneously being informed by local experiences situated within a particular context and moment in history. My sustained exploration of racial and ethnic socialization experiences of Caribbean American youth contributes to the understanding of the identities of 1.5- and second-generation youth as multifaceted and not simply developed in opposition to notions of blackness in America or Black Americans. Instead, this work has taken up the legacy of slavery in the Caribbean as well as the ways in which politics regarding race, ethnicity, and nationality mingle and merge with both the historical legacy and the modern-day experiences of Blacks in the United States. The socialization of 1.5- and second-generation youth is grounded in these distinct legacies and present-day realities, ultimately shaping the performance and embodiment of multiple—and often conflicting—identities. In particular, schools, families, and social networks play a central role in teaching children *how* to be and *who* to be as informed by sociohistorical and sociopolitical discourses reflected in socialization practices.

This study has endeavored to: (1) describe how Caribbean immigrant parents engaged in racial and ethnic socialization and the messages implied in these socialization practices; (2) examine the ways in which experiences in a mixed-race school, located in a middle-class community, contributed to the racial and ethnic socialization of Caribbean American youth; (3) highlight the means by which socialization experiences across home and school contexts shaped youth's racial and ethnic self-perceptions; and (4) share findings from the study, implications for these findings on policy, theory, and educational practice, as well as considerations and recommendations for future research. In this final chapter I will discuss research findings and share their implications for educational practice as well as recommendations for future research and public policy.

By drawing upon the in-school experiences of youth, the messages embedded in parents' life narratives, and youth's articulation of their identities as informed by school and home spaces, this book has highlighted themes reflected in experiences and processes related to the socialization of Caribbean American youth. Findings from this study have revealed how the racial ethnic socialization processes youth undergo at home and in school inform the racial and ethnic identities that 1.5- and second-generation Caribbean American youth develop. Socialization experiences allow students the space to both embrace and critique their parents', teachers', and peers' notions of who they are and who they ought to be. But, more importantly, they create a space in which these students define and re-define their identities. Understanding this process in a context fraught with racial tensions that relegate Blacks to the base of the racial hierarchy is essential. It helps us to understand both the risks students face and the processes that might serve to buffer the ill effects of these risks.

Study Findings

Several major conclusions can be drawn from this study illuminating the role of parents and schools in the racial and ethnic socialization of Caribbean American youth and the subsequent ways in which socialization messages are simultaneously internalized, rejected, and negotiated by students. Findings demonstrate that (1) parents mostly engaged in ethnic rather than racial socialization; (2) parental socialization took the form of narratives informed by transnational perspectives, class background, and early migration experiences; (3) youth's schooling experiences mediated parental socialization efforts; and (4) disjunctures in racial and ethnic socialization messages at home and in school created an alternate space for youth to (re-)define their identities.

Teaching What They Know

The data revealed that Caribbean immigrant parents tended to foreground ethnic socialization in lieu of racial socialization. Caribbean immigrant parents' ability to engage in racial socialization was partially constrained by their limited understanding of U.S. racial conventions and knowledge of the extent to which racial hierarchies are tied to structural barriers for Blacks. Rather, their analyses of race were informed by sociohistorical and sociopolitical discourses within the Caribbean context. Hence, several Caribbean immigrant parents did not position race as central to their own success or that of their children.

Despite the relative absence of explicit racial socialization practices in the homes of Caribbean immigrant parents, they did engage extensively in ethnic socialization. Parents supported transnational discourses that focused on the following ethnic values: hard work, educational achievement, community involvement and interdependence, and the demonstration of manners and respect for elders. These messages served as mechanisms to support the growth and development of Caribbean American youth and prepare them for successful participation in society.

Ethnic socialization messages were distinct from racial socialization that Blacks in the United States have typically used to prepare their children for the future by training them to identify racism, respond to interracial encounters, promote racial pride, and encourage healthy strategies for coping with race-related stress. Previous research has identified the aforementioned parental racial socialization strategies as central to the social and emotional health and well-being of Black youth in the United States as they contend with racially charged encounters and insidious structural forces.[1]

Ethnic socialization messages were generally shared through the telling of life narratives regarding family and community structures in the Caribbean, means of migration and integration into U.S. society, and parents' road to achieving middle-class status. Implicit in these life narratives were the parents' capacity to shape the trajectory of their own lives by working hard, being ambitious, persevering through trials, and developing academic competencies and practical skills. These narratives, however, did not address the implications of structural racism on Black immigrants' socioeconomic trajectories. The absence of race from their discourses on triumph and success demonstrated disjunctures between parents' perceptions of the world and their children's experiences in school.

The racial and ethnic socialization practices of several individual families have been documented in this book. Data drawn from these families suggest that Caribbean immigrant parents—particularly of Jamaican descent—engaged mostly in ethnic socialization strategies and seldom relied on racial socialization practices. In part, their reliance on and proactive employment of ethnic socialization strategies arose out of their limited experiences with and understandings of race in the U.S. context. More importantly, however, ethnic socialization strategies were most familiar to immigrant parents as the teaching of ethnic values was central to their upbringing in the Caribbean, where issues related to interpersonal racism rarely arose.

This distinction alone serves to explain why ethnic identities are often preserved among Caribbean immigrants' progeny. Mary Waters (1994, 1999) has argued that ethnic identities of Caribbean immigrants and their children are often formed in opposition to Black Americans, giving little consideration to distinctions in contextualized understandings and experiences related to race. Caribbean immigrants in this study had difficulty identifying issues related to race and the implications of racism. Issues such as length of stay in the United States, the characteristics of the communities into which families were integrated, and personal experiences with covert and explicit forms of racism guided parents' understandings of whether racism existed, how it is enacted, and the degree to which they were affected by racism. However, most parents did not perceive race as central to their lives or identities prior to migrating to the United States, and, in some instances, that never changed. If it did, the change was not significant enough to incite proactive measures of racial socialization.

Many Caribbean immigrants held closely to a national identity—as defined by one's place of birth—as a primary mechanism for determining the group to which they belonged. Parents' identities as Trinidadian or Antiguan supplanted racially derived affiliations. Descriptions of Black immigrants as oppositional toward Black Americans carries with it the underlying assumption and expectation that these groups should, in fact, readily cohere on the basis of race. However, the expectation that Caribbean migrants would readily join with Black Americans in racial solidarity is problematic.

Racial solidarity among Blacks in the United States is the fruit of a long history of having to fight against systemic oppression—a history of which many newcomers are unaware. The concept of African American unity as a movement has been developed over centuries of fighting together for equal rights. For generations, Black Americans have lived in a country where racial disparities and affronts have been a constant reminder of racial inequity. However, Black immigrants have little preparation for understanding why certain disparities exist in the United States. These distinctions influence the socialization messages Caribbean immigrant parents share with their children and add complexity to Caribbean American youth's racial and ethnic identity development.

The data yielded from this study suggest that Caribbean immigrant parents did not deny the existence of U.S. racism, but often dismissed its importance and potential impact on their lives and the lives of their children. Such viewpoints were shaped by the sociohistorical lenses that Caribbean immigrants brought with them, lenses that defied nationalistic boundaries, thereby transferring perspectives onto U.S. race politics that were a product of their experiences in the Caribbean context. Caribbean immigrants brought with them to the United States a distinctly different worldview—one that did not acknowledge the complexities of racial discrimination in a country known across the globe as the land of opportunity. This reputation might cause some to ask how there could be obstacles to upward mobility in a country where those willing to work hard are actually met with opportunities.

In an effort to buffer their children from impediments to success including, but not limited to, issues of race and racism, Caribbean immigrants generally promoted that which they knew best—ethnic values. Using personal narratives as a mode of ethnic socialization, Caribbean immigrant parents impressed upon their children the need to work hard, be mannerly and respectful (especially to elders), give back to their communities, and take seriously their education.

Value-laden narratives were also reinforced by parents' development and maintenance of domestic and international networks of other Caribbean-descended individuals. Youth were also encouraged to embrace their ethnic identities through participation in this insulated network. Sustained exposure to ethnic socialization increased the salience of youth's ethnic identities, which became primary identifiers for youth even in contexts outside of their home communities, where racial categorization and hierarchies prevailed.

As mentioned previously, explicit forms of racial socialization were far less apparent in parents' socialization practices as compared to ethnic socialization. Although parents proactively engaged in ethnic socialization, they assumed a more reactive approach in regard to racial socialization. In many instances Caribbean immigrant parents reported few experiences with racism and tended to be less adept at identifying incidents that were covert in nature. The data suggest that racial socialization occurred mainly in response to micro-level encounters with racism experienced by the child, parents, or close relatives. However, in many instances parents neglected discussions of their own personal experiences. These parents engaged in racial socialization that centered on racist media reports and portrayals and the experiences of individuals with whom their children did not have close personal relationships.

I would argue that exposure to micro-level racial socialization grounded in the personal experiences of close friends and family provided templates for identifying and coping with racist incidents for some of the youth in the study. Youth, whose parents relied mainly on macro-level examples of racism and issues disconnected from the daily lives of youth, were less apt to identify incidents of racism and tended to be ill equipped in the handling of such issues. Similarly, youth whose peer groups neglected to voice the seriousness of racially charged encounters generally dismissed those encounters rather than attempt to find a means to address them.

The degree to which parents and close friends and relatives were central characters in stories pertaining to race influenced youth's perspectives regarding the role of race in their own lives. Caribbean American youth whose parents either exposed them to or directly engaged them in dialogue regarding racial encounters tended to perceive more racist incidents at school. However, a more critical finding surfaced, which was documented in detail in Chapter 6. School-based peer groups seemed to mediate the influ-

ences of parental socialization messages. Students whose families
rarely discussed race but whose peers reported having experiences
with racism were more inclined to report experiences with racism.
The same was true for students whose parents did engage in discussions of race, but whose peer groups glossed over racially based
epithets. Due to the small sample size of the study, these themes
were documented across only a few students, yet the findings suggest the need to further interrogate the role of peer relationships
in shaping racial identity and racial socialization experiences.

I conclude that ethnic socialization provided for students a
framework by which they could interpret what it meant to be of
Caribbean descent. However, limited understandings of what it
meant to be Black and how racial conventions and hierarchies
might affect one's life led to inconsistent strategies and outcomes
among study participants. While youth's home experiences allowed
for the co-construction of Caribbean ethnic identities, there was
less consistency across families as it related to issues of race. This
is where class background and modes of incorporation into U.S.
society shaped parents' perspectives of racism and racialized others, and either supported or inhibited intraracial cohesion between
Black Americans and Black immigrants.

Parents whose initial incorporation into U.S. society thrust
them into low-income communities where resources were scarce
recalled tenuous relationships with their Black American counterparts. In some places the scarcity of resources, as well as the sociohistorical remnants of anti-Jamaican (and Caribbean)
sentiment owing to alleged drug and gang involvement, further
spurred conflict between the two groups.[2] More importantly, however, these conflicts shaped parents' perceptions of belongingness
to Black America as a racial or ethnic group. Parents whose incorporation experiences centered on building social networks with
Black Americans from middle-class backgrounds, or experienced
early on the ways in which they were implicated in racism by virtue of phenotype, readily acknowledged the ways in which they
were similar to Black Americans. I maintain that these incorporation trajectories were central to the racial socialization messages
that Caribbean immigrant parents chose to share with their children regarding intraracial and interracial relationships.

Disjunctures in Racial and Ethnic Socialization Messages Between Home and School

This study gives rise to important implications for how we conceive of the centrality of racial and ethnic socialization in the lives of Caribbean American youth and the role of home and school in socialization efforts. In particular, school-level socialization had a tremendous impact on the racial socialization of students in the study and served to perpetuate racist ideology that placed Blacks at the bottom of the racial hierarchy. Public schools are understood as sites of social reproduction whereby students are encouraged (and perhaps compelled) to continue in the socioeconomic direction of their parents—for better or worse. For students whose parents are middle class, this generally bodes well for them. However, that was not the case for Caribbean American students from middle-class families whose school experiences reinforced their marginality. The institutional socialization that occurred in the school engendered in students views about race that were divergent from those of Caribbean immigrant parents—ideas that effectively forced them into their role as marginalized other. Messages in the school environment were at odds with lessons learned at home that regarded Caribbean-descended Blacks in positive and uplifting ways, and in which parents used their own stories of success to motivate their children to succeed.

At school, Caribbean American students learned that there were grave consequences associated with the embodiment of blackness—a psychological and experiential reality seldom addressed by their parents. Although many Black students, regardless of ethnicity, were subject to racism by way of the institutionalized privileging of Whites and interpersonal interactions, social class distinctions mediated the types of racialized experiences to which students were exposed. School served as a space where high-achieving Black students learned that Whites were subject to privileges to which Black students had little access. While these Black students were academically capable, they were not expected to achieve at the same level as their White counterparts. Black youth in lower-level classes learned something a bit different. In addition to low academic expectations, they were often deemed dangerous and deviant. Because Caribbean parents engaged in very little racial socialization, Caribbean American youth were often left to their own devices when attempting to address, challenge, and cope with racist ideology embedded in school practices.

Although many racialized school experiences were not addressed by parents head-on, their descriptions of Caribbean Blacks as ethnically distinct, hard working, and able to succeed when given the opportunity—whether entirely true or not—created an imagined reality for Caribbean American students from which they were able to critique the negative depictions of Blacks they encountered in school and in society. In this way, socialization that was distinctly ethnic in nature and absent of racial critiques actually served as a means of racial socialization when internalized by Caribbean American youth. Youth viewed their parents' teachings about what it meant to be Caribbean also as a way to be Black or a Black person of Caribbean descent.

A central finding in this study indicated that the disjuncture between parental perceptions of blackness supported by ethnic narratives and racialized experiences at school created a space in which Caribbean American youth were able to critique negative depictions of Blacks and redefine self. At school, Caribbean American youth were primarily perceived as Black, and at home ethnicity was reinforced. Taken together, Caribbean American youth recreated identities that captured for them the amalgamation of what it meant to be *both* Black *and* Caribbean. The question, "How would you define your race?" yielded answers that were not predicated on race alone, but were defined by their ethnicity *and* their blackness. This trend was consistent across most of the student participants in the study. For them, their race and ethnicity were inextricably linked. The study participants who did not include ethnicity as central to defining their "race" were individuals who had little or no contact with their Caribbean immigrant parent.

Implications for Practice

Current research suggests that children need steady exposure to socialization purposed toward the formation of healthy self-identity, particularly in the areas of race and ethnicity (Nakkula & Toshalis, 2006; Stevenson & Davis, 2004). Given the potential for socialization forces to shape the perceived realities and academic outcomes of youth as documented by previous research (Nakkula & Toshalis, 2006; Waters, 1994, 1999), both parents and educators must engage in consistent and sustained attempts at racial and ethnic socialization that build up children and help them to imagine possibilities for their lives in spite of the obstacles they might encounter.

One of the more intriguing findings that emerged from these data gave evidence to the ways in which Caribbean American youth whose social networks were mostly White tended to report fewer experiences with racism and often disregarded racially charged epithets among their mostly White peer group as "jokes." In contrast, Caribbean American youth whose social networks were primarily Black reported more incidents of racism and could readily identify racial disparities in academic expectations and discipline. These distinctions demonstrate that in schools with diverse student populations, institutional structures such as tracking can have significant implications for students' peer group affiliations and racialized experiences.

Black students in high-level classes were treated more like their White peers and given greater access to school resources than their Black peers in low-level classes. However, students in high-level classes also had more opportunities to witness how White privilege operated in classroom spaces, privileges to which Caribbean American youth had no access. Youth in high-level classes were also subject to more covert forms of racism as compared to their Black peers in low-level classes. This also influenced Caribbean American youth's ability to identify racist incidents and shaped their responses to such incidents. High-achieving Caribbean American youth's investment in maintaining their preferential status among teachers and a mostly White peer group was reflected in their choices to overlook racially charged incidents.

This study suggests that schools reconsider tracking practices and seek to understand how these practices reinforce separate and unequal school experiences under one roof. Not only does tracking affect academic growth and development, but in this case it also influenced the way students experienced, identified, and responded to racism. Institutionalized tracking practices further divided groups of Black children on the basis of socioeconomic privilege and exposed students on the lower end of the academic and socioeconomic hierarchy to gross inequalities that negatively shaped their worldview and their potential to achieve success. Morristown Middle School played an integral role in the formation of racially homogeneous and heterogeneous social groups, as students in higher-level classes had greater opportunities to form diverse social networks as compared to their peers in lower-level classes that were skewed toward Blacks. Schools ought to contemplate seriously the consequences of institutional socialization in the form of tracking that serves to organize students along racial lines, not solely because of the potential for academic pigeonholing but also because of the social and psychological consequences of the tracking, which has been documented by other researchers (Hallinan, 1994; Mulkey, Catsambis, Steelman, & Hanes-Ramos, 2009).

Institutional socialization can either work to reinforce dominant hegemonic paradigms or promote global understandings and citizenry by acknowledging the diversity students bring to their educational contexts that transcends race. While the current NCLB legislation has encouraged the use of racial distinctions as primary tools for identifying students and marking their progress, schools must also work to understand the diversity that exists within groups and provide opportunities for these identities to be explored within the school context. According to Nakkula and Toshalis (2006), students who are given opportunities to explore a variety of identity options have the ability to choose that which aligns with their interests and future goals, something essential to healthy adolescent development.

While the experiences of Caribbean immigrants have been under-examined in research and scholarly literature overall, the same holds true for the acknowledgment of the experiences of Caribbean immigrants and their children in U.S. schools. The invisibility of Black immigrants is particularly pronounced in regions that have not been traditional immigrant gateways. The primary mode of identifying and categorizing students has centered on race and class distinctions, forcing ethnic distinctiveness to the periphery of school experiences. This work calls for an increased acknowledgment and sensitivity to the ethnic diversity of the U.S. Black population. Teachers' inability to see students as *both* Black *and* immigrants hinders opportunities for understanding how intersections of race and immigrant status lead to distinct school experiences for Caribbean American youth. Their relative invisibility prevents educators from identifying, assessing, and addressing needs and interests specific to this group.

To this end, educators must endeavor to be more purposeful in their attempts at racial and ethnic socialization. If the racial socialization messages reinforced in schools perpetuate racist ideology and hierarchies by default and without critical examination, immigrant and non-immigrant Blacks will continue to experience difficulty in adjusting to schools and achieving academic success. Additionally, teachers and curriculum developers must work to incorporate a wider array of people, cultures, and regions into the school curriculum. Several study participants made mention of the generally myopic perspective that Americans have of the world, something that also reflects schools' failure to produce knowledgeable global citizens.[3]

These findings also have implications for the types of professional development opportunities provided to educators. Teachers and administrators should be aware of the ways in which institutional socialization is enacted and the messages communicated to students through institutional socialization. Whether or not teachers agree with students' analysis of institutional socialization, schools should work to create a space in which students' perceptions and concerns can be addressed. Not only should teachers be engaged in these conversations, but parents should be as well. Parents can serve to support their children once they are made aware of schooling experiences and also work to hold teachers and administrators accountable for addressing the issues that are raised. In the case of Morristown, which is a seventh- and eighth-grade school, students attend for only 2 years. By the time parents are made aware of their children's challenges and organize around those challenges, their children are preparing for high school. Nonetheless, sustained organization of parental advocates across the elementary, middle, and high school levels can ensure the continuity of critical efforts.

Considerations for Future Research

Students in this study hailed from middle-class communities where the average annual homeowner tax was approximately $11,000. The narratives of parents who "made it" (that is, achieved middle-class status) despite initial experiences with poverty and a lack of formal education may not, in fact, represent the experiences of most Caribbean immigrants. Additionally, it was the middle-class status of study participants that increased the likelihood of their children attending school in a mixed-race community where they would regularly interact with middle-class Whites. This demographic distinction made Black-White comparisons more likely and served to color students' perspectives of race and racism, given a context that allowed direct experience with White privilege and Black disadvantage. However, in more racially homogeneous places, which often become the homes of recent immigrants, Caribbean immigrant students' comparison group might consist only of Black Americans, thereby decreasing the salience of race and increasing the centrality of ethnicity as an identifying marker. Furthermore, research should also examine racial and ethnic socialization and identity patterns across contexts with different ecological and demographic characteristics. This examination should occur in spaces that reflect the multiple lived realities of immigrants and their children.

Future research should also explore the experiences of Afro-Caribbean immigrants from a wider array of countries, especially those inhabited by speakers of languages other than English. Although Caribbean immigrants from English-speaking countries bring with them language needs, the language needs of non-English speakers shape tremendously the socialization of immigrants both at home and at school. The way in which language is also tied to power and culture has serious implications for how one is perceived and integrated into society and also influences the roles people play within their families, their ability to participate in particular peer groups, and the ways in which schools engage students around their language difference. Given these distinctions, socialization across home and school contexts might yield findings distinct from those related to the experiences of immigrants who hail from the English-speaking Caribbean.

Despite the overrepresentation of Haitian American students at Morristown Middle School, none of those students chose to participate in the study. The absence of Haitian and Haitian American students in the study, despite their presence in the school, is also indicative of larger issues with umbrella terms such as "Caribbean" that refer to a unique geographical region while at the same time disregarding the diversity within the region. The exploration of such tensions is essential, especially given the ways in which particular groups of people who inhabit the Caribbean differ in terms of identification and whose identities might have been shaped disparately by their respective colonizing countries and histories.

More recently, researchers have begun to critique findings regarding Black immigrants' success in the United States. According to Kalmijn (1996), the perceived success of Black immigrants does not hold up once social class, as a variable, is taken into account (Kalmijn, 1996). However, there has not been a critical examination of the distinctions between social class categories in the United States as compared to developing countries. Throughout this study it became evident that participants' perception of class status in the Caribbean varied greatly from class distinctions in the United States. Self-reports of class background prior to migration can be very problematic. This distinction adds a degree of complexity to Caribbean immigrants' interpretation of middle-class status—a perspective that might vary from that of U.S. conventions. Take, for instance, the case of Marcia, who lived in a one-room wooden house inhabited by five people. Marcia's grandmother resorted to the sale of illicit (but socially acceptable) drugs to support her family and others in the community, yet Marcia self-identified as having grown up in a middle-class family. Distinctions between her definition of middle-class status and that of Americans can have serious implications for how we determine the demographic profiles of immigrants prior to migration and whether the affordance of middle-class status or perceived middle-

CHAPTER SEVEN

class status holds up when compared to social class categories in the United States. Again, future research must account for such nuances, which have serious implications for data analysis, research findings, and related policies.

It has been argued that immigrant motivation also accounts for disparities in educational attainment and achievement as well as socioeconomic mobility (Kao & Tienda, 1995). Since the passage of the 1965 Immigration and Nationality Act, many Black immigrants from the Caribbean have migrated to the United States for the purpose of family reunification rather than economic mobility, although economic mobility might result from their migration (Suárez, 2002). All four parents whose narratives were profiled in Chapter 3 mentioned that they had no desire to come to the United States or remain in the United States for an extended period of time. In particular, Marcia, Kerry Ann, and Mark were forced to migrate to the United States once their parents filed for them and were essentially made to remain in the United States despite difficulties adjusting to life there and their desire to return to Jamaica. Similarly, Craig intended to return to Jamaica after graduate school but was encouraged by his then-fiancée to seek permanent residence in the United States. Moreover, Craig still held hopes of returning to Jamaica once his children enrolled in college. In addition to complicating research on immigrant motivation, such findings demonstrate the benefits of qualitative studies of Black immigrant groups as an integral piece in determining future research agendas.

Researchers must also try to understand the role of transnationalism in how Black immigrants make sense of their experiences in the United States. Transnationalism serves to inform how immigrants interpret, analyze, experience, and participate in the world. Black immigrants engage the U.S. context in ways that are marked by the history of and meaning-making processes derived from their native countries. The parents in this study chose to promote ethnic socialization over racial socialization despite their long residence in the United States, where racial socialization is said to be central to the parenting practices of Blacks (Stevenson & Davis, 2004). However, a transnational analysis demonstrates the porosity of national boundaries that allow the movement of not only people but also ideas, and adds nuance to past research that regards people's identity formation as oppositional rather than grounded in another lived reality or resistance to oppressive notions of blackness that are projected onto them.

The perpetuity of transnational ideology is further complicated by the passage of time. Concepts of child rearing and socialization that are linked to the past often serve to inform present-day parenting practices with little acknowledgment of the ways in which ethnic values have changed over time. In this way, socialization practices reflect the rituals of earlier generations that may have shifted in the Caribbean context, but remain imbedded in the minds of immigrants residing in the United States. Parents in the study held closely to ethnic scripts that were representative not only of the values of their community, but also of the time in which they were reared. Being away from their native contexts, however, suspends the natural occurrence of change over time that might otherwise be reflected in parental socialization practices. Transnationalism allows for a critical analysis of the suspension of space and time that is often reflected in the perceptions and practices of immigrants in an era when information and culture increasingly cross international boundaries.

Educational and Social Policy

When Craig, a study participant, mentioned that he was advocating for a census category that allowed Black immigrants to declare their place of birth as opposed to being confined to the category "Black, African American, or Negro," I felt conflicted. I was unsure if it was useful to make that distinction and if doing so would lead to resources being reallocated in ways that were detrimental to Blacks as a whole. However, my orientation has shifted as a result of this study. In particular, the study helped to call attention to the following: (1) the inability of Blacks to identify as immigrants further feeds essentialist notions of Blackness that reinforce racial marginalization and perpetuate stereotypes, and (2) immigration resources are rarely allocated to Black immigrants in need of language resources, job placement assistance, immigration services, and support in navigating mainstream institutions.

I contend that policies that affect schools and other social institutions can no longer render invisible this population. Policies must be implemented that accurately document the number of Caribbean immigrants and their children within particular institutions and geographic communities, assess their unique needs, and provide for those needs. However, the "model minority" label that has been ascribed to Black immigrants allows for public institutions to abdicate their responsibility for addressing the needs of the population and serves the political interest of polarizing groups of Blacks by blaming Black Americans for their victimization. This study calls for more visibility, more resources, more equity, and more access as it pertains to Caribbean immigrants and their 1.5- and second-generation children.

Conclusion

Racial and ethnic socialization is central to the experiences and identity development of Caribbean American youth. Both forms of socialization occur across home and school contexts to varying degrees, whether or not they are explicitly taken up by educators, caretakers, or the society at large. This study gives evidence to the ways in which both institutions and families contribute to youth's understanding of themselves, but also highlights youth's agency in making sense of the muddled messages they receive, thereby recreating and co-constructing their racial and ethnic identities.

In particular, disjunctures between mostly negative depictions of blackness and positive messages regarding Caribbean ethnicity helped Caribbean American youth to redefine their race and resist potentially damaging homogenizing notions of blackness. While youth in this study were left with little support in the form of parental racial socialization, parental ethnic socialization created a buffer against the internalization of racist depictions of Blacks by virtue of exposing their children to value-laden success narratives that contradicted mainstream stereotypes of blackness. While this does not imply that Caribbean American students are not subject to stereotype-related threats, it does recognize that ethnic socialization created enough dissonance for youth to reevaluate the messages they received. The relative absence of racial socialization on the part of Caribbean immigrant parents does not imply that racial socialization is not necessary for the healthy development of Black youth; instead it demonstrates that Black parents in the United States must work at preparing their children for racism and countering negative depictions of Blacks by all means, whether ethnic, racial, or otherwise.

While schools often resist taking up race and racism as central to their work beyond reporting students' race as it relates to standardized testing, this study calls for educators to reexamine the messages they send to students through implicit forms of racial socialization. Educators are invited to engage purposefully in racial socialization that uplifts rather than constrains students' potential and provides opportunities for healthy racial and ethnic identity development—factors that have been deemed essential to the long-term success of racial and ethnic minorities.

Notes

1. See discussion on racial socialization in Chapter 2.
2. See Chapter 4 for more information on presumed gang affiliation of Jamaican immigrants.
3. See interview with Kerry Ann in Chapter 2.

References

Abu El-Haj, T. R. (2007). "I was born here, but my home is not here": Educating for democratic citizenship in an era of transnational migration and global conflict. *Harvard Educational Review, 77*(3), 285–316.

Althusser, L. (2006). *Lenin and philosophy and other essays*. Delhi: Aakar Books.

Aratani, Y., & Chau, M. (2010). *Asset poverty and debt among families with children in the United States*. New York: National Center for Children in Poverty, Columbia University, Mailman School of Public Health.

Baptiste, D., Hardy, K., & Lewis, L. (1997). Family therapy with English Caribbean immigrant families in the United States: Issues of emigration, immigration, cultures, and race. *Contemporary Family Therapy, 19*(3), 337–359.

Bashi, V. (2004). Globalized anti-Blackness: Transnationalizing Western immigration law, policy, and practice. *Ethnic and Racial Studies, 27*(4), 584–606.

Bashi, V., & McDaniel, A. (1997). A theory of immigration and racial stratification. *Journal of Black Studies, 27*(5), 668–682.

Bates, L. M., & Teitler, J. O. (2008, April). *Immigration and low birthweight in the US: The role of time and timing*. Paper presented at the Population Association of American (PAA) Annual Meeting, New Orleans, LA.

Bell, D. (1995a). Intellectual precursors: Early criticisms of conventional civil rights discourse. In K. Crenshaw, N. Gotanda, G. Peller, & K. Thomas (Eds.), *Critical race theory: The key writings that formed the movement* (pp. 5–19). New York: The New Press.

Bell, D. (1995b). Brown v. Board of Education and the interest convergence dillemma. In K. Crenshaw, N. Gotanda, G. Peller, & K. Thomas (Eds.), *Critical race theory: The key writings that formed the movement* (pp. 20–29). New York: The New Press.

Bentley, K. L., Adams, V. N., & Stevenson, H. C. (2008). Racial socialization: Roots, processes, and outcomes. In H. A. Neville, B. M. Tynes, & S. O. Utsey (Eds.), *Handbook of African American psychology* (pp. 255–267). Thousand Oaks, CA: Sage Publications, Inc.

Bloom, V. (1988). Tables. In G. Nichols (Ed.), *Poetry jump-up: A collection of Black poetry collected by Grace Nichols* (p. 42). London: Puffin Books.

Bonilla-Silva, E. (2002). We are all Americans! The Latin Americanization of racial stratification in the USA. *Race and Society, 5*(1), 3–16.

Bowles, S., & Ginits, H. (1976). *Schooling in capitalist America: Educational reform and the contradictions of economic life*. New York: Basic Books.

Brookings Institution Center on Urban and Metropolitan Policy. (2003). *Philadelphia in focus: A profile from Census 2000*. Washington, DC: Brookings Institution Press.

Bryce-Laporte, R. S. (1979). New York City and the New Caribbean immigration: A contextual statement. *International Migration Review, 13*(2), 214–234.

Caughy, M. O., Randolph, S. M., & O'Campo, P. J. (2002). The Africentric home environment inventory: An observational measure of the racial socialization features of the home environment for African American preschool children. *Journal of Black Psychology, 28*(1), 37–52.

Césaire, A. (2000). *Discourse on colonialism.* New York: Monthly Review Press.

Chang, J., & Le, T. N. (2010). Multiculturalism as a dimension of school climate: The impact on the academic achievement of Asian American and Hispanic youth. *Cultural Diversity and Ethnic Minority Psychology, 16*(4), 485–492.

Charles, C. (1992). Transnationalism in the construct of Haitian migrants' racial categories of identity in New York City. *Annals of the New York Academy of Sciences, 645*(1), 101–123.

Coleman, C. (2006). *Exploring the nuances of racial socialization: A beginning to understanding and designing race related curriculum.* [Class paper].

Conley, D. (1999). *Being Black, living in the red: Race, wealth, and social policy in America.* Berkeley: University of California Press.

Creswell, J. W. (2004). *Research design: Qualitative, quantitative, and mixed methods approaches* (2nd ed.). Thousand Oaks, CA: Sage Publications.

Crosnoe, R., & López Turley, R. N. (2011). K–12 educational outcomes of immigrant youth. *The Future of Children, 21*(1), 129–152.

David, R. J., & Collins, J. W. Jr. (1997). Differing birth weight among infants of US-born Blacks, African-born Blacks, and US-born Whites. *New England Journal of Medicine, 337*(17), 1209–1214.

Davis, J. (1991). *Who is Black? One nation's definition.* University Park: The Pennsylvania State University Press.

Delpit, L. (1995). *Other people's children: Cultural conflict in the classroom.* New York: The New Press.

Dickson, L. (1993). The future of marriage and family in Black America. *Journal of Black Studies, 23*(4), 472–491.

Dominiquez, T.P., Strong, E.F., Krieger, N., Gillman, M., & Rich-Edwards, J.W. (2009). Difference in self-reported racism experiences of U.S.-born and foreign-born Black pregnant women. *Social Science and Medicine,* 1–8.

Du Bois, W.E.B. (2007). *The souls of Black folk.* Oxford: Oxford University Press.

Fang, J., Madhavan, S., & Alderman, M. (1999). Low birth weight: Race and maternal nativity—impact of community income. *Pediatrics, 103*(1), 1–5.

Feagin, J. R., & McKinney, K. D. (2003). *The costs of racism.* Lanham, MD: Rowman & Littlefield.

Foley, D. (2005). Elusive prey: John Ogbu and the search for a grand theory of academic disengagement. *International Journal of Qualitative Studies in Education, 18*(5), 643–657.

Foster, K. M. (2005). Narratives of the social scientist: Understanding the work of John Ogbu. *International Journal of Qualitative Studies in Education, 18*(5), 565–580.

Fouran, G. E., & Glick-Schiller, N. (2002). The generation of identity: Redefining the second generation within a transnational social field. In P. Levitt & M. C. Water (Eds.), *The changing face of home: The transnational lives of the second generation* (pp. 168–208). New York: Russell Sage.

Franklin, J. H., & Moss, A. (1994). *From slavery to freedom: A history of African Americans* (7th ed.). New York: McGraw-Hill.

Freeman, A. (1995). Legitimizing racial discrimination through antidiscrimination law: A critical review of Supreme Court doctrine. In K. Crenshaw, N. Gotanda, G. Peller, & K. Thomas (Eds.), *Critical race theory: The key writings that formed the movement* (pp. 29–46). New York: The New Press.

Freire, P. (2004). *Pedagogy of the oppressed.* New York: Continuum.

Gafar, J. (1998). Growth, inequality and poverty in selected Caribbean and Latin American countries, with emphasis on Guyana. *Journal of Latin American Studies, 30*(3), 591–617.

Gasparini, L., Gutierrez, F., & Tornarolli, L. (2007). Growth and income poverty in Latin America and the Caribbean: Evidence from household surveys. *The Review of Income and Wealth, 53*(2), 1–86.

Gibson, M. (2005). Promoting academic engagement among minority youth: Implications from John Ogbu's Shaker Heights ethnography. *International Journal of Qualitative Studies in Education, 18*(5), 581–603.

Gibson-Davis, C. (2011). Mothers but not wives: The increasing lag between non-marital births and marriage. *Journal of Marriage and Family, 73*(1), 264–278.

Gladwell, M. (1996, May 6). Black like them. *The New Yorker,* pp. 74–80.

Hall, S., & Carter, R. (2006). The relationship between racial identity, ethnic identity, and perceptions of racial discrimination in an Afro-Caribbean descent sample. *The Journal of Black Psychology, 32*(2), 155–175.

Hallinan, M. T. (1994). Tracking: From theory to practice. *Sociology of Education, 67*(2), 79–84.

Hammersley, M., & Atkinson, P. (1995). *Ethnography: Principles in practice* (2nd ed.). New York: Routledge.

Harrell, S. P. (2010). A multidimensional conceptualization of racism-related stress: Implications for the well-being of people of color. *American Journal of Orthopsychiatry, 70*(1), 42–57.

Harris, C. I. (1993). Whiteness as property. *Harvard Law Review, 106*(8), 1707–1791.

Harris-Britt, A., Valrie, C.R., Kurtz-Costes, B., & Rowley, S.J. (2007). Perceived racial discrimination and self-esteem in African American youth: Racial socialization as a protective factor. *Journal of Research on Adolescence, 17*(4), 669–682.

Headley, B. D. (1988). War ina "Babylon": Dynamics of the Jamaican informal drug economy. *Social Justice, 15*(3/4 [33–34]), 61–86.

Heath, A. F., & McMahon, D. (1997). *Education and occupational attainment: The impact of ethnic origins.* London: HMSO.

Helms, J. E. (1995). An update on Helms's White and People of Color racial identity models. In J. G. Ponterotto, J. M. Casas, L. A. Suzuki, & C. M. Alexander (Eds.), *Handbook of multicultural counseling* (pp. 181–198). Thousand Oaks, CA: Sage.

Herrnstein, R., & Murray, C. (1994). *The bell curve: Intelligence and class structure in American life*. New York: Free Press.

Horst, H. (2007). "You can't be in two places at once": Rethinking transnationalism through Jamaican return migration. *Identities: Global Studies in Culture and Power, 14*, 63–83.

Huff, C.R. (1989). Youth gangs and public policy. *Crime & Delinquency, 35*(4), 524–537.

Hughes, D., & Chen, L. (1999). The nature of parents' race-related communication to children: A developmental perspective. In L. Balter & C. Tamis-LeMonda (Eds.), *Child psychology: A handbook of contemporary issues*. Philadelphia: Taylor and Francis.

Hughes, D., Rodriquez, J., Smith, E., Johnson, D., Stevenson, H., & Spicer, P. (2006). Parents' ethnic-racial socialization practices: A review of research and directions for future study. *Developmental Psychology, 42*(5), 747–770.

Jacobson, R. (2006). Characterizing consent: Race, citizenship, and the new restrictionists. *Political Research Quarterly, 59*(4), 645–654.

Jensen, A. (1969). *How much can we boost IQ and scholastic achievement?* Cambridge, MA: Harvard University Press.

Johnson, K. (1997). "Aliens" and the U.S. immigration laws: The social and legal construction of nonpersons. *The University of Miami Inter-American Law Review, 28*(2), 263–292.

Kalmijn, M. (1996). The socioeconomic assimilation of Caribbean American Blacks. *Social Forces, 74*(3), 911–930.

Kao, G., & Tienda, M. (1995). Optimism and achievement: The educational performance of immigrant youth. *Social Science Quarterly, 76*(1), 1–19.

Karunungan, M. (2001). Chasing hope through culturally responsive praxis: One master teacher and her African American eighth grade readers. In J. Irvine (Ed.), *In search of wholeness: African American teachers and their culturally specific classroom practices* (pp. 113–137). New York: Palgrave.

Kasinitz, P., Mollenkopf, J., & Waters, M. (2002). Becoming American/becoming New Yorker: Immigrant incorporation in a majority minority city. *International Migration Review, 36*(4), 1020–1036.

Kellecioglu, D. (2010). Why some countries are poor and some rich: A non-Eurocentric view. *Real-world Economics Review, 52*, 40–53.

Kozol, J. (1991). *Savage inequalities: Children in America's schools*. New York: Harper Perennial.

Kusow, A. (2003). Beyond indigenous authenticity: Reflections on the insider/outsider debate in immigrant research. *Symbolic Interaction, 26*(4), 591–599.

Ladson-Billings, G. (1994). *The dreamkeepers: Successful teachers of African American children*. San Francisco, CA: Jossey-Bass.

Leipziger, D. (2001). The unfinished poverty agenda: Why Latin America and the Caribbean lag behind. *Finance and Development, 38*(1), 38–41.

Lopez, G. (2003). The (racially neutral) politics of education: A critical race theory perspective. *Educational Administration Quarterly, 39*(1), 68–94.

Loveless, T. (1999). *The tracking wars: State reform meets school policy*. Washington, DC: Brookings Institution Press.

Lynn, M. (1999). Toward a critical race pedagogy. *Urban Education, 33*(5), 606–626.

Martinez, G. A. (2006). Immigration and the meaning of United States citizenship: Whiteness and assimilation. *Washburn LJ, 46*, 335.

Massey, D., Mooney, M., Torres, K., & Charles, C. (2007). Black immigrants and Black natives attending selective colleges and universities in the United States. *American Journal of Education, 113*, 243–271.

McHale, S. M., Crouter, A. C., Kim, J. Y., Burton, L. M., Davis, K. D., Dotterer, A. M., & Swanson, D. P. (2006). Mothers' and fathers' racial socialization in African American families: Implications for youth. *Child Development, 77*(5), 1387–1402.

McIntosh, P. (1989, July/August). White privilege: Unpacking the invisible knapsack. *Peace and Freedom*.

McIntosh, P. (1998). White privilege: Unpacking the invisible knapsack. In P. S. Rothenberg, *Race, class, and gender in the United States: An integrated study* (4th ed., pp. 165–169). New York: St. Martin's Press.

Meeks, B. (2009). The rise and fall of Caribbean Black power. In M. West, W. Martin, & F. Wilkins, *From Toussaint to Tupac: The Black international since the age of revolution* (pp. 197–214). Chapel Hill: University of North Carolina Press.

Memmi, A. (2006). *Decolonization and the decolonized*. Minneapolis: University of Minnesota Press.

Mickelson, R. A. (1993). Review essay: Minorities and education in plural societies. *Anthropology and Education Quarterly, 24*(3), 269–276.

Miller, D. (1999). Racial socialization and racial identity: Can they promote resiliency for African American adolescents? *Adolescence, 34*(135), 493–501.

Model, S. (2008). *West Indian immigrants: A Black success model?* New York: Russel Sage Foundation.

Montagu, A. (1997). *Man's most dangerous myth: The fallacy of race* (6th ed.). Lanham, MD: AltaMira Press.

Morris, J. E., & Monroe, C. R. (2009). Why study the US South? The nexus of race and place in investigating Black student achievement. *Educational Researcher, 38*(1), 21–36.

Mulkey, L. M., Catsambis, S., Steelman, L. C., & Hanes-Ramos, M. (2009). Keeping track or getting offtrack: Issues in the tracking of students. *International Handbook of Research on Teachers and Teaching*, 1081–1100.

Nakkula, M., & Toshalis, E. (2006). *Understanding youth: Adolescent development for educators*. Cambridge, MA: Harvard Education Press.

Nichols, G. (1988). *Poetry jump-up: A collection of Black poetry*. London: Puffin Books.

Oakes, J. (2008). Keeping track: Structuring equality and inequality in an era of accountability. *Teachers College Record, 110*(3), 700–712.

Ogbu, J. (1991a). Immigrant and involuntary minorities in comparative perspective. In M. Gibson & J. Ogbu (Eds.), *Minority status and schooling: A comparative study of immigrant and involuntary minorities*. New York: Garland Publishing.

Ogbu, J. (1991b). Low school performance as an adaptation: The case of Blacks in Stockton, California. In M. Gibson & J. Ogbu (Eds.), *Minority status and schooling: A comparative study of immigrant and involuntary minorities*. New York: Garland Publishing.

Ogbu, J. (1992). Adaptation to minority status and impact on school success. *Theory into Practice, 31*(4), 287–293.

Ogbu, J. (2003). *Black American students in an affluent suburb: A study of academic disengagement*. Mahwah, NJ: Lawrence Erlbaum Associates.

Ogbu, J., & Simons, H. (1998). Voluntary and involuntary minorities: A cultural-ecological theory of school performance with some implications for education. *Anthropology and Education Quarterly, 29*(2), 155–188.

Ogletree, C. (2000). America's schizophrenic immigration policy: Race, class, and reason. *Boston College Law Review—Student Publications, 41*(4), 755–770.

Pallotto, E. K., Collins, J. W., & David, R. J. (2000). Enigma of maternal race and infant birth weight: A population-based study of US-born Black and Caribbean-born Black women. *American Journal of Epidemiology, 151*(11), 1080–1085.

Papademetriou, D., & Jachimowicz, M. (2004). *Immigrants and homeownership in urban America: An examination of nativity, socio-economic status and place*. Washington, DC: Migration Policy Institute.

Peller, G. (1995). Race-consciousness. In K. Crenshaw, N. Gotanda, G. Peller, & K. Thomas (Eds.), *Critical race theory: The key writings that formed the movement* (pp. 127–151). New York: The New Press.

Pennsylvania Department of Education. (2006–2007). *2006–2007 PSSA and AYP Results*. Retrieved April 28, 2013 from http://www.education.state.pa.us/portal/server.pt/community/school_assessments/7442/2006-2007_pssa_and_ayp_results/507511

Perlmann, J. (2002). Second-generation transnationalism. In P. Levitt & M. C. Water (Eds.), *The changing face of home: The transnational lives of the second generation* (pp. 216–220). New York: Russell Sage.

Perry, T., Steele, C., & Hilliard, A. G. (2003). *Young, gifted, and Black: Promoting high achievement among African-American students*. Boston: Beacon Press.

Peters, M. F. (1985). Racial socialization of young Black children. In H. P. McAdoo & J. L. McAdoo (Eds.), *Black children: Social, educational, and parental environment* (pp. 159–173). Newbury Park, CA: Sage Publications.

Pierre, J. (2004). Black immigrants in the United States and the "cultural narratives" of ethnicity. *Identities: Global Studies in Culture and Power, 11*(2), 141–170.

Pinder, P. J. (2012). Cultural, ethnic differences, parental involvement differences, and educational achievement of African heritage students: Towards employing a culturally sensitive curriculum in K–12 classrooms, a literature review. *Journal of African American Studies*, 1–13.

Portes, A., & Rumbaut, R. G. (2001). *Legacies: The story of the immigrant second generation.* Berkeley: University of California Press; New York: Russell Sage Foundation.

Portes, A., & Rumbaut, R.G. (2005). Introduction: The second generation and the children of immigrants. Longitudinal Study. *Ethnic and Racial Studies, 28*(6), 983–999.

Portes, A., & Zhou, M. (1993). The new second generation: Segmented assimilation and its variants. *Annals of the American Academy of Political and Social Science, 530*(1), 74–96.

Putnam, L. (2009). From Toussaint to Tupac: The Black international since the age of revolution. In M. West, W. Martin, & F. Wilkins (Eds.), *From Toussaint to Tupac* (pp. 107–129). Chapel Hill: University of North Carolina Press.

Rogers, J., & Freelon, R. (2012). Unequal experiences and outcomes for Black and Latino males in California's public education system. Retrieved March 21, 2013, from http://pathways.gseis.ucla.edu/publications/201209_rojersfreelonRB.pdf

Rogers, R. (2006). *Afro-Caribbean immigrants and the politics of incorporation: Ethnicity, exception, or exit.* Cambridge: Cambridge University Press.

Rong X. L., & Brown, F. (2001). The effects of immigrant generation and ethnicity on educational attainment among young African and Caribbean Blacks in the United States. *Harvard Educational Review, 71*(3), 536–566.

Rong, X. L., & Brown, F. (2002). Immigration and urban education in the new millennium: The diversity and the challenges. *Education and Urban Society, 34*(2), 123–133.

Rong, X. L., & Brown, F. (2002). Socialization, culture, and identities of black immigrant children: What educators need to know and do. *Education and Urban Society, 34*(2), 247–273.

Rong, X. L., & Fitchett, P. (2008). Socialization and identity transformation of Black immigrant youth in the United States. *Theory into Practice, 47*(1), 35–42.

Rubin, B. (2008). Detracking in context: How local constructions of ability complicate equity-geared reform. *Teachers College Record, 110*(3), 646–699.

Sakamoto, A., Woo, H., & Kim, C. (2010, March). Does an immigrant background ameliorate racial disadvantage? The socioeconomic attainments of second-generation African Americans. In *Sociological Forum, 25*(1), 123–146).

SchoolDigger. 2007. *Pennsylvania middle school rankings*. Retrieved November 13, 2007, from http://www.schooldigger.com/go/PA/schoolrank.aspx?Level=2 &findschool=1863000119

SchoolMatters. (2007). Retrieved November 14, 2007, from http://www.school matters.com/schools.aspx/q/page=sp/sid=14718

Scott, L. D. (2003). The relation of racial identity and racial socialization to coping with discrimination among African American adolescents. *Journal of Black Studies, 33*(4), 520–538.

Seaton, E. K., Caldwell, C. H., Sellers, R. M., & Jackson, J. S. (2008). The prevalence of perceived discrimination among African American and Caribbean Black youth. *Developmental Psychology, 44*(5), 1288–1297.

Seminara, D. (2010). Dirty work: In-sourcing American jobs with H-2B guest-workers. Retrieved from http://www.cis.org/h-2b-guestworkers

Singer, A., Vitiello, V., Katz, M., & Park, D. (2008). *Recent immigration to Philadelphia: Regional change in a re-emerging gateway.* Washington, DC: Metropolitan Policy Program at Brookings.

Solorzano, D. G. (1995). The Chicano educational experience: Empirical and theoretical perspectives. In S. K. Rothstein (Ed.), *Class, culture, and race in American Schools: A handbook.* Westport, CT: Greenwood Press.

Stanton-Salazar, R. D. (1997). A social capital framework for understanding the socialization of racial minority children and youths. *Harvard Educational Review, 67*(1), 1–40.

Steele, C. (1997). A threat in the air: How stereotypes shape intellectual identity and performance. *American Psychologist, 52*(6), 613–629.

Stevenson, H. C., Cameron, R., Herrero-Taylor, T., & Davis, G. Y. (2002). Development of the teenager experience of racial socialization scale: Correlates of race-related socialization frequency from the perspective of Black youth. *Journal of Black Psychology, 28*(2), 84–106.

Stevenson, H. C., & Davis, G. (2004). Racial socialization. In R. Jones (Ed.), *Black psychology* (pp. 353–382). Hampton, VA: Cobb & Henry Publishers.

Stevenson, H. C., McNeil, J. D., Herrero-Taylor, T., & Davis, G. Y. (2005). Influence of perceived neighborhood diversity and racism experience on the racial socialization of Black youth. *Journal of Black Psychology, 31*(3), 273–290.

Stevenson, H. C., Reed, J., Bodison, P., & Bishop, A. (1997). Racism stress management: Racial socialization beliefs and the experience of depression and anger in African American youth. *Youth & Society, 29*(2), 172–222.

Stewart, S. (2012). Problematizing racism in education. In M. Vicars, T. McKenna, & J. White (Eds.) *Discourse, power, and resistance down under* (pp. 199–213). Rotterdam, The Netherlands: Sense Publishers.

Stinchcombe, A. (1995). *Sugar island slavery in the age of enlightenment: The political economy of the Caribbean world.* Princeton, NJ: Princeton University Press.

Suárez, C. T. (2002). Making up for lost time: The experience of separation and reunification among immigrant families. *Family Process, 41*(4), 625–643.

Suárez-Orozco, C. (2000). Identities under siege: Immigration stress amid social mirroring among the children of immimigrants. In A. Robben & M. Suárez-Orozco, *Cultures under siege: Collective violence and trauma* (pp. 194–226). New York: Cambridge University Press.

Suárez-Orozco, C., Onaga, M., & Lardemelle, C. D. (2010). Promoting academic engagement among immigrant adolescents through school-family-community collaboration. *Professional School Counseling, 14*(1), 15–26.

Suárez-Orozco, M. (2001). Globalization, immigration, and education: The research agenda. *Harvard Educational Review, 71*(3), 345–365.

Sue, D. W., Capodilupo, C., Torino, G., Bucceri, J., Holder, A., Nadal, K. L., et al. (2007). Racial microaggressions in everyday life: Implications for clinical practice. *American Psychologist, 62*(4), 271–286.

Thomas, A. J., & Speight, S. L. (1999). Racial identity and racial socialization attitudes of African American parents. *Journal of Black Psychology, 25*(2), 152–170.

Thomas, K. J. (2012). Migration processes, familial characteristics, and schooling dropout among Black youths. *Demography, 49*(2), 477–498.

Thornton M. C., Chatters, L. M., Taylor, R. J., & Allen, W. R. (1990). Sociodemographic and environmental correlates of racial socialization by Black parents. *Child Development, 61*, 401–409.

Trulia: Real Estate Search. (2007). *Cheltenham, PA Real Estate Guide.* Retrieved January 11, 2008, from http://www.trulia.com/real_estate/Cheltenham-Pennsylvania/

Vickerman, M. (1999). *Crosscurrents: Caribbean immigrants and race.* New York: Oxford University Press.

Vickerman, M. (2001). Tweaking a monolith: The West Indian immigrant encounter with "Blackness." In N. Foner (Ed.), *Islands in the city: West Indian migration to New York* (pp. 237–256). Los Angeles: University of California Press.

Watanabe, M. (2008). Tracking in the era of high stakes state accountability reform: Case studies of classroom instruction in North Carolina. *Teachers College Record, 110*(3), 489–534.

Waters, M. (1994). Ethnic and racial identities of second-generation Black immigrants in New York City. *International Migration Review, 28*(4), 795–820.

Waters, M. (1999). *Black identities: West Indian immigrant dreams and American realities.* Cambridge, MA: Harvard University Press.

Weiss, R. (1994). *Learning from strangers: The art and method of qualitative interview studies.* New York: The Free Press.

Wells, A. S., & Serna, I. (1996). The politics of culture: Understanding local political resistance to detracking in racially mixed schools. *Harvard Education Review, 66*(1), 93–118.

Willinsky, J. (1998). *Learning to divide the world: Education at empire's end.* Minneapolis: University of Minnesota Press.

Woodson, C. G. (1933). *The mis-education of the Negro.* Trenton, NJ: Africa World Press.

Yoon, B. (2012). Junsuk and Junhyuck: Adolescent immigrants' educational journey to success and identity negotiation. *American Educational Research Journal, 49*(5), 971–1002.

Yosso, T. (2002). Toward a critical race curriculum. *Equity and Excellence in Education, 35*(2), 93–107.

Zhou, M. (1997). Growing up American: The challenge confronting immigrant children and children of immigrants. *Annual Review of Sociology, 23*, 63–95.

Index

ROCHELLE BROCK &
RICHARD GREGGORY JOHNSON III,
Executive Editors

Black Studies and Critical Thinking is an interdisciplinary series which examines the
intellectual traditions of and cultural contributions made by people of African descent throughout the world. Whether it is in literature, art, music, science, or academics, these contributions are vast and far-reaching. As we work to stretch the
boundaries of knowledge and understanding of issues critical to the Black experience, this series offers a unique opportunity to study the social, economic, and
political forces that have shaped the historic experience of Black America, and that
continue to determine our future. Black Studies and Critical Thinking is positioned
at the forefront of research on the Black experience, and is the source for dynamic,
innovative, and creative exploration of the most vital issues facing African Americans. The series invites contributions from all disciplines but is specially suited for
cultural studies, anthropology, history, sociology, literature, art, and music.

Subjects of interest include (but are not limited to):

- EDUCATION
- SOCIOLOGY
- HISTORY
- MEDIA/COMMUNICATION
- RELIGION/THEOLOGY
- WOMEN'S STUDIES

- POLICY STUDIES
- ADVERTISING
- AFRICAN AMERICAN STUDIES
- POLITICAL SCIENCE
- LGBT STUDIES

For additional information about this series or for the submission of manuscripts,
please contact Dr. Brock (Indiana University Northwest) at brock2@iun.edu or Dr.
Johnson (University of San Francisco) at rgjohnsoniii@usfca.edu.

To order other books in this series, please contact our Customer Service Department:

(800) 770-LANG (within the U.S.)
(212) 647-7706 (outside the U.S.)
(212) 647-7707 FAX

Or browse online by series at www.peterlang.com.